D0443965

THE GREAT AMERICAN VIDEO GAME

Also by Martin Schram

RUNNING FOR PRESIDENT 1976:
THE CARTER CAMPAIGN

THE PURSUIT OF THE PRESIDENCY 1980

THE GREAT AMERICAN VIDEO GAME

PRESIDENTIAL POLITICS IN THE TELEVISION AGE

MARTIN SCHRAM

WILLIAM MORROW AND COMPANY, INC.
New York

Library of Congress Cataloging-in-Publication Data

Schram, Martin.
The great American video game.
Includes index.
1. Television and politics—United States.
2. Presidents—United States—Election. 3. United States—Politics and government. I. Title.
E839.5.S35 1987 324.7′3′0973 86-31225
ISBN 0-688-05881-7

Printed in the United States of America

First Edition

1 2 3 4 5 6 7 8 9 10

BOOK DESIGN BY RICHARD ORIOLO

This book is dedicated, with love, to my parents,
Neece and Marlo Schram

■

ACKNOWLEDGMENTS

The Great American Video Game would never have become a book without the encouragement and unswerving support of Pat Golbitz, who is vice-president and senior editor of William Morrow & Company, Inc. Her belief in the project, faith in its author, and continued common-sense advice were essential and deeply appreciated. She knows how I valued her counsel and friendship; the rest of the world should know it as well.

The Gannett Center for Media Studies, located in Columbia University's School of Journalism, was most generous in sharing its resources and support for this project. I am thankful to the advisory board and staff of the Gannett Center, its executive director, Everette E. Dennis, and my colleagues-in-fellowship for their many kindnesses and friendship while I was working on my book there.

I am also most grateful to the Washington Journalism Center and its director, Julius Duscha, and the Schumann Foundation and its president, William B. Mullins, for their strong support in the research that led to this book. William Mullins was among the earliest and most enthusiastic advocates of a project of this sort, and he was of great help in getting the research started.

No project such as this can be undertaken without strong and reliable research support. I was fortunate to have the assistance of three fine researchers over the course of the project. At the Gannett Center for Media Studies at Columbia, David Bushman, who is now a freelance journalist, proved a most thorough and resourceful pursuer of facts; Charles Elder, who now works in the publishing industry, was also an eager and able assistant. In Washington, Claude Marx, now a reporter on *The Nashua* (New Hampshire) *Telegraph*, was most energetic and helpful in his researching of politics and journalism.

At William Morrow & Company, Randee Marullo was as insightful and caring in copyediting my manuscript as if the reporting and the writing had been her own. I am most appreciative of the work she put into this project and the spirit with which she went about her work.

A project such as this cannot be completed without the cooperation of people in the television industry, network and local, in politics, in print journalism, and in academia. The list of those who gave so unselfishly of their time and their knowledge would fill pages. Let me just thank all who helped me in this one paragraph, in the hope that I'll be able to thank them personally in the near future.

Twenty-two years of marriage should leave little room for surprises, yet it was not until I had finished this manuscript and handed it to my wife, Pat, that I came to realize that she has still one more talent that I'd never seen. She was a magnificent editor of the first draft, offering strong and most-appreciated suggestions. She was also a wonderful companion, confidante, and friend throughout the entire effort.

Throughout the project, no task seemed too large or too small (or too inconvenient) for our sons, Kenneth, who is studying engineering at Washington University in St. Louis, and David, who is a junior at Walt Whitman High School in Bethesda, Maryland. They tended to the complexities of keeping the word processor running and handled a variety of tasks—mechanical, clerical, and familial—all of which were essential to getting this project done. They were helpful to have on call, and wonderful to have around the house.

CONTENTS

PART FOUR

THE GREAT AMERICAN VIDEO GAME

INTRODUCTION

"Politics," said Mister Dooley, "ain't beanbag."

Saloonkeeper and sage, Mister Dooley was created just before the turn of the century by Chicago newspaperman Finley Peter Dunne to give voice to views that were high on muckraking, low on politics, and unencumbered by subtlety or refinement, which of course could be excused since Mister Dooley did his speaking for the common man in Irish dialect. Looking at the rough-and-tumble ways of politics in the 1880s and '90s, Mister Dooley counseled:

"Politics ain't beanbag. 'Tis a man's game; an' women, childher, an' pro-hybitionists'd do well to keep out iv it."

If Mister Dooley were tending bar today, pouring Chablis and mixing Daiquiris and putting bits of fruit on burger platters, he would no doubt tell us how, in the past century, politics had changed even more than bartending.

"Politics is video games," Mister Dooley might say. " 'Tis an actor's game—an imagemark'r's an' illusionist's game—an' women, childher, an' politicians'd do well to keep out iv it."

Presidential politics has evolved in quadrennial leaps and bounds since television first made its presence felt in the battles for the White House in 1952, bringing the Democratic and Republican national conventions into America's living rooms a scant six months after the coaxial cable had been laid from coast to coast.

Every four years, the candidates and journalists who cover the conventions have scrambled to catch up to the revisions in communications technology and campaign theology. Leaps and bounds: First the pols would leap at the new tools of their trade, crafting new strategies to fit; eventually the media would catch on; and together they would rewrite the books on running and winning.

Over the years, America has come to know the major progressions by the literary landmarks along the way. The grandest and most enduring of all was set into place after the 1960 campaign by the late Theodore H. White, when he set the standard for all political reporters to come with the first of his *The Making of the President* series. White showed us all how to report the story within the story of how the presidency is sought, how strategies are shaped, and how power in America is shared or snared.

There were other milestones. In *The Selling of the President, 1968,* Joe McGinniss celebrated the ability of Richard Nixon's campaigns to use television ads to mold a popular and winning image for its candidate, a view McGinniss saw from his position on the inner fringe of the Nixon team. Four years later, Timothy Crouse took the nation along for a ride with the press corps, as *The Boys on the Bus* showed how the other half lives and works on the road in a presidential campaign, with heavy emphasis on the lions of print journalism.

It was only fitting that the circle would come around once again to Teddy White. After decades of chronicling campaigns, each more dependent on television than the one before, White came to feel that this relationship of videos and politicos was the one area of presidential politics that most needed exploring. He encouraged this study and his counsel was greatly appreciated. In 1985, at a University of Chicago round table on the role of television in presidential politics, a session distilled into a public-television program, White began by talking of the video evolution that had happened around him. He explained it in a context that was both political and botanical.

"There are certain plants that take root under a porch or in a dark place," White concluded. "And then they will reach up and turn toward the sun. These are called heliotropic plants. All American politics today are videotropic. Every candidate turns or pitches his entire campaign to the sun of television."

But while the politicians have become videotropic, the coverage of them has remained mainly in the shade. Reporters would talk about the emergence of the Television Age, but would cover the campaigns just about the same way they had always covered them. As the campaign of 1984 approached, a certain unfortunate consistency had developed in media coverage of primary elections in the television age: Each year, one candidate would come surging out of the ranks of the unheralded and underreported to defeat a front-runner in an early contest for the Democratic or Republican presidential nomination. Each year, we in the media would be caught in our traditional role of surprise. So we would call it a stunning upset and proclaim the race more volatile than in any past. We would then shift into overdrive and proceed directly to overkill.

The reason all this seemed to be happening each year was that voters were not really focusing on the candidates as early as the journalists were. Voters paid little attention to what the candidates were saying until the last week or so before the election. And when voters then began to make up their minds, it wasn't that they were suddenly running out to attend candidates' rallies. They were focusing on the race by focusing on their television sets.

With that in mind, and with the encouragement of the editors of *The Washington Post*, I covered the 1984 presidential campaign differently than I had covered campaigns in the previous two decades. I carved out what could be called a "messages beat." The idea was first to understand the candidates' strategies for getting their messages across to voters, then look at the race from the other end of the funnel, as the messages of the various candidates in their television news appearances and television ads were viewed in the living rooms, rec rooms, and barrooms. At times, I would go to a television station and watch a week's worth of news coverage in a single sitting, just to get a sense of the campaign story as it was unfolding nightly.

Watching the campaigns this way was like watching a short story played out an episode at a time. Some candidates clearly succeeded in getting their messages out, others clearly failed. It had to do with the decisions of the candidates and their aides, the television correspondents and their producers, and the voters themselves, whose opinions would often shift markedly based on what they saw in news and ads.

All of that gave a reporter a sense of what was happening and why—quicker and more viscerally than public-opinion polls could. It is not a substitute for polls, but an added tool. And it is surely a better way to learn about a campaign than to traipse after the candidates, in a procession of planes and buses and motorcades, seeing everything up close and yet seeing nothing at all.

The end of the 1984 campaign marked the beginning of what this book is really about: the decisions that determine what our view of campaign reality is, and who our presidents will be. It is an effort to show what has really been going on.

This book looks at the decisions that have been shaping—and will continue to shape—the outcome of America's presidential campaigns in the 1980s and beyond. It looks at the decisions that are made in the headquarters of the candidates—how they try to manipulate the television news, when they succeed, and when they fail.

It looks at the decisions that are being made at the same time in the control rooms of television's local stations and the networks—decisions of the correspondents, producers, anchors, local-station managers, and network-news presidents—that determine the reality that the voters will see.

And finally, it looks at the decisions that are being made at the other end of the funnel, as all of that information that is poured into the funnel comes flowing out the narrow end and into the living rooms of people who watch the news and make up their minds and vote.

They are the ultimate players in the Great American Video Game.

During the 1980s, two organizations made major strides toward expanding the scope and depth of the news that is available throughout America in the Television Age.

The Cable News Network greatly expanded television's ability to serve as a purveyor of nonstop news. At all hours, CNN provides viewers with news that is as up-to-date and complete as ABC, CBS, or NBC provide at their morning, noon, and nighttime public feedings. And their weekly analysis and interview shows provide important forums for politicians and policies to be examined in depth. CNN's audience ratings are nowhere near those of the three major commercial networks, but the nonstop nature of their news offering assures them a sizable audience and a significant role in keeping America informed.

The Public Broadcasting System provides the nation with television's finest example of consistent depth in examining public policies and the officials who make and administer them. The *MacNeil/Lehrer Newshour* gives America sufficient breadth, greater depth, and a refreshingly nonhuckstering approach to the nightly news. Other shows such as *Frontline* are often masterful and deserving of the accolades that come their way. The ratings show that the PBS programs are not molders of mass opinions, but the quality of what they offer assures those who do watch of thoughtful coverage.

In examining the sort of decisions that are crucial to the way we pick our presidents, I found for the sake of structure and control that I too had to make a few difficult decisions. Hardest of these was the decision to limit this study to a few local stations in the major primary states, plus the three major commercial-television networks. But that was essential to permit a sufficiently closeup look at the decisions that drive the Great American Video Game.

PART ONE

ONE

MARXISM ON THE POTOMAC

Lesley Stahl, one of television's greatest stars of network news, sat in silence, listening to an ominous sound she feared could seal her fate at the White House. From the speaker of a small Sony television set wedged between plastic coffee cups and old press releases in the cramped CBS cubicle at the White House press room, about three hundred feet from the Oval Office, she sat listening to the sound of her own voice. She heard herself saying things she had long thought about Ronald Reagan and his aides, but had never dared say publicly before.

For almost four years, Reagan and his advisers had been using television newscasts to create an image of the Reagan presidency that just did not square with the policies of the Reagan presidency. Now Stahl was telling America precisely that—in the most toughly worded piece she had done in her six years of covering the White House for *The CBS Evening News.*

Night after night, Reagan had had his way with the television news. He had succeeded in setting their agenda and framing their stories by posing for the cameras in one beautiful and compelling setting after another. (Reagan officiating at the handicapped Olympics; Reagan dedicating a senior-citizens housing project.) And the networks had duly transmitted those scenes to a grateful nation on the nightly news, even though the pictures of the president conveyed impressions that were quite the opposite of the policies of the president. (Reagan actually had proposed cutting the budget for the disabled; Reagan actually had proposed cutting federal housing subsidies for the elderly.)

The president couldn't control what the correspondents would be saying; but, due to the unintended compliance of the networks, he could certainly control what America would be seeing while they said it.

Now, for five minutes and forty seconds—about three times longer than most stories she got on the air—Stahl told America all about it. Her piece had been the subject of much internal concern and even tension within CBS. "I went over that script as intensely as any script I've ever gone over," recalled Lane Vernardos, who was executive producer of the *CBS Evening News with Dan Rather* in that era. "This was a very sensitive piece. It certainly was a sensitive issue. . . . I thought, 'This is a tough piece. I know I'm going to take a lot of flak for this—not CBS flak, but the phones ring off the hook and Larry Speakes [the White House deputy press secretary] will call.' Larry calls every three or four weeks to complain about something. Larry will be on the phone with this one."

In her script, Stahl told it like it really had been:

> How does Ronald Reagan use television? Brilliantly. He's been criticized as the rich man's president, but the TV pictures say it isn't so. At seventy-three, Mr. Reagan could have an age problem. But the TV pictures say it isn't so. Americans want to feel proud of their country again, and of their president. And the TV pictures say you can. The orchestration of television coverage absorbs the White House. Their goal? To emphasize the president's greatest asset, which, his aides say, is his personality. They provide pictures of him looking like a leader. Confident, with his Marlboro Man walk. A good family man. They also aim to erase the negatives. Mr. Reagan tries to counter the memory of an unpopular issue with a carefully chosen backdrop that actually contradicts the president's policy. Look at the handicapped Olympics, or the opening ceremony of an old-age home. No hint that he tried to cut the budgets for the disabled and for federally subsidized housing for the elderly. . . .
>
> Another technique for distancing the president from bad news—have him disappear, as he did the day he pulled the marines out of Lebanon. He flew off to his California ranch, leaving others to hand out the announcement. There are few visual reminders linking the president to the tragic bombing of the marine head-

> quarters in Beirut. But two days later, the invasion of Grenada succeeded, and the White House offered television a variety of scenes associating the president with the joy and the triumph. . . . President Reagan is accused of running a campaign in which he highlights the images and hides from the issues. But there's no evidence that the charge will hurt him because when people see the President on television, he makes them feel good, about America, about themselves, and about him.

And as she spoke, to illustrate her sharply worded points, viewers were treated to four years of Reagan videos:

The president basking in a sea of flag-waving supporters, beaming beneath red-white-and-blue balloons floating skyward, sharing concerns with farmers in a field out of Grant Woods, picnicking with Mid-Americans, pumping iron, wearing a bathing suit and tossing a football . . . more flags . . . wearing faded dungarees at the ranch, then a suit with Margaret Thatcher, getting a kiss and a cake from Nancy, getting the Olympic torch from a runner, greeting wheelchair athletes at the handicapped Olympics, greeting senior citizens at their housing project, honoring veterans who landed on Normandy, honoring youths just back from Grenada, countering a heckler, joshing with the press corps, impressing suburban schoolchildren, wooing black inner-city kids, hugging Mary Lou Retton . . . more flags . . . red, white, and blue smoke emissions from parachutists descending, red-white-and-blue balloons ascending.

Stahl turned off the Sony, and as she sat alone in the silence of that cubicle in the nearly deserted press room on the night of October 4, 1984, a certain occupational tenseness—a mix of nervousness and apprehension—began to build within her. Reporters are an internally contradictory lot; on the one hand we want to be tough, ever-vigilant as we pursue our subjects, yet we know that the reward for tough reporting is often a deep freeze. Phone calls go unreturned, scoops suddenly drop into the laps of competitors.

And so it is understandable that this concern, which can be defined as journalistic fear of freeze-out, began to well within Stahl as she thought about what she had just told the nation in this extraordinarily long piece. ("I was worried," she recalled later. "It was a tough piece—it insinuated that the campaign wasn't being totally honest about the president's record, and I did have to go back there the next day. And, you know, it's never pleasant if they're angry at you.")

The ringing of the telephone startled her. As she reached to pick it up, she knew what to expect. It was, just as she feared, one of the president's assistants. The Reagan man had wasted no time in punching up the number of the CBS phone at the White House; he couldn't wait to give Stahl a piece of his mind after having monitored with the rest of America her evening's journalism.

"Great piece," the Reagan man said.

Stahl thought she was not hearing right.

"We loved it," he continued.

"You what?" Stahl said.

"We loved it!" he said.

"What do you mean you loved it?" Stahl asked. (It should be pointed out that, for a journalist, there is perhaps one weapon a subject-victim can use to retaliate that is worse than a deep freeze—it is high praise.) "How can you say you loved it—it was tough! Don't you think it was tough?"

"We're in the middle of a campaign and you gave us four and a half minutes of great pictures of Ronald Reagan," said the Reagan assistant. "And that's all the American people see."

Stahl, a veteran on the White House beat and star moderator of CBS's Sunday news showcase *Face the Nation*, was suddenly in no mood to take yes for an answer—she went on to repeat all the tough things she had said in her piece.

The president's man listened to this off-the-cuff replay, and then replied. "They don't listen to you if you're contradicting great pictures," he said, patiently explaining a truth his White House had long held to be self-evident. "They don't hear what you are saying if the pictures are saying something different."

So it is that Ronald Reagan has been able to maintain his public support and dominate America's politics in the 1980s, even when all the public-opinion polls were showing that Americans had seemingly fundamental differences with many of their president's policies, both foreign and domestic. He succeeded because he was able to employ an appeal more fundamental than government policies. He skillfully mastered the ability to step through the television tubes and join Americans in their living rooms; and together they would watch these policies of Washington's and shake their heads—and occasionally their fists—at Washington's policymakers. Americans came to understand that if they were happy with Reagan's policies, the president deserved the credit; and if they were unhappy with them, the president was right there with them, plainly disgusted too.

Reagan accomplished all that because he was able to have his way with a television medium that is represented on the air by journalists who, in many cases, are considered to be decidedly more liberal than he. He did it not by catering to them or debating with them—he did it by making America's most famous television stars irrelevant. He stepped right past these stars and took his place alongside the Americans in their living rooms, and together they paid no great mind to what these media elites were saying.

This is a nation of nonstop news: morning news and noontime news and afternoon news and evening news and nighttime news and late-night news and then early-morning news again. The three major networks had been making it so in the 1970s, and the growth and popularity of the Cable News Network (CNN), pioneered by multimillionaire Ted Turner, has only accelerated the logical course of events. Television watching has become America's true national pastime, and Ronald Reagan has shown the nation's political strategists how it is possible to reduce the pronouncements of the medium's news stars to mere dugout chatter.

Reagan accomplished this in part—but only in part—because he was a former actor who has essentially played the same aw-shucks-cum-John-Wayne part throughout his careers in Hollywood, Sacramento, and Washington. He mainly accomplished it because of the careful strategy-making by top advisers who, especially in his first term as president, made the making of the President's image their prime political task and highest presidential calling.

A whole new generation of political advisers has now gone to school on the teachings of Reagan and his videologists, most notably Michael K. Deaver, who functioned for more than four years in the White House as the creator and protector of the president's image.

It is the second great lesson that America's pols have learned in the last two decades. In the 1970s, they learned that the key to politics was poli-techs: the computer basics that enabled them to make the leap from precinct canvasing to computerized phone banks and direct mail. Not surprisingly, the Republicans learned it first, largely out of necessity, since their vote was not in the cities, where it was easiest to go door-to-door and where ward-healer politics had machined the urban vote for the Democrats for decades. The Democrats, meanwhile, felt no such necessity because they had relied on organized labor for so long to provide the political machinery that would run their cause. Only belatedly did the Democrats learn that their blue-collar machinery could be outperformed by the mix of blue chips and microchips that the Republicans had put together.

Now, in the 1980s, the political strategists have gone to school again—only this time they have gotten an education in video politics. They have learned from Ronald Reagan and his advisers that it is possible to master the greatest of America's video games: the artful manipulation of television news.

Ever since the television age of politics was born in the 1952 campaign of Dwight Eisenhower versus Adlai Stevenson, the ability to use the medium has been increasingly essential to electoral success. In 1960, John F. Kennedy's video persona in his televised debate with Richard Nixon proved his margin of victory. In 1968, Joe McGinniss captured America's political imagination with his book *The Selling of the President*, which unfolded from the inside the machinations of Richard Nixon's television advertising campaign. In 1976, Jimmy Carter co-opted television in the Democratic primaries to help him create a candidacy that was larger than life, and then failed to master that medium and went on to appear as president smaller than the office he held.

And in 1984, the Democrats in their primaries and Ronald Reagan throughout his presidency proved that the visual medium had become the political message. Success on the TV news has come to overshadow success with TV ads; and in the primaries, success on the local newscasts in the primary states has come to overshadow the much shorter network evening news shows as shapers of electorate opinion.

In all the presidential primaries of that year, it was the candidate's ability to get his daily message out on the nightly television news that unquestionably was the single greatest factor in determining the winner. This was even true in the caucus states, where traditional political punditry maintained that machine organization was key and television impact was minimal.

When people vote for president, they are most interested not in policy specifics but in taking the measure of the candidate—what kind of leader will he or she be? How will the candidate react in the crisis to come, which involves issues unknown? That is the greatest service television performs in this democracy's rites of succession. Television's greatest disservice is its difficulty in dealing with governmental policies and their consequences and showing that they are in fact very much a part of the candidate's real leadership skills.

In the years of the Reagan presidency, the White House advisers have succeeded in getting the television news shows to do their bidding whether the electronic journalists realized it or not. They were able to do this in part because of the nature of the medium. And they were able to do it because there are some pols who understand TV better than the TV people themselves.

They understood early that in areas of government policy and global complexity the nature of the medium is tedium. And so by controlling the pictures, they could control the pacing—and the entertainment quality—of the news shows.

For the first three years of the Reagan presidency, Democrats had put aside their varied ideological passions and plotted to overthrow the leader of the Reagan Revolution. But in 1984 the president and his brain trust quashed Democratic plans for the Year of the Comeback by convincing the nation that America *was* back. He turned aside the Democrats' era of pragmatic feeling with a campaign grounded in feel-good imagery and economic fact. "It's morning again in America," the Reagan campaign of 1984 had proclaimed each day. And on Election Day, for the Democrats, it was mourning again in America.

Reagan owed his landslide victory and his public-opinion success that endured long afterward not to a secret campaign strategy but to a fundamental shift in the way he and his advisers conducted his presidency from the moment they arrived at 1600 Pennsylvania Avenue. Ronald Reagan's White House worked its image-making wonders—and may well have set a standard for a new generation of presidential strategists—by borrowing liberally from an old Marxist philosophy.

"Yes, it was definitely Marx," Woody Allen is saying at a table in Manhattan's Michael's Pub. He has finished his last hot licks of "South Rampart Street Parade" on that old Albert system clarinet of his that had gone out of fashion years before Benny Goodman had had his first taste of licorice but which he is reviving now, with firm tone and earthy glissando, at this watering hole most every Monday night. Allen is taking a break between sets on his weekly excursion into Dixieland, and I have sought him out because I need an expert's citation for an old quotation that I only vaguely remember, but which I know will most accurately define the political-science theory that underlies Ronald Reagan's skill as a visual communicator.

"Yes, I remember the quotation—and you're right—when it comes to Reagan's politics, that says it all," says Allen, with the grace and clarity of an NYU professor who is moonlighting by conducting a tutorial on Poli Sci 101. "It's Marx, all right. I feel sure Groucho said it, but I can't give you the citation of just where he said it. Try Dick Cavett. He really knows his Marx better than I."

The call is made and the trail gets warmer; Cavett too recalls the line, but he can't come up with the citation either. He suggests a call to Groucho Marx's former personal secretary and archivist, Steve Stoliar.

Bingo!—Stoliar knew the line well: It was Chico, not Groucho, who uttered the line. He said it in *Duck Soup*. Plot summary:

Groucho is Rufus T. Firefly, ruler of tiny Fredonia; and at the moment he is being impersonated by two spies—Harpo and Chico—who have donned greased moustaches, eyeglasses, white sleeping gowns, and stocking nightcaps in the hopes of deceiving the indubitably straightlaced dowager, Margaret Dumont. They want to convince her to give them Fredonia's war plans, which Groucho, as ruler, had turned over to her for safekeeping.

So these two bogus Grouchos slip separately into the lady's boudoir—but there is a foul-up. No sooner does she see one Groucho run out of her bedroom than another climbs out from beneath her bed. It is really Chico—and as she speaks, he goes into his act.

"Your Excellency," says the startled grande dame, "I thought you'd left."

"Oh, no," says Chico. "I no leave."

"But I saw you with my own eyes," she says. Chico is undeterred.

"Well," he says, in a burst of logic and triumph, "who are you gonna believe, me or your own eyes?"

"Who are you gonna believe, me or your own eyes?"—that Marxist thought from the 1930s was the Reagan strategy of the 1980s. Their approach to the public came down to this: What are you gonna believe, Reagan's policies or Reagan's videos? Reagan's advisers had concluded early on that their best plan for dealing with policies that were undeniably tarnished and even failed was not to duck them, but to meet them head on—and make the public think the president was on their side all along.

James A. Baker III, who was Reagan's chief of staff during his first term and his treasury secretary during his second, recalled the early planning days in the White House when the president's advisers sat in his office and decided the thing to do was not run away from the politically troubling issues, but run to them.

"I remember sitting in here and we'd be talking about the need to deal with the environmental problems, the need to deal with the gender gap, the need to deal with fairness," Baker said. ". . . And what we did was we carved periods of time out, maybe it was for women, maybe it was for Hispanics, maybe it was for environment, maybe it was for education—we did that extremely successfully. . . . The education thing succeeded beyond our wildest dreams."

Baker reflected back on the listing of the president's visually compelling performances that were aimed at countering political problem areas. And he recalled that so many of the efforts had worked well, but one, he conceded, clearly had not.

"Nothing really was seen as phony, with the possible exception of . . . the environmental things," said Baker. "They bombed. Okay? We went out and we looked at eagles and ospreys in the Patuxent River Wildlife Refuge or something. . . . I really don't think we had the substance to support it, and I think that's why [it bombed]. . . . We believe in clean water and air, and at the same time I think we have to acknowledge we made some mistakes in the administration of some of the environmental programs, and this wasn't going to appeal to the professional environmentalists."

The credit and glory for all the cameos and videos that have worked so surprisingly well for Ronald Reagan throughout his White House years should go, Baker said, to two men: Michael Deaver, whose title was White House deputy chief of staff but who functioned really as the chief caretaker of the president's image; and William Henkel, whose title was chief of the presidential advance office but who was mainly in charge of setting up all those cinematic Reagavision spectaculars. Henkel took his cues each day from Deaver.

"It was obvious to us that as long as we could make people feel good about themselves, about the economy, and about the country, we were going to win," said Michael K. Deaver. He was sitting in offices as sprawling and lavish as Lesley Stahl's was spare and cramped. To say that Deaver is a Washington lobbyist now is to say that Babe Ruth was a professional baseball player; it is accurate enough, but it doesn't quite tell the story. Deaver, after creating years of images of reflected glory for his boss, the president, retired to what passes for private enterprise in Washington, where he became a megalobbyist and promptly fell on his own petard. He quickly capitalized on his friendship with his former employer to make himself millions of dollars in lobbying fees. And that, in turn, brought him the Washingtonian rewards of fame and scandal—complete with congressional inquiries into the propriety of his contacts with his old pals at 1600 Pennsylvania Avenue, and questions about the truthfulness of the answers he gave at a congressional hearing while under oath.

Out of office, he succeeded in making himself a very rich man. In office, he succeeded in bringing to the president the sort of public-relations riches Reagan could never have bought on the open market but which he could always cash in on election days or those Washington judgment days that come so often when a president is of one party and a branch of the legislature is of another.

Deaver was the designer of Ronald Reagan's famous Teflon coat, that protective bit of PR sheen that has meant that no policy failures or political scandals—not even Deaver's own—can stick to him. Throughout the first four years of the Reagan presidency, it was Deaver who guided the president and pulled the invisible strings that put the network-news stars through their nightly paces.

"It was really just instinct as far as I was concerned," said Deaver. "I'm not sure it works for everybody, but I think it would help ninety percent of them [the presidential candidates and incumbents]. . . . The visual is so important, always has been. To have a man standing up in front of a microphone talking—boring! The only guy who can get away with that is Ronald Reagan, with a straight head-on in the Oval Office . . . but even at that point, you are talking about losing fifty to sixty percent of your audience after the first three or five minutes. Even with Ronald Reagan!" And so the White House would arrange the sort of visually compelling backdrops—action scenes, as often as possible—so as to make the story irresistible to the networks.

Deaver has no doubt that much of what Ronald Reagan is today he owes to what he was decades ago. "We've got a guy who has been in front of a camera for fifty years or so. He is at ease with himself physically, mentally, spiritually. He doesn't have to worry about where his hand is going to be. He doesn't have to stick them in his pocket like the royals do. . . .

"Jimmy Carter, inspecting the troops, was worried about where he was going to put his next foot—I'm serious. And so was Richard Nixon. Watch Richard Nixon walk through a room—I mean, it was incredible."

Deaver recalls one of the first times Reagan, as president, was reviewing the troops of the four military branches at a ceremony in the south grounds of the White House. A little stage direction in the name of image-making was discreetly called for. "There's a general standing next to him, and as the troops passed by, the president returned their salute. And the general said, 'Sir, you should never return a salute without your head covered.' And I turned to the president and I said,

'Ahh-hmmm! You're the Commander in Chief. You can salute anytime you want to.'

"And he salutes anything that moves now."

Long after the 1984 campaign had become history, Lesley Stahl recalled in great detail how that phone call from the White House assistant on the evening of October 4 had taught her a crucial lesson about the nature of her workaday medium, a medium that she had never truly understood before. It was the lesson about how the pictures on the screen could drown out her audio reporting.

"What I never really thought was that the public wasn't going to listen to me," Stahl said. "I thought if I did say something tough, they'd hear me. . . . Can I say something tough—yes or no? The question is, even if I do, it doesn't make any difference. . . .

"I have to tell you that it never dawned on me."

It had, however, dawned on one of Stahl's colleagues at CBS News, senior political producer Richard Cohen. A tall, slim man with sandy-colored hair, Coke-bottle-lens eyeglasses, and an engaging, professorially absentminded way, Cohen had sat in the network headquarters in New York while the Lesley Stahls of the organization worked the fields of politics. Cohen coordinated the campaign coverage. And when it was over, he took a sabbatical at Harvard and spent much of that time reviewing tapes and contemplating the year that had rushed through his fingers and out into America's living rooms.

Cohen came to a personally and professionally painful conclusion about the way his network—and all the other television networks—had covered the presidential campaign of 1984 and the entire Reagan presidency.

"Do you know who was the real executive producer of the television network news? Michael Deaver was the executive producer of the evening news broadcasts—yes he was," said Cohen, who is now back at the network in his role as senior producer.

"Michael Deaver decided what would be on the evening news each night. He laid it out there. I mean, he knew exactly who we were, what we went for.

"He suckered us."

INTERLUDE: THE OTHER END OF THE FUNNEL

The family room in Michael and Susan Talbot's bi-level in Hanover Park, Illinois, is a comfortable place, with a tweedy rust-colored sofa, a sturdy, reddish-brown La-Z-Boy recliner, and two more rust-colored chairs, all of which afford a fine view of the wall units at the end of the room and the twenty-three-inch Zenith TV console that sits between them.

The Talbots' family room is the Other End of the Funnel. It was here, in the fall of 1984, that Mondale could be seen losing the race for the presidency, night after night, while Ronald Reagan continued to glide comfortably in video cruise control. And it was here, as the Talbots and fourteen of their friends and neighbors watched the campaign unfold on television in this pleasant middle-class suburb well northwest of Chicago, that the video approach to politics and governance of Reagan, Deaver, Henkel & Company could be tested and seen to work.

The success of the Reagan team's emphasis on visual imagery could be seen as the Talbots and their neighbors and friends watched a mix of campaign newscasts and campaign ads. And it could be seen as well as the group watched tapes, including Lesley Stahl's tough piece on Reagan's image machine—with the sound off, they thought those clips from the television newscasts were Reagan campaign commercials, and very effective ones at that.

But first, a word about the Funnel. Pouring into the wide end of the Funnel each day are decisions made by an elite but far-flung few. They are the decisions made by the candidates and their handlers on the campaign trail; and the decisions made by the strategists and TV ad specialists in Washington headquarters; then there are the decisions made by the television correspondents and producers traveling with the candidates; and the decisions made by the network anchors and producers in the New York control rooms; and the decisions made by their local television station counterparts in the control rooms of each city.

All of these decisions tumble together through the Funnel and spill out the narrow end in the form of *news*—where it is consumed in the living rooms, family rooms, rec rooms, bedrooms, dining rooms, dens, and kitchens of 98 percent of the population of the only nation on earth that can boast of having more television sets than it has telephones or bathtubs or flushing toilets.*

*America stands indebted for that wonderful statistic to New York University professor and *New York* magazine media critic Edwin Diamond, who used it in his book *The Tin Kazoo*.

The Talbots and their friends and neighbors pulled themselves up to the Zenith to watch a couple of videotapes. First they were shown a number of Mondale campaign ads—but without the sound. Then they were shown that CBS News piece done by Lesley Stahl that is composed of a series of scenes of Reagan that had aired previously in news stories about the president—also without sound.

They were asked for their impressions of what they had just seen (but not yet heard). They spoke as though they had just been watching Reagan ads, not Reagan news footage. And they were quite specific about their feeling that the Reagan "ads" were more effective than the Mondale ads.

"Reagan's ads are kind of uplifting . . . all red, white, and blue, apple pie and no issues," said Mike Talbot, who runs a truck-parts company from his home. "Mondale's ads are kind of a downer. You get depressed watching them." Talbot especially got depressed comparing the two videotapes he had just seen because he is a registered Democrat who came to the campaign clearly supporting Mondale and unhappy with Reagan and his administration.

Bud Cherry, a Republican who is in brake parts and does business with Talbot daily, focused on the same appeal and found it much to his liking. "Sure it was red-white-and-blue balloons in the Reagan ads—and it was how I felt about the Olympics. Uplifting! Great!"

"Reagan's ads were very well staged—a little theatrical," said Dian Johnson, an artist who is an Independent and had come to the fall campaign undecided. "There was a lot of the actor, a lot of the flags."

Dian's husband, Sandy, who does marketing for a chemical firm, saw Reagan's "ads" as a rather skillful attempt to deflect the age issue. That prompted Judy Cherry, who keeps the books for the family's brake-parts shop and who is a Democrat, to note: "He looked pretty good on the Nautilus, a little flabby in that beach scene." And that led her husband, Bud, to say that either way, the Reagan "ads" added up to one thing: "He looked young enough to be president."

Chris Evans, a young blue-collar worker in Bud Cherry's brake-parts shop and an Independent, was struck by the fact that "Reagan's ads are very careful to always show him with the people—people who are for him and who like him." And that was viewed as a shrewd ad strategy by Monty Clark, who is a schoolteacher, a Democrat, a former local president of the teachers federation that had endorsed Mondale, but who approached 1984 as a voter leaning toward Reagan for the sake of economic prosperity. He explained: "It shows the reaction for

Reagan that they want you to have for Reagan. All of the people around him, the hoopla and everything—it's all very positive and happy. I don't get the feeling anybody's smiling in the Mondale ads. They're very austere."

Added Sandy Johnson: "A majority of the people would rather watch the Reagan ads than the Mondale ads."

Then the videotapes were reshown—this time with sound. And the Talbots' family room erupted in laughter, for everyone discovered that those Reagan ads were not ads at all, but were in fact the background scenery for some very pointed and critical comments about the video gamesmanship of the Reagan campaign.

But when they talked about how they felt about Reagan now that they had heard Stahl's commentary and critique that went along with the pictures, they found that it didn't really change the way they felt.

"Does it make a difference? Not at all," said Bud Cherry, who had liked Reagan all along. "It was just marketed well."

"It was just a smart strategy," said Monty Clark, the schoolteacher Democrat, who leaned just as much toward Reagan in the talkie as he did when Reagan was on the silent screen. "I don't think the American people were duped by this or any other . . . campaign maneuver."

Sandy Johnson, who had been leaning toward Reagan anyway, found himself liking Reagan even more after he heard what Lesley Stahl was saying—because he also heard what Reagan was saying as he sparred in a couple of scenes with an occasionally combative press corps. "Sometimes journalists ask cutting questions, and he kind of puts them in their place, but in a nice way. You kind of cheer him on for that."

And Judy Cherry, a Democrat leaning toward Mondale, explained that as she saw it, the script that CBS decision-makers had studied with such caution really had not told people things they did not already know anyway. "I don't think that this was any revelation," she said. "We all knew that he was a media star. It wasn't 'news.' It was something we already knew."

She paused and another thought occurred to her about the president she had just watched in the Stahl report. "He kind of gives you the impression you could have him over for dinner," she said. ". . . The mere fact that we thought that they were Reagan commercials shows that [in effect] that's what they were—commercials."

TWO

A VIDEO CLASSIC IN RED, WHITE, AND BLUE

The images of July 4, 1984, remain vivid long after the television set has clicked off and the fireworks have echoed their last, glorious ka-boom.

Here is Ronald Reagan: He is telephoning aboard Air Force One, celebrating America's holiday with America's stockcar enthusiasts down South, basking in winner Richard Petty's reflected glory, beaming as Tammy Wynette first serenades him with "Stand by Your Man" and then seals it with a Fourth of July kiss. He is ever the president, ever the man of the people, ever the down-home patriot.

Here is Walter Mondale: He is surrounded by demanding Democratic women pushing one of their gender for vice-president, meeting with the Hispanic-American mayor of San Antonio as the television screen graphically lists the special-interest blocs whose favor he could curry with that choice, and conceding once again that he hasn't made up his mind. He is ever the politician, ever the man of the special interests, ever the organization pol. And he is never seen celebrating—or even indicating an awareness of—the fact that this is patriotic America's Independence Day.

July 4, 1984, lives on as the all-American classic, an example of what presidential campaigning has become in the television age. It shows the basic differences in the ways two famous politicians and their strategists approach (or are even aware of) their ability to use television to communicate and manipulate messages and images.

And it shows the differences in the ways the television and print news organizations often approach a day's campaign news. Reporting on the events of that day, *The New York Times* and *The Washington Post* built their stories around what the president said. ABC, CBS, and NBC built theirs around what the president did in his daylong photo opportunities.

Remember, as July 4, 1984, is relived here, that both the Reagan and the Mondale strategists accomplished precisely what they set out to do on that day. So this is not the tale of fundamental screw-ups. It is the tale of how winners and losers are made in the Great American Video Game.

THE REAGAN MESSAGE

As seen by the nation's two most influential newspapers, the news coming from the president was that he had lashed out for the first time against Democratic presidential candidate Jesse L. Jackson, who was achieving much media attention for his ongoing efforts to travel the globe, freeing political prisoners and dissidents in distress. The two newspapers played it hard and they played it straight; clearly they were in the business of reporting news, not fostering image.

REAGAN CONTENDS JACKSON'S MISSIONS MAY VIOLATE LAW

by Francis X. Clines
Special to The New York Times

> DECATUR, Ala., July 4—President Reagan has questioned the legality of the Rev. Jesse Jackson's missions of personal diplomacy and cautioned against his traveling to Moscow to seek the release of Andrei D. Sakharov, the dissident Soviet physicist.
>
> The President, in an interview recorded Monday and released today, said the "law of the land" prohibits private citizens from negotiating with foreign governments.
>
> [It was fully Six paragraphs later that the newspaper mentioned the scene that television had used as the focus of its story.] Mr. Reagan's comments were offered to three regional broadcasting stations in advance of his Fourth of July visit to the Spirit of America festival here this evening and the Pepsi Firecracker 400 stockcar race in Daytona Beach, Fla., earlier today.
>
> . . . Mr. Reagan's comments contrasted with remarks he made

last January after Mr. Jackson flew to Syria and gained the release of Lieut. Robert O. Goodman Jr. of the Navy, a captured American flier. At the time Mr. Reagan said, "Reverend Jackson's mission was a personal mission of mercy and he has earned our gratitude and admiration."

REAGAN HAILS DEMOCRACY, ASSAILS TOTALITARIANISM

by David Hoffman
Washington Post Staff Writer

Daytona Beach, Fla., July 4—President Reagan today combined criticism of "totalitarian" governments with a warning to Democratic presidential candidate Jesse L. Jackson not to "intervene" with the Soviet Union in an effort to win freedom for dissident Andrei Sakharov.

Opening a three-day campaign swing on a patriotic note, Reagan contrasted the "beacon" of democracy in the United States with the "iron fist of dictators" in such places as Cuba and East Berlin. . . .

The *Post* story went on in the same hard-news vein as the *Times* story. (Reagan's comments about Jackson were made in an interview with Florida TV reporters two days earlier, and the White House carefully delayed the release and broadcast of it to coincide with this campaign trip to the South, to the Daytona International Speedway and the Independence Day rally in Decatur, Alabama.)

Both newspapers concentrated on the hard news of the president's criticism of Jesse Jackson while leaving it to the photographs accompanying the story to supply the presidential stockcar flavor. The *Times* story led the newspaper, in the upper right-hand corner of the front page, and beside it was the photo of Reagan alongside winning driver Richard Petty, who, as the *Times* article noted in its very last paragraph, was "a regional hero among auto worshipers who has endorsed the President for reelection." The *Post* used an Associated Press photo of Air Force One swooping in low on its landing approach and passing over the speedway directly above one of the cars racing around the track—it was, as luck would have it, Number 44, Richard Petty.

While the newspapers went for the news, the three major television networks went for the White House bait. It was a video lure that was a half year in the making. For it was that long ago that the president's chief political adviser and campaign manager, Ed Rollins, and his deputy, Lee Atwater, had urged that Reagan attend a race at the Daytona speedway to ensure his political fortunes. It had to do with securing their Southern base. In 1976, Jimmy Carter had won the presidency because he had had more support from Southern whites than any Democratic nominee since Lyndon B. Johnson; and in 1980, Ronald Reagan defeated Carter because he had brought many of those white Southerners back to the Grand Old Party presidential ticket. Now, in 1984, Reagan's strategists planned to hold the presidency by first securing the South, which in their position meant playing to Dixie's red, white, and blue: red necks, white faces, and blue collars.

So the Daytona speedway seemed a politically noble thing to do, and it was way back in November when White House chief of advance William Henkel put advance man Stephen M. Studdert on the case, who reported back in a memo to Henkel and White House scheduling chief Frederick Ryan. It was the first of a series of memos in this most meticulously planned day of political public relations, a triumph in messagery for the Reagan officials, with a little help from their friends at the speedway.

THE WHITE HOUSE
Washington

November 17, 1983
MEMORANDUM to William Henkel, Frederick Ryan
FROM: Stephen M. Studdert
SUBJECT: Daytona International Speedway

Yesterday I made an on-site survey of the Daytona speedway at Daytona Beach. A presidential event is possible but not easy. Attached hereto are:

* A schedule of events for 1984.
* A track diagram.
* A track diagram whereon I have indicated options.

. . . According to speedway officials, there is generally a capacity crowd for all events. I am also aware that the track general manager/owner [Bill France] was in 1972 one of the major backers of George Wallace's presidential campaign. He did attend the 1980 Reagan-Bush Inaugural . . . and will probably be most supportive. This could be a very good event, and one the president could enjoy.

[Undated]
MEMORANDUM for William Henkel
FROM: James L. Hooley [White House advance man]
SUBJECT: Daytona Speedway Appearance

As we discussed yesterday I would like to bring up for consideration one more time the issue of the President greeting the winning driver at the speedway before departing. Bill France Jr. feels very strongly that this would be an important gesture . . . as much for the President's standing with racing supporters as it would the speedway. So important, in fact, that France is building a road to facilitate the President's departure from the grandstand area following the greeting. . . .

France is a strong supporter (he attended the Bohemian Club with Jim Baker and has attended a State Dinner) and has the President's best interests in mind.

[NOTE: At the top of the memo, in blue pen, is written "Approved!"]

THE WHITE HOUSE
Washington

MEMORANDUM for Michael K. Deaver
June 20, 1984
FROM: William Henkel
SUBJECT: Trip of the President to the Pepsi Firecracker 400 Race at Daytona International Speedway, in Daytona Beach, Fla., Wednesday, July 4, 1984.

. . . The President will participate in the start and finish of the Pepsi Firecracker 400 race. . . . Approximately 60,000 people will be in the grandstands and several thousand more on the infield. ABC will be taping the race to be aired the following weekend.

The President will start the race with a call to "start your engines" via radio-telephone from Air Force One. Upon arrival, the President will proceed to a suite located above the grandstands from which he will watch the last half hour of the race. While in the "sky suite" the President will take part in five minutes of a live broadcast going out to 300 radio stations across the United States. . . . After the race is complete . . . the President will make brief informal remarks and present the trophy. ABC will then conduct a brief, light, sports-oriented interview with the President in the Winner's Circle.

[NOTE: Deaver checked his approval on a list of options and across the top of the memo, in blue pen, he wrote: "Excellent!"]

On the evening of July 4, all three major networks found the president's day newsworthy, and all focused on the lure of compelling pictures, which became the framework of their evening news reports. The NBC and CBS stories began, in fact, with the same visual scene—just as Henkel had described it in his memo to Deaver.

NBC NIGHTLY NEWS

[VISUAL: The president is aboard Air Force One, the Commander in Chief on the Fourth of July, a white telephone to his ear.]

CHRIS WALLACE: It was one of the most unusual phone calls ever made from Air Force One. The president, eight thousand feet over Virginia, starting the Firecracker Four Hundred stockcar race in Daytona Beach, Florida.

THE PRESIDENT: Gentlemen, start your engines.

[VISUAL: The stockcar gentlemen start their engines and roar down the track.]

WALLACE: Before the race was over, Mr. Reagan was in the stands himself, watching cars racing at two hundred miles per hour. The president, who used to broadcast baseball games, had a little trouble when he tried to announce the race.

[VISUAL: Reagan in the booth, microphone in hand, is doing radio play-by-play.]

THE PRESIDENT: Oh, wait a minute here. Somebody just went past somebody, right out here in front of us.

CHRIS WALLACE: But by the end he was as involved as everybody else in a close finish. And it turned out the winner, Richard Petty, had organized stockcar drivers backing Mr. Reagan's reelection.

[VISUAL: Petty wins the race; there are shots of the festive Fourth of July crowd, and one of those "heart" signs that says: WE LOVE RON.]

CHRIS WALLACE: There was a lot of politics today. White Southerners are a key group for the president, especially conservative blue-collar Democrats. In 1980, Mr. Reagan won seven Southern and border states by a total of 108,000 votes. With Jesse Jackson registering thousands of blacks this year, the Reagan campaign says it needs white Southerners more than ever. Aides say a white backlash against Jackson is helping the president in the South. In a Florida TV interview, Mr. Reagan said Jackson is breaking the law with his private diplomacy, and opposed Jackson's new plan to get Andrei Sakharov out of the Soviet Union.

[VISUAL: The president is speaking in that Florida TV interview.]

THE PRESIDENT: To intervene, for example, on this very delicate matter on Sakharov ignores things that might be going on in quiet diplomatic channels that we have going forward.

[VISUAL: Blond and attractive Tammy Wynette materializes beside the president; her strong singing voice fills the audio channel as she sings "Stand by Your Man." She is, indeed, standing by her president as she sings, pressing against the left side of his light sport jacket and blue open-necked sport shirt. As she finishes, she turns his way, presses a bit closer, and, at her initiation, their lips meet in a Firecracker 400 kiss.]

CHRIS WALLACE: This afternoon the president went to a picnic at the speedway, where country singer Tammy Wynette sang for him. Mr. Reagan praised the race drivers.

[VISUAL: Reagan is addressing his supporter, Petty, and his fellow drivers.]

THE PRESIDENT [He has assumed his best aw-shucks, almost embarrassed acting manner, which he does quite well.]: I know how you all feel too, because, ah, I'm in, ah, a little race myself this year. [The drivers laugh and roar.]

CHRIS WALLACE: Despite the obvious campaign benefits today, the president's trip here was paid for by the taxpayers—a spokesman . . . [explained] that Mr. Reagan did not ask for any votes.

TOM BROKAW: In criticizing Jesse Jackson's foreign excursions, the president raised the Logan Act; it's a federal law which prohibits private citizens from undertaking diplomatic negotiations without official sanctions. It is a law rarely enforced, however. In fact, it wasn't even raised when Jackson negotiated the release of Lt. Goodman in Syria last fall.

THE CBS EVENING NEWS

CBS's report was constructed much like that of NBC, opening with the same footage and using most of the same cuts and sound bites throughout. It was preceded by anchorman Dan Rather's introduction:

"Mr. Reagan's campaign swing through the South started today at the stockcar races in Daytona, and Lesley Stahl reports it included a blast at Jesse Jackson." The piece opened, however, with the Air Force One race-starting, and scenes of the Fourth of July crowd at Daytona.

Stahl did not tie the attack on Jackson to the day's events or the president's political motives. But she did note, at one point: "Today, Mr. Reagan joined eighty thousand stockcar fans, mostly conservative Southern whites." And Stahl closed her piece by saying: " 'These are the voters we're after,' said a Reagan aide. 'They're workers and they're anti-Communist.' Mr. Reagan's campaign staff has advised him to avoid scenes with tuxedos and Cadillacs and to attend more events with folks like these."

ABC WORLD NEWS TONIGHT

With Ted Koppel sitting in on holiday duty as anchor, ABC chose to combine this story with the president's reaction to the fact that the Soviet Union detained two American diplomats who had talked to dissidents. But even as they used that news story, their pictures were of the president and the crowds in Daytona.

[VISUALS: Reagan in a hat, waving at crowd]

SAM DONALDSON: The president was doing some Fourth of July campaigning in a stockcar race in Daytona Beach today, when he commented publicly about the Moscow incident.

[VISUALS: The president is then shown, pausing while walking from one place to another, to say the Soviet action was a "major annoyance."]

SAM DONALDSON: The race was the Pepsi Firecracker 400. Mr. Reagan had come not so much to see it as to be seen seeing it, by blue-collar voters who are stockcar fans.

[VISUALS: Daytona crowd cheering . . . Reagan's stint at stockcar radio broadcasting . . . Petty's narrow victory . . . Petty with his political hero, the president . . . Reagan with a gift T-shirt.]

SAM DONALDSON: . . . Even though the White House maintains this trip was not political, and the taxpayers picked up the bill for it, political overtones were everywhere. In a prerecorded television interview for an Orlando station, the president took a swipe at Reverend Jesse Jackson, saying it would not be helpful for Jackson to go to the Soviet Union to try to free the Sakharovs.

[VISUALS: Reagan speaks, then Jackson, who says if Reagan has a plan to free the Sakharovs he should use it, if not he should not object to others trying.]

[VISUALS: Tammy Wynette, serenading, hugging, kissing.]
SAM DONALDSON: The powers of incumbency—and the joys.

THE MONDALE MESSAGE

Walter Mondale's Fourth of July message received just about the same treatment from all branches of the media. Television, radio, newspapers—it really didn't matter, for there were no special videos, no memorable cameos, nothing but the straight news to tell and to sell at the Mondale home in North Oaks, Minnesota. The straight news was about the ongoing search for a vice-presidential running mate; the message that came with it was about interest groups and politics as usual.

To celebrate the Fourth of July, Mondale had arranged for the sixth in a running series of vice-presidential hopefuls to come a-courtin'—this one was Mayor Henry Cisneros of San Antonio. Later, Mondale met with twenty-three activist Democratic women, headed by then–New York City Council President Carol Bellamy and featuring National Organization of Women President Judy Goldsmith in a supporting role. Cisneros and Mondale talked before the cameras while standing on the grounds of the Mondale home; the twenty-three women sat surrounding Mondale around a large table. For Walter Mondale and his well-machined strategy corps led by his campaign chairman and alter ego, James Johnson, the Great American Video Game might just as well have been about radio.

The Washington Post and *The New York Times* both opted to lead their articles with the meeting of the women. They produced front-page stories with laughably different headlines, but both said the same things. The *Post:* DELEGATION VISITS MONDALE, URGES WOMAN AS NO. 2. The *Times:* 23 PROMINENT WOMEN TO SUPPORT MONDALE EVEN IF HE PICKS A MAN.

For television, the top of the story was that Mondale met with Cisneros—perhaps because it happened earlier in the day, and perhaps because two people strolling down a walkway and standing in front of green trees looks marginally better than twenty-four people sitting at a table in a room.

The CBS report was, as usual, a bit deeper and showed a bit more reporting and extra work. It emphasized the various interest groups

Mondale was courting. For Americans who had just seen Ronald Reagan celebrating the Fourth of July with his countrymen, and could perhaps feel at one with him, this was what Walter Mondale had to offer.

CBS EVENING NEWS

DAN RATHER: In his high-pressure effort to be seen searching for a running mate, Walter Mondale has interviewed blacks and whites, Easterners, Westerners, and Southerners. Today, he interviewed a candidate of Hispanic heritage. But as Susan Spencer reports, that interview was almost overshadowed by the upping of pressure from feminist groups to make Mondale's number-two spot a no-man's-land.

[VISUAL: Mondale and Cisneros and his young family are on the grounds of the Mondale home.]

SUSAN SPENCER: Henry Cisneros's entire family showed up for his interview, Mondale's sixth vice-presidential meeting so far. Cisneros, the popular thirty-seven-year-old mayor of San Antonio, could solidify Mondale's support among Hispanic voters, among the young, and perhaps help Democrats carry his native state of Texas, rich in electoral votes.

[VISUAL: A graphic now covers the screen, and as the Mondale report has evolved into a lesson on interest-group politics, the voting blocs are listed as Spencer speaks: "Hispanics, Young, Texans."]

SUSAN SPENCER: But as Mondale interviews numerous minority candidates, the most pressure continues to come from women's groups. Today, twenty-four female politicians met with him to repeat the claim that a woman on the ticket is the best way to win.

[VISUAL: Mondale is shown with the group of women who are pressuring him. Then the screen becomes another graphic about voting blocs.]

SPENCER: . . . Despite pressure from women's groups, a growing number of conservative Democrats thinks a woman might actually cost Mondale votes.

BEN WATTENBERG [Editor of *Public Opinion* magazine and a syndicated columnist]: Particularly from the more conservative areas, particularly among less-educated people, particularly in the South, particularly from sort of the lower strata of the industrial working class in the United States.

And then the Mondale piece is over—and the way a viewer can tell is that the screen is suddenly alive again with the Fourth of July, which of course is what the viewer has been celebrating all day and is looking forward to celebrating that night. There is march music and a grand hailing of the red, white, and blue—it's a holiday extravaganza in Boston.

IN REFLECTION: THE POLITICIANS

"We did a super event!"

Bill Henkel's eyes dance and his palm goes skyward, as though he is looking for a jock to slap him a high-five for having just won the Super Bowl, or maybe even the Firecracker 400. He has erupted in enthusiasm even though it is many months after the election that he is being asked to recall the highlights of his Daytona Beach classic.

"Daytona was originally the idea of Ed Rollins, himself . . . and Lee Atwater, who's a good ol' boy and Southern. We were looking for . . . Independence Day, motherhood, apple pie, patriotism, families. All manner of means of different ideas for July the Fourth. . . . And we did a tremendous event!"

The television networks were exactly right that day, says Ronald Reagan's chief of advance. The newspapers? They just don't matter in this scheme of things. "We were looking out for what we call our base constituency—all around the country, but particularly the South."

It comes down to a matter of priority, he says, speaking with all the reverence of a man who has made a political living out of creating votes out of beautiful pictures. "Priority number one is the network evening news. I'd say priority number two is to play for the morning —*Good Morning America*, *Today*, and *CBS Morning News*. And I think with all due deference, you've got to include the emergence of CNN—they'll cover practically anything. All I know is they'll cover anything. So you don't really have to worry about some of their [needs]. . . . And we never lost sight of the local regional media TV."

As Reagan, Deaver, Henkel & Company see it, the Fourth of July, 1984, was a day bursting with political riches. "We knew we were getting a double bang for our buck on media play there," says Henkel. There were the TV nightly news shows, then there was the radio network live broadcast, and finally there was the replay of the race on *Wide World of Sports*—complete with a brief all-sports interview with Reagan that had been negotiated in advance with ABC. "And then Petty wins!" Henkel's eyes are bouncing again, like headlights on a jeep negotiating a bumpy road, as he recalls the *Wide World of Sports* interview in which Petty heaped a stockcarful of praise upon the president one more time. "And Petty says things that ABC didn't cut out. . . . I give them some credit. They could easily edit it out on a sports show, because Richard said some very nice things about the president."

Bill Henkel has a few mental merit badges of which he is proud, and one of them, he says, is the memory of when he and campaign manager Ed Rollins talked after watching the television news that night. "He just said to me, 'You know, you've done more today to help us than anything,' " recalls Henkel. But he also thinks there were forces even greater than those of good advance people that made the day. "I mean, did you see that picture? The plane [Air Force One] was coming in as Petty's car Fourty-four is just going over that high bank. . . . I'd love to say that was brilliant advance work—I mean, we did know where the airport was and everything else. But I mean you can chalk that one up to God. He was on our side, I think, a lot during this campaign."

Within Walter Mondale's camp, July 4, 1984, is remembered variously. Robert Beckel, who was Mondale's campaign manager and who in fact has a television and message savvy that belies his 1984 employment, remembers the Fourth of July with a clenched fist and a heap of envy. "They created the American mood of 1984," says Beckel, who is a political consultant in Washington, and who spent a lot of time in the post-1984 period wishing he had paid more attention to the image and message subtleties of the presidential campaign and less time on boiler-room basics. "They sensed it and they created it." He recalls all too well that midsummer Saturday when he tried to get away from the tensions of the campaign by watching a little *Wide World of Sports*. He wound up experiencing the agony of defeat. "I mean, Richard Petty drove into victory lane," he recalls, "and there was the lady with the victory champagne. And his first words were: 'God Bless Ronald Reagan!' It was all part of the American psyche—and Walter Mondale was trying to break the American psyche."

Michael Deaver is sitting in his Washington-lobbyist office suite, contemplating the video games of the Fourth of July, 1984. He is, of course, ever-respectful of the camera skills of his former boss. But he is being asked now whether a candidate other than Ronald Reagan could have registered such significant gains on that day—say, perhaps, even a Walter Mondale. Could Mondale have registered what Deaver would call a successful day of video politics, given the right kind of event and the right kind of advance work?

"Let me just tell you something—it could have worked if Walter Mondale had talked, not only have taken that kind of a visual, but rolled his shirt sleeves up, led a hometown parade and then got up there and talked about how great this country is. But the problem is that Walter Mondale constitutionally couldn't have done that. What he would have done is taken that beautiful visual and kicked the shit out of Ronald Reagan—okay? And he'd have ruined it. But Reagan could get up there and paint that and say, 'You can fly as high as you want to in this country. That's what's great about this country. Don't let anybody ever tell you there is anything wrong with America.' And he'd never mention Mondale by name!"

IN REFLECTION: THE NETWORKS

There is not quite unanimity within television journalism in support of the networks' decision to build their news stories around Ronald Reagan's Fourth of July pictures instead of building them upon the hard-news attack on Jesse Jackson and playing down the videos. There is not quite unanimity—but it is close.

At ABC News, the executive producer of *World News Tonight*, William Lord, has only one regret as he looks at videotapes of his network's coverage, which featured the hard news of the day at the top of the piece, and that of the other two networks. He wishes he had packaged his Reagan piece the way the other two did—opening with that scene of the President on the telephone in Air Force One. He wishes he had done that because it looked better. "I liked the way CBS started on the plane, and then down to the cars," Lord says. "That was neat. . . . Our job is to take the viewer on this trip—to be where the president is, to be where Walter Mondale is.

"Our job is to take tens of millions of viewers with us on this event. Therefore, to run a couple of sound bites [of Reagan attacking Jackson] is not fulfilling what I would define as our purpose."

And one of Lord's bosses, ABC News vice-president David Burke, agrees. "I'll tell you why that [Reagan's photo-opportunity day] is news," says Burke, who in a past professional incarnation served as a top adviser to Senator Edward Kennedy of Massachusetts. ". . . That was an enormous piece of news. He [Reagan] did an awful lot in his effort to be leader of this nation again that day. And another guy did an awful lot to guarantee that he couldn't lead this nation that day. And *that's* news. . . . And the fact that one guy takes a hype road to his ultimate success cannot be, I don't think, editorially handicapped by us because we don't want to be caught hyping him. He made a choice in a campaign context that was ultimately the correct choice. Walter Mondale made a choice in a campaign context that would make you cry. That's news."

At CBS, it is not possible to raise the discussion of the Fourth of July coverage without being aware of the strongly held views of Van Gordon Sauter, then overseer of CBS News. The reason it is impossible to be ignorant of his strong views on the subject of Daytona Beach and the Firecracker 400 is because he makes it clear up front that he is one of America's staunchest racing-car fans.

Van Gordon Sauter seems proud to be an eclectic fellow. He has a background of newspapering and broadcast, he is a stockcar enthusiast whose office looks like a ship captain's, and he keeps his newspapers in a cradle with *The Times* of London on top. He has a full, graying beard. He likes his politics conservative, which he points out puts him at frequent conversational odds with his wife, the sister of former California governor Edmund G. (Jerry) Brown. After years of serving as the president of CBS News, he moved on to a grander corporate job only to come back again to run the news division. He left the network after the 1986 corporate shake-up.

Ask Van Gordon Sauter about the CBS coverage of the Fourth of July, then sit back and hang on for the ride. "There is a category of male viewers out there . . . for whom this is a major event. You walk into North or South Carolina or Georgia and say, 'Hey, I know the Petty family,' and that's consequential. You can walk in and say you know Bella Abzug and they're going to get the tar and feathers and away you go! And I just thought it was absolutely marvelous that he did that. . . .

"People would say, 'Well, my goodness, that's playing to the media.' But that's what candidates do. I mean, they have every right to do that and it's a sensible thing for them to do. And we should not say, 'Oh-oh, we're being exploited here and therefore we're not going to show Tammy Wynette and we're not going to hear the president say 'Gentlemen, start your engines' because it's exploitive or whatever. I mean, that's what the guy is doing. And I think he's smart to do it. And I think it's our responsibility to say to the public, 'This is what he's doing.' As it's our responsibility to have Lesley Stahl say, 'These are the images, these are the facts.' I mean, it's all part of that total, cumulative picture we funnel into these houses across the country where people make up their minds."

When it comes to the presidential campaign of 1984, and the way the candidates communicated their message to America, Sauter agrees that the Fourth of July reports were most telling—even as he defends so vigorously television's coverage of the day. "That one day crystallized everything," he says. "I think the candidate has the right to run any form of campaign he or she wishes, and it's our job to cover it. . . . These are not dumb people who suddenly are waking up, coming out of a deep sleep, and they're saying we're going to pay attention for three months and make this decision. They know what's going on. They understand instinctively what's going on. They understand the balloons and the parades and Tammy Wynette. It's all part of their experience. They get sold constantly. They get sold by rock singers and book promoters and television stations and newspapers, and soap people. They know this better than anybody. And they factor it in. . . . They don't care that the pictures are contradictory to the facts. They made a decision a long time ago that this is the persona that they want running this country. And by God, they're going to vote for it."

Meanwhile, the man who served during the campaign year as the executive producer of *The CBS Evening News with Dan Rather*, Lane Vernardos, who formerly covered political campaigns as a field producer, sees things he likes and dislikes in his own network's coverage of the Fourth of July. The problems he sees in the piece are technical, not conceptual.

And what about the larger question of the news value of putting the television piece together that way—the basic concept of building the news story around the strongest video rather than the strongest hard-news story? "I don't see any way around it," says Vernardos. "We're here to cover what's going on. That sounds so basic and so simple, and yet that's a big part of our life around here. We're a sort of wire service and a news magazine simultaneously."

But that view in defense of the television-news coverage of Reagan on July 4—with the story constructed upon a scaffolding of strong video content—is not a view that is unanimously held within the industry, or even within the CBS network. So it is that senior producer Richard Cohen looks at the same story that has been praised by Sauter and Vernardos, and says simply: "That Daytona thing . . . the Fourth of July . . . is an example of a story that we shouldn't have on the air. . . . It's jelly-bean journalism. . . . My argument . . . is that you don't put meaningless pictures on. You don't put Ronald Reagan chopping wood, riding a horse endlessly, kissing his wife."

Those, then, are the parameters that are applied variously in the daily decision-making at the nation's television networks, as America's communications leaders shape their coverage of America's political leaders. In his office in Rockefeller Center, NBC's John Chancellor, who has built a career of distinction in television as a correspondent, an anchor, and now a commentator, draws deeply on his pipe and draws heavily on his decades of experience in the worlds of electronic and print news, plus an interlude in government, when he is asked to put into perspective television's daily struggle with the news. He offers a view that is, in a sense, as tough on television as it is in praise of it.

"Television is very good at conveying experience, and not very good at conveying facts," says Chancellor. "Television is weaker than print at resisting manipulation. . . . If *Life* magazine were a daily newspaper, its coverage would have looked very much like television's."

INTERLUDE: THE OTHER END OF THE FUNNEL

Walter Mondale and Ronald Reagan celebrated the Fourth of July with Mike and Sue Talbot and their neighbors and friends in the far suburbs of Chicago. The mere fact that it was autumn and they were actually viewing old videotapes of the network newscasts of Independence Day, 1984, did nothing to dampen their ability to get into the midsummer spirit of things. But the message they saw Mondale putting out on the network newscast from that July Fourth dampened their political ardor indeed.

Walter Mondale was not their sort of fellow.

Mike Talbot found it disheartening, he being staunchly Democratic and a confirmed Mondale man. "Reagan's news is upbeat. Everything's good, it's wonderful. He's having a good old time. Mondale just comes off very bad, interviewing someone from each group—the Mexicans, the women, the Jews, and so on."

To Sandy Johnson, the marketing specialist, the newscasts reaffirmed the correctness of his inclination to vote for Reagan. "Mondale seems to be showing an inability to make a decision on his own, with all the interest groups involved," he said. "It's showing what politician is the smartest politically instead of the most capable." Reagan, he conceded, was also not demonstrating great presidential capability on that day—but that's okay, Johnson said, because "after all, he was celebrating the Fourth of July."

"That's the point," Talbot interjected. "Everything Mondale was doing was a downer. He was not out there smiling, having a good time on the Fourth of July. Everything he gave the news to work with was down—it wasn't up. Everything Reagan got was up and everything Mondale got was down. And people get tired of the down part of it."

The Reagan supporters, the Mondale supporters, the uncommitted, the unconvinced, and the unenthused all seemed to think that while Reagan may not have given them anything of substance that Independence Day, it was not the sort of day when they really want that from their president. And what Walter Mondale gave them on that holiday they would not really want on any day.

"I look at it as a businessman," said Bud Cherry, proprietor of Cherry's Brake and Parts shop. "When there's a customer standing over the counter, I'm not going to let them see the disorganization. I'm not going to let them see the problems. I'm not going to let them see me sweat. I portray nice soft music, nice mood, nice everything. All organized, all façade. Mondale lets you see him sweat, lets you see his disorganization."

THREE

SYMBIOSIS

None in the media can claim immunity, but there is a reason that television journalists are particularly susceptible to manipulation by politicians—especially White House politicians. It is because they suffer from a severe case of symbiosis. It is an affliction that is both epidemic and endemic to the profession. And it befalls even the finest in the field.

Susan Zirinsky is of that rank. In 1984, as the CBS News producer assigned to the White House beat, she served as the journalist-colleague of veteran correspondents Bill Plante and Lesley Stahl, and ofttimes, if it ever came down to the crunch of giving orders, as their de facto field boss. At the age of thirty-two, she had already earned credits and accolades that stood far grander than her own five-foot-two proportions, having earned her way to the top of a career that had its beginnings in a job she defines as "researcher/caseworker/sludge" for two New York Democratic congressmen who were making a bit of a reputation of their own in the seventies: Allard Lowenstein and Edward Koch.

She had earned, as well, a reputation for pursuing her profession with great enthusiasm and enterprise—like the time she jumped a moving freight train to get her film to a station in time for the evening news. And in the process of her work, she has earned a reputation for expressing her opinions in a manner saltier than that of a sailor who's been six months at sea. Now, however, she is waxing philosophical as she discusses the nature of her work.

"In a funny way, the [White House] advance men and I have the same thing at heart—we want the piece to look as good as [it] possibly can," she said. "That's their job and that's my job. . . . I mean, I'm looking for the best pictures, but I can't help it if the audiences that show up, or that are grouped together by the Reagan campaign, look so good. I can't think of that. I can't factor that out of the piece.

"I show whatever is there. I show who shows up. I can't help it if they're great-looking people and it looks like a commercial."

That is what White House video experts like William Henkel are counting on. Offering television's professionals pictures they could not refuse was at the core of the Reagan officials' efforts to shape and even control the content of the network newscasts.

"I've always accepted that these people . . . the correspondents . . . are professionals, that the [television field] producers have a unique journalistic and artistic balance, but that deep down the cameramen . . . view themselves as artists," said William Henkel, a man whose angular features convey a handsomeness, whose intensity of manner conveys a sense of Sammy Glick, and whose dedication to his president and his conservative political principles is unswerving, just as it was in the Nixon White House, where he also served. The distinction between the journalistic and the artistic instincts of television people is what makes it possible for him to shape television news, he believes. It is, in part, a distinction between the correspondents, who he thinks are the least desirable to deal with, and the field producers and camera people, who are the other part of the network-news teams, he says.

"There's a relationship that gets very close. And we do a lot to cooperate with them. Make their jobs easier—because, believe me, it's one of the most unique relationships you'll ever see. From an artistic and journalistic standpoint, they want good pieces. And I think the emphasis they may not admit to, but there's an artistic element."

Zirinsky admits to that artistic inclination. It is born out of a mix of professional pride and competitive fear. "Each advance man knows the question I would ask," she said. "At every event, I would ask, 'Is there a prize shot? Is there an unusual shot that I should send a third crew in for?' And I'll tell you this—a couple of times that I didn't ask for it and the shot existed, it was suddenly brought to my attention [by the White House aides] that there was this great high shot. . . .

"You see, I'm going to protect myself. I'm going to go in for the best video no matter how I get it. I'm not compromising myself if I ask if there's a high shot. . . . So I work with the advance man. . . . You want to protect yourself so that you have the best picture possible—that shows you have all of your bases covered."

Henkel knows well how to play on the network producers' mutual fear of being "beaten" by the competition—not on a news story, but on a more beautiful picture. His ability to exploit that for his boss's political purposes is what makes him good at the job he does. Says Henkel:

"I've played that out a lot. I mean on my end, by knowing that the artist in them is going to compel them to take these [shots]—and that's why we do so many cutaways and we'll spend a tremendous amount of time on an event, analyzing it with . . . a whole system of different shots. . . . Again, knowing that that appeals to the artistic thing . . . when they set up to edit, that's what they want. They take tremendous satisfaction out of . . . piecing together a visually appealing piece. That's what we were good at creating.

". . . So we have a very unique relationship with these associate or assistant producers. There is very little that this office knows about that they don't. [He said they are told of major presidential travel plans well before the trips are announced to the rest of the news corps.] I mean weeks in advance. And I can honestly say we never had a conflict between us . . . the journalistic side, they never violated that. I mean . . . we got into some pretty sensitive stuff about what we would be doing."

Campaigns are extra-special times in the bonding of politicians and political journalists, and in the case of the television journalists, what was once impossible often proves easily done. "Sometimes we'd want to use helicopters for high shots, but security was a problem," Zirinsky said. "But suddenly, during the campaign, if you wanted a helicopter for a high shot, for the first time the Secret Service wasn't telling the people at the White House how to run the operation. The White House was telling the Secret Service, 'We want them to have this shot. This is not a matter for discussion. We want it. . . . Put a goddamned agent in that helicopter . . . [and it] will happen.' And it did."

Ronald Reagan is walking down a street in Buffalo in the middle of the 1984 campaign. It is just a routine event, with just a routine photo opportunity. Zirinsky wants more. She has hired a freelance camera crew for $60,000 and has asked the White House to let her crew take pictures of the president walking down the street from an open window in a building; the White House has agreed and has told the Secret Service it wants this. Zirinsky has just had an argument with the White House because she has been told she must "pool" her videotape, share it with the other networks.

"I used to fight tooth and nail because why, if it is my idea, do I have to goddamned give it to the likes of CNN, who wouldn't do it anyway because they can't afford the [extra] crew. But you have to buy off and do these kinds of deals," Zirinsky says.

"So we go up to Buffalo. The crew comes down. And the Secret Service won't let them open the windows. So they had to shoot through the glass and that's a waste of time. And I was really pissed off. The shot was terrible. And I complained and complained."

Back in Washington, Henkel says he was furious too. It was just a local agent, he says. Everything had been cleared with Secret Service in Washington.

In a campaign, the Henkels and the Zirinskys of politics and television come to function as a team. And like teammates who saw their routine double play blown by an umpire's call, that move in Buffalo left them united in their anger—and yelling at the ump.

Among network television's leading on-camera news stars and its off-camera executive luminaries, there is a grudging recognition that William Henkel and the Reagan White House news managers had it about right when they talked about what amounts to a journalistic schizophrenia within television news. For the television-news business creates a sort of split professionality that turns its people into part journalist and part artist, and allows the politicians to play to the instincts of the latter.

They are aware of it, they are concerned about it; but they do not really know what to do about it. This is an industry populated by people who are conscientious and professional. It is represented at its highest level of visibility by three men who have a number of common traits. They are the network anchors—Tom Brokaw of NBC, Peter Jennings of ABC, Dan Rather of CBS. Each considers himself first and foremost a professional news journalist, and a damned good one (and years of covering stories both with them and against them led me to realize long ago that they are indeed that). They have done their time in the trenches, in places where makeup artists do not tread, but they are working now for news outlets where the ultimate success is measured in Nielson points—the calibration there being in terms of people lured, not people informed.

So it is that television newscasts have gone increasingly for what the industry recognizes as *news that wiggles*. And while they talk about their desire for news in depth, the problem is that the deeper it gets, the less it can wiggle.

"I think television is afraid of being dull," Peter Jennings, anchor of ABC News's *World News Tonight*, said with considerable candor. "I think that it is a very general basic dilemma about television. You see it in the entertainment schedules. They're afraid of being dull [in television news] and so the parachutist [a reference to the Reagan campaign's penchant for having sky divers drop in on political rallies], who may or may not break his leg when he lands on the Astroturf, is taken to be a necessary part of the package.

"Now when you challenge some of those in television and say, 'Well, what about that?' I think we will say to you in person, 'Yikes! Is that what we do?' The truth is it is what we do. We are a little afraid of—for some reason in this country we've grown up with the belief that talking heads are dull. And I don't think talking heads are dull. . . . Transpose that to the political process . . . and I think people in television get very nervous. They say, 'Oh, my God, we're going to have eight months of talking heads here and they're all going to want to talk about the issues.' And there's more to politics than that—and so I think we probably get a bit defensive."

And so, Jennings said, the White House in the years of Reagan hit upon an essential truth about television news that television newspeople had not sufficiently focused upon—the fact that television journalists are artists too. "Television appreciates it, but hasn't analyzed it," he said. "The role of the cameraman is perhaps the most underappreciated role in photojournalism. The role of the cameraman is also the most underanalyzed role in photojournalism. . . . On a political campaign, or in any situation, the cameraman comes back with the pictures—and in television to a very large extent you're obligated to write to the pictures, and should write to the pictures."

Jennings paused and pondered the classic television dilemma that he had just framed. "I haven't thought that one through," he said with a smile. "An interesting contradiction."

"We were conscious of that," Tom Brokaw said when the Reagan White House view of television's professionals as journalists/artists was put before him, "and tried not to let the Reagan media-manipulation machine overrun us." He has a favorite example of one time when NBC did not do a lengthy campaign piece that the Reagan advance team had crafted as a stage-managed string of visuals. It was when Reagan went to Waterbury, Connecticut, a campaign stop where John

F. Kennedy had once made a famous campaign speech and where the Republican president was now making a pitch for the votes of Kennedy Democrats. "We did not put that on the air [they gave it just the briefest mention]," Brokaw said. "The reason we didn't put that on the air is that it was short on form, no substance. We didn't give him the full-blown treatment. . . . It struck us as the sheer exploitation of our medium. So we were the gatekeepers then."

Many other days, and many other events, he conceded, Reagan's video gamesmanship triumphed and worked its way onto the *NBC Nightly News with Tom Brokaw*. Brokaw acknowledged that those pictures carefully prepared for the networks by the Reagan White House could speak louder than any of the network-news correspondents who may have been explaining that the facts were at variance with what the pictures seemed to be saying. The former NBC White House correspondent in the Nixon years said: "Now you're quite right when you say that . . . for all the description that we could get from Chris Wallace or Lisa Myers or the Sam Donaldsons of the world, they cannot, if you will, be an effective counterweight to the enormous force of those pictures, well crafted."

But there is always the concern, Brokaw conceded, that the other networks will be using a story with its compelling and memorable pictures; and that, too, is a subtle factor in news decisions. "We're always going one-on-three," said Brokaw. "You know, the fast break is developing and it's a one-on-three proposition for the networks against that kind of sophisticated campaign management."

"The Reagan people saw the whole campaign as a movie," Dan Rather said. "The campaign is a movie. They saw it that way. And they thought as movie directors do, of shooting sequences—we have our star, this is our sequence, now how . . . do we want the shot framed?

"The Mondale people—at best—saw it as a series of quick sound bites."

CBS went through the 1984 campaign with the most clearly conceptualized plan for coverage among the three major networks. It was a plan devised during months of meetings, attended by top and mid-level decision-makers, to try to gain control over the content of the news pieces and not let them be shaped as much by the campaign image-makers. It was a plan based on the recognition that news ought to be something that happened that is *new*, and not something that happened that was packaged with pretty pictures. And CBS set the pace in the fall for declining to do lengthy newscast pieces on events that were pretty but not new.

The so-called CBS plan was based on a recognition that the Reagan White House had become expert at designing movie-quality campaign videos, and that the symbiotic nature of network-news fieldwork was to get the most perfect-looking visuals that could be had—which of course only added to the quality of the Reagan videos. And so Rather came to see his job as that of anchor and managing editor and chief of resistance, all rolled into one. He explained:

"Their job—these staff members and publicity people, public relations, advertising—their job is to get us, insofar as they can, to be a receptacle and conveyor of free advertising for their candidate. There's nothing wrong with that. There's nothing vile about their taking that attitude at all, as far as I'm concerned. That's their job.

"My job is to resist that as best I can. And my job is to sit and say, 'What's news here?' They're doing their job. I'm doing my job."

"I think we always feel used to a degree," Roone Arledge said. He is one of the giants of network television, an innovator in his own way every bit as creative a force in his era as Edward R. Murrow was in his. By the sheer dint of his creative talents, Roone Arledge has changed the scope and thrust of nonentertainment network television. He was the creator and producer of *The Wide World of Sports*, a formula the other networks have copied in decades since. He was the creator of ABC News's *Nightline*, that show born out of the desire to do nightly reports on the crisis of the U.S. Embassy hostages in Iran and which has remained, under the exceptional on-air stewardship of Ted Koppel, to become network television's best (and, most nights, only) bow to regular-depth discussion of serious issues. And he pioneered the use of graphics as he made *ABC's World News Tonight* a competitive force in the network-news business, and has seen the look and tone of his shows copied by the other two networks.

Time and again in 1984, Reagan's advisers generated captivating television visual scenes, Arledge said. "Mondale was particularly unable to generate situations like that. . . . We just sat back and thought, 'Dammit, we're not going to cover those and be a conduit for image-building. And then you say, 'Well, how can you not cover it?' . . ."

It all has to do, in part, with the nature of ABC News's uniquely forceful and journalistically unabashed White House correspondent, Sam Donaldson, Arledge explained. "When you have a correspondent like Sam, who we allow a certain leeway to, I think we bend over backwards to give the administration their shots—pictures—and what they want to say. Because you know Sam's going to be tough on them. And there's a kind of subconscious balance. If we're going to have Sam saying whatever he's going to say, then we ought to let them have their shot unencumbered. Lesley Stahl and Bill Plante [of CBS] and Chris Wallace [of NBC] are not going to be perceived by the American public as being essentially adversarial toward the presidency to the degree that Sam does. . . . He just has a louder voice and presence."

If Sam Donaldson did not exist, Ronald Reagan's image-makers would have had to invent him. The veteran ABC White House correspondent is a thoroughly skilled, ever-aggressive television journalist who has made himself the best known—and perhaps the absolute best—in his field. He is also a thoroughly irrepressible, ever-entertaining figure who sometimes leads people to think he matriculated at the Don Rickles School of Charm, and other times appears to have graduated with honors from the Al Capone Academy of Tactful Inquiry, but who has always gone about his job with great determination if not great dignity.

And Sam Donaldson also can be a perfect foil for Ronald Reagan. Not despite his hard-hitting aggressiveness, but because of it. For Donaldson has made it his journalistic duty to shout questions at the president as he walks from the executive mansion to his helicopter or poses for a photo opportunity with a visiting world leader. To many viewers, it seems as if the press is being rude and disrespectful to the president of the United States—a shrill air-raid siren in a poison-ivy patch—and so the president just gets their sympathy and support with a shrug that is meant for the cameras and a Gee, What's a Guy to Do? look on his face.

But Donaldson says a television person has to do all he can to get the president to talk to the cameras. And Lesley Stahl of CBS defends him mightily on that. "I'm glad Sam's that way," she said. A broadcaster, she explained, has "a responsibility to ask, shout, interrupt, get a question—because for television it is important that they have a sound bite. And you're not fulfilling your responsibility unless you make the effort. The president always has the option of ignoring you, saying 'No comment,' making a joke."

An alternative, one that used to be standard press fare but is now not done, would be for a reporter to ask simply whether the president would come over and talk to the press corps for a few minutes. That too would get a yes or a no, depending on the president's purposes, and the matter could be disposed of with a modicum of civility.

Donaldson viewed his role and that of the network newscast differently than did Dan Rather and his colleagues at CBS. "It is correct that [you like to have] . . . compelling pictures," he said. "You like to work at your craft and perform your work. . . . But we had an obligation to cover it. If it was nonsubstantive, if it was nothing but photo opportunities . . . I still maintain that we had an obligation to put that on the air. It was their campaign. A shrewder Mondale, a Mondale with better instincts and forces, could have perhaps demolished that kind of campaign. . . .

". . . I would call in [to ABC News headquarters in New York] and say, 'Today I have nothing more than I had yesterday. I have the flags. I have singing "God Bless the U.S.A." I have the fireworks. I have the standard lines of when he has a knee-jerk reaction we get kicked.' But I would say, 'That was the president's campaign today and we ought to put it on the air.' And it was not that I had once again compelling nine-thousand-foot American flags billowing. It was that that's what they called the presidential campaign, from their standard.

"And then, of course, we'd stick in where we'd yell at him questions that he couldn't answer or refused to answer. And we would feel real noble that we'd done a little bit more than just—" Donaldson paused for a breath and came back on a new tack: "It's very frustrating to cover that kind of campaign for television. I think newspapers can do a different job. They can take the position that the candidate didn't say or do anything today that was new; therefore our campaign coverage today will be an analytical piece on X, Y, or Z."

That is also precisely the sort of piece that network television could do on a day without news that is new. Instead they opt for news that wiggles. That is how the campaign of 1984 was stage-managed so successfully by those strategists who did it best. And if that ABC thinking prevails, it is why future campaign managers will be able to mold the television-news-show coverage, at least on ABC, in presidential races to come.

Sam Donaldson is a veteran of two landings at Normandy: Jimmy Carter's in January 1978, and Ronald Reagan's in June 1984. The two landings have come to symbolize, for him, the difference between a one-term president who will be voted out of office and a president who wins reelection.

Sam Donaldson: "I'll never forget—God love him . . . Jimmy Carter, as little liked as he was and is, but there he was—he walked into the picture, the first time after we got to Normandy and we saw him. He's walking with Giscard [French President Giscard d'Estaing]. Giscard, the politician, of course was coatless. Here's Jimmy Carter with his tan gabardine. There he is. Oh, come on, give me a break, folks. I'm here to make you an historic figure and here you are walking along with something that you've bought in Americus [the little Georgia town near Plains]. I mean it's all those things. And who made the most memorable speech that day? It wasn't Carter, it was Giscard."

A look back at the video footage shows Donaldson is being accurate, and just a little kind. Carter, shuffling along in that round-shouldered posture of his, draped in his tan gabardine as he reviewed the troops and walked with the president of France, was a most unimposing figure.

Ronald Reagan's landing at Normandy was something else. "Mike Deaver's magnificent triumph to me was Normandy," said Sam Donaldson, with all the reverence he could muster.

Ronald Reagan landed at Normandy in June 1984 with the veterans of the original Normandy invasion, and he played the role of a proud leader of the free world for all it was worth. During the time of the actual invasion of Normandy, Reagan had been stateside, making movies for the military. But on that day in June 1984, Reagan was there on the bluff overlooking the beach, fighting back tears, paying true tribute, with the blue of the sea behind him and the wind blowing just a bit, biting his lip and saying in a way that only makes us all proud of our country and our president: "These are the boys of Pointe de Hoc."

In with the men who landed at Normandy was one young woman; her father had wanted to make this reunion trip but had died of cancer, and so she had written the president a letter about it, and the White House saw to it that she would be there too. And in one of the most touching moments in any man's presidency, Reagan read the letter, voice choking, fighting back tears as she cried, and soon the men of Pointe de Hoc were crying, and television recorded it all.

Donaldson had read the president's advance text. "I felt here's some woman whose father had been dead of cancer eight years. Forgotten her name; you know who I'm talking about. I thought, 'Hell, they've blown it this time.' Not only was it schlock, it wasn't compelling. And yet, when Reagan said it and Reagan's tears came and [he read], 'Dad, I'll never let them forget'—oh, I mean, we put three pounds of that in [the ABC news story that night]—I'll admit it to you. . . . I put three pounds of it in because it was a compelling, dramatic moment.

"I mean, that was D day. And there are some things on which you don't urinate. . . . I got back to London [to put the nightly news piece together] . . . and I sat there thinking, 'I can't trash D day. I'm sorry. They've got me. They have me. They have me today. Yesterday I put it in. Tomorrow I'll put it in—so it's not that my audience is never going to hear from me how slick this bunch is. But they've got me today. They got me. That's it. You win, Deaver. Here, take it.' " And ABC's star of the nighttime news put his hands around his own neck in a grimacing gesture of choking as he slid slowly off his chair and toward the floor.

Months later, in September, the Mondale/Ferraro campaign headquarters in Washington is awhirl in clutter and confusion, trademarks of any presidential race. In a television screening room, a group of young campaign workers have gathered around a TV set to screen some enemy propaganda. They are watching the half-hour Reagan campaign film, for which the Republicans paid dearly to have shown in prime time. As the film starts, there are the expected catcalls and caustic comments from the young Mondale workers—they are duly derisive of the man they say is their rich man's president with his rich candidate's treasury and his cornball-communicator ways. It goes like that.

But soon there is silence. The Reagan ad is showing that news footage from Normandy, in all its poignant length, with the president . . . and the young woman . . . and the old soldiers . . . and the sea. The president is crying, and the young woman is crying, and the old soldiers are crying.

And there are tears in the eyes of some of these Mondale workers; and then tears are streaming down their cheeks, as they watch what, after all, is just a television commercial from the camp of their enemy.

INTERLUDE: THE GREAT COMMUNICATORS

The mantle of Great Communicator and the malady of symbiosis did not start with the inauguration of Ronald Reagan. Throughout America's history, the nation's greatest political leaders proved to be the ones who were best able to master the mass-communications technology of their times, and to foster mutually convenient symbiotic relationships with the practitioners of that communications industry.

John F. Kennedy ushered America into the era of the television presidency. But the nation had learned to heed the call of its great communicators long before the pursuit of the presidency became a video game. Franklin Delano Roosevelt dominated the country's politics by mastering the political potential of radio and motion-picture newsreels. The camera people and photographers, in turn, respected his wishes and never used their lenses to capture his crippled gait, his wheelchair, or the times when he would be lifted from place to place.

A century earlier, Andrew Jackson defied long odds and the Establishment power of banking and commerce by creating a new, friendly newspaper to enunciate and defend his policies—*The Washington Globe*—and installed his old Kentucky friend, Francis P. Blair, as its editor. And to reach those who could not read, Jackson and his advisers created a new campaign art form in his fight for reelection in 1832—spectacular torchlight parades through the cities and towns, the first political extravaganzas of the young nation. As a visual image sure to remind people of the man known as "Old Hickory," the parades featured huge hickory poles. And for a dash of patriotic symbolism, live eagles were tied by the feet to the tops of the poles—giving the spectacle a theatric aura of patriotic celebration not unlike Ronald Reagan's most memorable rallies of 1984, featuring those skydivers with their red-white-and-blue parachutes and smokestreams, and of course the balloons.

The Jackson processions were credited as brilliant political strategy in his stunning landslide victory, since somewhere between one third and one half of the voting public then could not read. They went to the colorful political processions and came away feeling good about Old Hickory.

In the spring of 1898, forty years before the birth of Michael K. Deaver, an ambitious and energetic assistant secretary of the navy named Theodore Roosevelt had to tend to his own details of public relations. It was a task for which Roosevelt was well suited, for he was on his way to becoming the Great Communicator of his time.

Theodore Roosevelt
Assistant Secretary
NAVY DEPARTMENT
Washington
April 30, 1898
Brooks Brothers
Twenty-second St. & Broadway, New York

Can you make me so I shall have it here by next Saturday a blue cravennet [sic] regular lieutenant-colonel's uniform without yellow on collar, and with leggings? If so make it.

[signed]
Theodore Roosevelt

Charge Mr. Roosevelt [handwritten postscript]

Theodore Roosevelt
Assistant Secretary
NAVY DEPARTMENT
Washington
April 26, 1898
E. Petbury, Esq.
524 15th St., City

Dear Sir:
Have the cavalry yellow stripe put on my trousers.

Yours truly,
[signed]
Theodore Roosevelt

TELEGRAM

NAVY DEPARTMENT
WASHINGTON, D.C.
APRIL 27 1898
R. SHERIDAN.
47 BROADWAY, NEW YORK.
SEND ME A DOZEN PAIRS OF STOUTEST BOOT LACES.
THEODORE ROOSEVELT

(CHARGE MR. ROOSEVELT)

Teddy Roosevelt was on his way to war. On his way, as well, to the governorship of New York, the vice-presidency, and the presidency.

Today, all of America knows the story of how Roosevelt went to war in Cuba, leading his Rough Riders in the famous charge up San Juan Hill against the Spanish troops. What few Americans realize today—or realized in 1898—is that the mounted volunteers were not really Roosevelt's Rough Riders; He was not their leader, and the "famous charge" was not really much of a charge at all. Roosevelt had worked hard to give Americans that perception of reality.

When it came to mastering the media of the masses, the benchmark was set by the builder of the bully pulpit. Theodore Roosevelt was "nineteenth-century America's greatest master of press relations," proclaimed biographer Edmund Morris in his painstakingly researched and impressively written book, *The Rise of Theodore Roosevelt*. (Morris is on his way to becoming something of an expert on great communicators. Most recently, he has been given the run of the White House by the latest of that line, Ronald Reagan, who has authorized Morris to be the official chronicler of his presidency.)

In the spring of 1898, Americans were brimming with patriotic fervor. They were of a mind to remember the Maine, and their memories were repeatedly refreshed and their emotions refueled not only by newspaper headlines but by a newborn medium: newsreels, which were longer on melodrama than they were on fact and which were playing to full theaters everywhere.

And, in the spring of 1898, assistant secretary of the navy Roosevelt was eager to have a full and well-publicized role in the Spanish-American War that he had worked hard to foment in his speeches—one mentioned the word *war* sixty-two times in the course of his speech. His address received widespread newspaper attention and much acclaim. The *New York Sun* applauded the speech as "manly, patriotic, intelligent, and convincing."

Shortly after the declaration of the Spanish-American War, one of the nation's three major newsreel producers, the Vitagraph Company, scored triumphantly with its short film *Tearing Down the Spanish Flag*, which was made on April 21 and was being cheered by audiences days later, just about the time the assistant secretary of the navy was writing to his tailors.

The climactic moment of the newsreel came after the camera had panned in on a flagpole from which the Spanish flag was flying. Suddenly the Spanish flag was torn down (never mind that the hand doing the tearing was one of the newsreel's directors) and an American flag was run up in its place. "Projected on a thirty-foot screen, the effect on audiences was sensational and sent us searching for similar subjects," wrote one of Vitagraph's founders and cameramen, Albert E. Smith (as noted in Raymond Fielding's book *The American Newsreel*). "The people were on fire and eager for every line of news. The

New York Journal sold a million copies in a single day. The circulation of Pulitzer's *New York World* rose to five million a week. . . . With nationalistic feeling at a fever pitch we set out to photograph what the people wanted to see."

Roosevelt had resigned his navy office to join the First U.S. Volunteer Cavalry; his rank was lieutenant colonel, and he was second in command to Colonel Leonard Wood. But as biographer Morris noted, "The President and the Congress might imagine Wood to be the true commander of the regiment, but the American public was not fooled." Newspapers were already pouring forth labels of alliteration: "Teddy's Terrors," "Teddy's Riotous Rounders," and after their namesake put out the word that he was not fond of their use of his nickname, "Roosevelt's Rough 'Uns," and finally, "Roosevelt's Rough Riders." It is not surprising that a majority of the twenty-three thousand applications for volunteers had come to Washington addressed to Roosevelt. And it is no wonder that the *New York Press* felt moved to observe: "Colonel Wood is lost sight of entirely in the effulgence of Teethadore"—Roosevelt had made himself so well known that even his piano keyboard of a grin was a trademark by then (this being twenty-six years before Jimmy Carter cut his first teeth and almost one hundred years after George Washington's dentist whittled his last).

Roosevelt had an eye for the lens. When the Rough Riders assembled in San Antonio and posed for the official regimental photograph, on their mounts in full dress uniform, biographer Morris noted with delightful understatement, "The picture was marred by a slight irregularity of drill: Lieutenant Colonel Roosevelt had absent-mindedly allowed his horse to stand a few feet in advance of Colonel Wood's."

Then it was on to Tampa, Florida, the staging area for the grand war. When Roosevelt heard in Tampa that the last available ship had already been assigned to two other units he ran the Rough Riders at full tilt, boarded the boat first, and then held the ship against the protests of the other two units. Left standing on the docks, Roosevelt noticed, were two cameramen with their equipment.

"What are you young men up to?" he asked.

One replied: "We are the Vitagraph Company, Colonel Roosevelt, and we are going to Cuba to take moving pictures of the war."

The cameramen were promptly escorted onboard. "I can't take care of a regiment," said nineteenth-century America's greatest master of public relations, but I might be able to handle two more."*

*Edmund Morris, *The Rise of Theodore Roosevelt*, p. 629.

Once in Cuba, Colonel Wood and Lieutenant Colonel Roosevelt carried out the famous charge up San Juan Hill as might be expected. They made their way up the terrain, Morris noted, with Wood flanked by three military aides and Roosevelt flanked by his two favorite reporters, Richard Harding Davis of the *New York Herald* and Edward Marshall of the *New York Journal*, who had written favorably about his work as New York City's police commissioner and who he was courting anew in the hopes that they would cover him with glory as they covered his war campaign. They did—a clear case of rampant journalistic-political symbiosis. Banished to the rear of the contingent was a newsman whom Roosevelt did not like and could not expect to pay him journalistic tribute, one Stephen Crane of the *New York World*.

Richard Harding Davis, ever-immaculate in a white suit, was a friend of the family and was the sort of journalist who responded in kind to friendly treatment, Morris notes. And so it was that Davis wrote of Roosevelt, the lieutenant colonel in the dashing blue scarf, "Mounted high on horseback, and charging the rifle-pits at a gallop and quite alone, made you feel that you would also like to cheer."

Stephen Crane, viewing the tough, slow journey to the top from a different, distant angle, wrote that the Rough Riders looked like "brown flies" as they swarmed up the bluff. Roosevelt had also marveled at the cooing and cuckoo calls he had heard; but Crane, who had been in Cuba longer, recognized the calls for what they were, according to Marshall. Crane wrote: "Ah, the wood dove! The Spanish guerrilla wood-dove which had presaged the death of gallant marines at Guantanamo!"

It was indeed an ambush and it took a heavy toll among the Rough Riders. The whole long and tortuous ordeal had been filmed by the grateful men from Vitagraph, Albert E. Smith and J. Stuart Blackton. Smith later wrote that at one point during the so-called charge up San Juan Hill, Roosevelt had paused to pose so the newsreels could better capture his heroic efforts and preserve them for posterity. "It was not until then that we began to appreciate the full scope of his perception in the field of public relations," Smith noted. He also wrote of "the camera's hypnotic effect on Mr. Roosevelt."*

Their film showed a slow and undramatic ordeal and they were astonished upon returning to New York to find that America already

*Morris, p. 845.

had a mental picture of a cavalry charge far more dramatic than the pictures their camera saw. Wrote Smith:

"The thin line of Rough Riders halted, fired, advanced slowly, more picking their way through the heavy thicket than charging. This was the assault. Nothing glamorous or hip-hip-hooray. . . . It was not until Blackton and I returned to New York that we learned we had taken part in the celebrated 'charge' up San Juan Hill."*†

Theodore Roosevelt came home to find that he had become the most famous man in America. The battles in Cuba, especially those of San Juan and Santiago Bay, had overshadowed even Admiral Dewey's victory in Manila. "One object at least was accomplished," wrote correspondent Burt McIntosh of *Leslie's Magazine*, who, according to Morris, was among the journalists Roosevelt left behind. "The names of several men were in the newspapers before the names of several others, and a number of newspapermen, who were sure to write things in the proper spirit, were given the necessary 'tip.' " They were also

*Fielding, p. 31.

†So glorious was this war, in the public perception, that they vowed to improve upon the dramatics of their newsreel film. And they did just that, bringing all due glory to this little war by producing a fraudulent representation of the crucial Battle of Santiago Bay. The battle sequence that brought America's victory in Cuba home to the mainland was captured by Vitagraph's war correspondents like this, as reported by Smith himself:

"At this time street vendors in New York were selling large sturdy photographs of ships of the American and Spanish fleets. We bought a set of each and we cut out the battleships. On a table, topside down, we placed one of Blackton's large canvas-covered frames and filled it with water an inch deep. In order to stand the cutouts of the ships in the water, we nailed them to lengths of wood about an inch square. In this way a little 'shelf' was provided behind each ship, and on this shelf we placed pinches of gunpowder—three pinches for each ship—not too many, we felt, for a major sea engagement of this sort.

"For a background, Blackton daubed a few white clouds on a blue-tinted cardboard. To each of the ships, now sitting placidly in our shallow 'bay,' we attached a fine thread to enable us to pull the ships past the camera at the proper moment and in the correct order.

"We needed someone to blow smoke into the scene, but we couldn't go too far outside our circle if the secret was to be kept. Mrs. Blackton was called in and she volunteered, in this day of nonsmoking womanhood, to smoke a cigarette. A friendly office boy said he would try a cigar. This was fine, as we needed the volume.

"A piece of cotton was dipped in alcohol and attached to a wire slender enough to escape the eye of the camera. Blackton, concealed behind the side of the table farthermost from the camera, touched off the mounds of gunpowder with his wire taper—and the battle was on. Mrs. Blackton, smoking and coughing, delivered a fine haze. . . .

"The film and lenses of that day were imperfect enough to conceal the crudities of our miniature, and as the picture ran only two minutes there was not time for anyone to study it critically. . . .

"Pastor's [theater] and both Proctor [theater] houses played to capacity audiences for several weeks. Jim and I felt less and less remorse of conscience when we saw how much excitement and enthusiasm were aroused by 'The Battle of Santiago Bay.' " (Fielding, p. 32)

Vitagraph's coverage of the famous battle, in the famous war that made Teddy Roosevelt's career, cost the company $1.98.

given the necessary flattery, author Morris went on to note. Roosevelt cited the *New York Herald*'s Davis in his official report, and tried to get the Associated Press to mention Davis's own war exploits—he'd grabbed a gun and begun firing it at one point in the battle.*

On August 15, 1898, the troopship carrying Roosevelt's Rough Riders docked at Montauk Point, Long Island, conveniently in Roosevelt's home state. And while there were huge cheers for all, correspondent Edward Marshall of the *New York Journal* wrote, "When 'Teddy and his teeth' came down the gangplank, the last ultimate climax of the possibility of cheering was reached."† The casualties of his regiment had been the heaviest of any regiment in the campaign; Roosevelt had seemed proud of that fact, not dismayed by it, his chroniclers have noted. And while the troops looked bedraggled and beset with tropical diseases, Roosevelt looked jaunty as ever; he wore a fresh uniform and gaiters and scuffed boots and fairly sprinted down the gangplank. Morris noted that Roosevelt stopped courteously to greet his greeting party, but soon spotted a group of newspaper reporters and strode to them. He dismissed talk about being the next governor, saying he just wanted to talk about his regiment—"It's the finest regiment there ever was, and I'm proud to command it."

He happily brandished a 1980s-style visual prop that he had brought with him for the occasion. "This is a pistol with a history," Roosevelt said, showing his sidearm. "It was taken from the wreck of the Maine. When I took it to Cuba I made a vow to kill at least one Spaniard with it, and I did. . . ."**

It was a touch worthy of John Wayne in the movies or Ronald Reagan in the television news. Teddy Roosevelt was on his way.

Once in the White House, Theodore Roosevelt quickly earned a reputation as the most cooperative and easy-to-photograph president America had, at that time, ever known. No official ceremony was so official or so solemn that it could not be interrupted for a wave and a smile for the cameras. So, too, Roosevelt took great interest in the proper care and watering of the press, seeing to it that personal relations with the reporters were direct and friendly, and that their professional thirst was always quenched by a carefully regulated flow of news.

Theodore Roosevelt's accessibility as president did not stop the news-

*Morris, p. 645.
†Morris, p. 664.
**Morris, p. 665.

reel producers from trying just a bit harder, and embellishing just a bit more. So it was that when the president went on a headline-making safari to Africa and bagged a lion, the news of which was carried at length in the press, one newsreel company—Selig Polyscope of Chicago—found it too good a trip to miss. So Selig Polyscope hired a toothsome actor who impersonated Roosevelt, and obtained what has been described as an "aged, peevish lion," which as it turned out was indeed killed on the set in a moment of uncontrol, according to historian Terry Ramsaye's account, which was said to have been based on his acquaintance with Colonel William Selig.* When the re-creation was released to the theaters, the film never mentioned Roosevelt's name—it was just called *Hunting Big Game in Africa*—and, after all, the newsreel company could scarcely be blamed if theatergoers somehow thought this was the actual film of the presidential safari they had been reading about in their newspapers. *Hunting Big Game in Africa* became a big money-maker, which only further angered the great White House hunter himself, since he had made a deal with the Smithsonian Institution, giving them the film rights to the real thing.

If faking a president's safari can be said to have enraged Roosevelt, then the faking of a president's family can be said to have pushed him beyond all limits of public-relations endurance. And that is precisely what happened when a newsreel company unveiled its film *Princess Alice* to a nation of theatergoers anxious for a glimpse at America's royalty. The fact that the offending newsreel company was none other than Vitagraph—whose bogus recreations had popularized Roosevelt's pet war—did not matter. Vitagraph's otherwise respectful *Princess Alice* so angered the First Father, he demanded that all prints of it be recalled from the theaters. They were, and Roosevelt then severed his cordial relationship with this newsreel company that had played such an important early role in his making.

A FAILURE TO COMMUNICATE

For a quarter-century after the years of Theodore Roosevelt, the presidency was beset by a failure to communicate. Presidents Taft and Coolidge and Hoover did not have the inclination. President Wilson had the inclination but not the persona. President Harding was otherwise occupied.

Of them, only Woodrow Wilson tried. His advisers completed the

*Fielding, p. 51.

machinery for the government management of public information and opinion. Wilson set the precedent for regularly scheduled press conferences, a precedent that his successors have followed when it suited them, forgotten when it didn't. Wilson also began the government's own use of motion pictures, and he created the Committee on Public Relations as a vehicle for coordinating and expanding the government's ability to manage its own news.

But communication with the masses did not come easily to this college president who sought to govern the national campus as he did Princeton's. Purity of policy alone does not sell in a democracy. And in the end, even the best advice of his secretary, Joseph P. Tumulty, could not salvage his fondest hopes. Tumulty apparently understood the levers of public opinion and could have functioned as the Michael Deaver of his time, if only he had had the pleasure of serving, say, a Franklin Delano Roosevelt (or perhaps even a Francis X. Bushman). But Tumulty had to make do with Wilson, as he worked to make his boss a good if not great communicator.

When Wilson went to the Paris Peace Conference at the end of World War I—it was the first trip to Europe by a sitting president—Tumulty stayed in Washington and cabled Deaveresque advice to the traveling party. Tumulty saw that Wilson needed to inject some human touches and warmth into his public relations to best sell his efforts abroad at home, and that, according to George Juergens in his book, *News from the White House,* was the theme of his steady stream of cables to Europe. He attended to the sort of detailed instructions—complete with names of reporters and staging suggestions—in the manner that under Theodore Roosevelt would have been superfluous, and under Franklin Roosevelt or John F. Kennedy or Ronald Reagan would have been executed, but under the more personally constricted Wilson was mainly wasted.

Among the Tumulty cables:

DECEMBER 16, 1918

IF THE PRESIDENT VISITS HOSPITALS HAVE THE PRESS REPRESENTATIVES WITH HIM TO GET HUMAN INTEREST STORY. DO NOT LET HIS VISITS BE PERFUNCTORY. LET HIM SIT BESIDE BED OF COMMON SOLDIERS. KEEP PRESIDENT IN TOUCH WITH LAWRENCE, SEIBOLD, SWOPE, PRESS ASSOCIATIONS, HILLS AND GILBERT. DONT FORGET MOVIE MEN.

> January 16, 1919
>
> Stories . . . only show . . . President as an official living in a palace and guarded by soldiery. . . . Try to get newspapermen Probert, Bender and Levin to inject some emotion in stories. Can't President meet poilus and American soldiers face to face. . .? President's smile is wonderful. Get this over in some way. . . .

In the end, Wilson proved unable to get over to the American people his wonderful smile or his League of Nations.

It is a telling point about the evolution of the American presidency that today it remains hard to imagine Ronald Reagan having the intellect or ability to forge a League of Nations in Europe; but it is just as hard to imagine Reagan failing to communicate in human terms while overseas, or failing to sell the treaty back home once the deed was done.

HIS MASTER'S VOICE

A quarter-century of governmental incommunicado reached its silent peak with the presidency of Herbert Hoover. He responded to the collapse of the economy by building a wall of silence, becoming, as historian Richard Steele noted, "uncommunicative, hostile, and ultimately all but totally estranged from the press."

But the flow of news out of Washington, having been halted by the Hoover Dam, began to gush from all channels at once upon the inauguration of Franklin Delano Roosevelt.

> We soon discovered that in Franklin Delano Roosevelt we had the greatest single attraction. Announcement of his fireside chats, which were always filmed, brought hundreds of patrons to the theater. Anti–New Dealers came to hiss.
>
> —W. French Githens,
> an editor of *Movietone News* in the 1930s*

VISUALS: FDR playing with his grandchildren at Hyde Park, landing a fish on a cruise, playing water polo with fellow polio patients at Warm Springs, and of course his stewardship of the New Deal.

The warmth of the new president's love of humanity and the vigor

*Fielding, p. 201.

of the new president's love of sports life beamed out at Americans from the giant screens of their friendly neighborhood theaters each week. A night at the movies was also a night of communing with the president, as the newsreels revealed to the nation a leader who was at once active and caring and human—a marked contrast to the reclusive view they had had of Hoover.

The newsreels were news as entertainment, and the president was ever-entertaining as he was seen in scenes arranged to be photographed by his top information advisers, Marvin McIntyre and Stephen Early, who were both former newsreel-company officials.

These were genteel days of censorship of a sort, a censorship imposed by the news organizations—the newspapers, magazines, radio, and the newsreels. So the public never saw President Roosevelt being pushed in his wheelchair or being lifted into his car or walking in his slow, crippled, but courageous way. (It was a policy far unlike that which in a more contemporary era was accorded Alabama's George Wallace, who was crippled by an assassination attempt while running for president and was shown at various times by the news media being lifted—and, at least once, even dropped—by his aides when he campaigned again in a subsequent election.) It was a policy of self-censorship imposed to the benefit of many personalities, not just the president. The newsreels, for example, withheld the slapstick footage of the Duke of Windsor tripping over a sound cable at his wedding, and Italy's midgetlike King Victor Emanuel being lifted upon his horse.

While photogenic cousin Theodore won his way into the hearts and lenses of the newsreels through personal attention to the care and stroking of all camera-carrying humans, Franklin Roosevelt found another, even more surefire method for convincing them to record his successes on the silver screen. He paid them.

In 1936, with Roosevelt's first try for reelection just months away, trusted New Dealer Harry Hopkins invited forty-one filmmakers to bid for a government contract to produce a series of thirty movies heralding the success of Roosevelt's Works Progress Administration (WPA). Five companies submitted bids and Pathé was awarded the contract for $4,280. Pathé also agreed to distribute, free of charge, a WPA newsreel to its contracted theaters as part of its own regular newsreel programming.

One storyline (proposed by the WPA itself): A mother of four is living from handouts and her children are hungry. The WPA provides her with a job as a weaver; she sells what she produces and earns enough money to feed her children and support herself. All ends well, thanks to FDR and his WPA.

Predictably, Republicans howled that this was an improper use of federal funds, which of course it was. And Hopkins's contracting effort proved a one-time thing. But the Roosevelt flair for government filmmaking was not deterred, just detoured. The Resettlement Administration (RA) sponsored the production of two motion pictures that were documentaries about the Dust Bowl: *The Plow that Broke the Plains*, made in 1936, and *The River*, made in 1937; the latter was so well received, artistically and popularly, that Paramount Pictures decided to distribute it.

Franklin Roosevelt managed over the years to get along well with most print reporters. He was fond of spontaneity in his regularly scheduled press conferences, which were themselves informal affairs around his desk in the Oval Office. He did away with the policies of his predecessors, who required questions submitted in advance. And he was fond of punctuating his comments to reporters with instructions about how he thought they should write the news he was giving them, as in, "If I were writing the story, I would put it this way . . ." But he also railed privately—and not so privately—that the problem with the newspapers was that too often what the reporters wrote was dictated by the publishers, who were overwhelmingly Republican and had opposed him all of his political life.

Radio became Franklin Roosevelt's favored medium of great communication. Radio had no editorial page and presented the news as the White House served it, unencumbered by analysis that might muddle the government's prose by pointing out errors of omission or fact. Historian Richard Steele has noted: "While newspapers never matched the President's ideal, radio would exceed his most extravagant expectations. Everything the administration had to say went over the airwaves without the intercession of reporters, editors, or publishers. Not only did radio carry the government's message without adulteration, it carried it farther, more immediately, and more effectively than newspapers."*

Radio networks operated in fear that government disapproval could manifest itself in regulatory intervention; indeed, Roosevelt's Radio Commission overseers made it clear that theirs was a partisan purpose and they did not place a premium on the political independence of their regulatory role.

*Steele, p. 21.

And radio, for its part, was a willing supplicant, playing its role of fallen virtue with impunity, in the hopes of immunity. CBS's executive in charge of White House liaison was Henry Bellows, who was a Democrat and former Harvard classmate of the president's and a former Federal Radio Commission member. Shortly after FDR's inauguration, according to Steele, Bellows told White House press secretary Stephen Early, "The close contact between you and the broadcasters has tremendous possibilities of value to the administration, and as a life-long Democrat, I want to pledge my best efforts in making this cooperation successful." NBC's vice-president for political affairs, Frank M. Russell, also made promises to Roosevelt of network cooperation. The networks proved indeed cooperative, with CBS being considered a special favorite of the White House.

The networks devoted hundreds of hours to government "public service" broadcasts. In addition, there were commercial radio specials. CBS chose to celebrate the second anniversary of the New Deal, in 1935, by creating a program entitled *Of the People, By the People, For the People*, which featured professional actors portraying administration figures enacting the great moments of the administration's early successes. Military bands provided the music, and civics and government classes throughout the country were encouraged to listen in and were given supplementary materials. NBC had done a similar, but less dramatic, show celebrating the New Deal a year earlier.

There was much more. FDR's secretary, Louis Howe, possessor of a rich and resonant voice, was given his own radio show on NBC for the first nine months of the administration. He was the star of a fifteen-minute interview-format show in which he answered questions about what the government was doing; but the questions and answers were scripted in advance and were often, in fact, cleared by FDR himself. He was, by the way, "generously remunerated" for his performances, according to historian Steele.*

Steele notes that what the radio networks decided *not* to air was at least as significant as what they did broadcast. For example, their decision to adopt a stance of "neutrality" was taken as a sign that while they would carry government information, they would discourage broadcasting of criticism of the government.

When Roosevelt ordered the closing of the banks just hours after taking office, NBC implemented a policy in which statements about the banking policy were to be made only by the president and his officials. NBC promised the president that they would air twelve and

*Steele, p. 23.

a half hours of such administration pronouncements in the first week, while giving no time at all to the administration's critics.

Also, in 1933, NBC informed the Massachusetts American Legion that it would not permit their broadcasts to undermine public confidence in the president, as Steele noted. And in 1933 CBS denied time to people planning to criticize the administration's recognition of the Soviet Union; and a year later it rejected people who sought to criticize the National Recovery Administration (NRA).

Great Communicatorship was part of being a Roosevelt, and so it was that the First Lady, Eleanor Roosevelt, played a significant role in the family's drive to reach the masses. She wrote a syndicated newspaper column, "My Day," which was carried in hundreds of newspapers. And she did a series of radio broadcasts over NBC and CBS networks—mainly aimed at women and always commercially sponsored.

Pond's cold cream sponsored twelve broadcasts by the First Lady during the months just before and after Roosevelt's 1933 inauguration, in which she talked about such topics as child rearing and family relations. In one broadcast she noted that a young woman "faces the probability of learning, very young, how much she can drink of such things as whiskey and gin, and sticking to the proper quantity."

After editorial criticism about the commercialization of the First Lady, Mrs. Roosevelt announced she was no longer going to do paid broadcasts. But in 1934 she resumed her commercial broadcasts, announcing in an off-the-record press-conference comment, which has since been widely quoted, that she was going to "get the money for a good cause [charity] and take the gaff." A roofing company paid her $500 per minute, as did the Simmons mattress company. The American typewriter industry sponsored more shows, as did the Selby shoe company, which paid her $4,000 a broadcast, of which her agent received $1,000.

Not all the money she received went to charity, although quite a lot of it did. The American Friends Service Committee—they are a Quaker social-service organization—was reported variously as having received $66,000 and $72,000 from the First Lady's broadcast revenue.

Ever the master communicator, Franklin Roosevelt created a message vehicle that was uniquely his. He did it by taking the greatest mass-communications technology of the day—radio—and shaping it to fit his political talents and needs. He created the fireside chat and became not just America's president but the head of the American household.

A Roosevelt fireside chat was more than just a radio speech to the nation; in fact, it really was not that at all. It was a conversation between every American and their president. It was vivid and compassionate television to a nation that had no video screens, just radio speakers. It was his way of showing leadership that was larger than life and showing that he understood the hardships of Americans' everyday lives at the same time. Roosevelt's presidency was everything that Herbert Hoover's never was.

Roosevelt knew the medium enough not to overuse it. He spoke on radio just about twenty-five times a year, and of those, just two or three each year were his fireside chats, and none was more than a half hour in length. He wanted the chats to be special and meaningful—and attention-getting—and they were. Those who watched him give his radio fireside chats marveled at how Roosevelt would ignore the microphone and begin to talk conversationally, gesturing as he spoke, as though engrossed in conversation with people he was visualizing but who were in fact not there. It was a speaking style that an acting professional who became a political star would turn to his great communicating advantage in the White House in the 1980s. (So too, Roosevelt's first fireside chat of 1934, entitled "Are You Better Off Than You Were Last Year?" rings reminiscent of the debate snapper that Reagan used so skillfully on his way to the White House in 1980, when he asked: "Are you better off now than you were four years ago?")

Like the Great Communicator who would occupy that same Oval Office a half-century later, Roosevelt's gift for communicating was his ability to reduce the complexities of national economic and international policies to common, easy-to-visualize everyday situations. So it was that he explained the intellectually unwieldy Lend-Lease program for helping European friends confronted with the threat of war by talking about how it was like lending a garden hose to a neighbor to help him fight his fire.

Like that Great Communicator of the 1980s, Roosevelt was fond of talking about the situations of just plain people. He repeatedly pressed his wife and aides and his labor secretary, Frances Perkins, into service as reporters who would gather examples for him to use as needed.

And like Reagan, Roosevelt was not above inventing people and occurrences if it would help him communicate his point. (This may be of little comfort to those who have despaired at Ronald Reagan's fondness for anecdotes that were only the product of an inventive mind—a welfare cheater who rides in a Cadillac, a food stamp chiseler who uses the stamps to buy an orange and uses the change to buy vodka. Reagan was never disturbed by the inconsistency of this last mean-spirited little story of his: The anecdote, which he always presented as fact, simply cannot happen according to the way the law and the program work.)

Roosevelt's flights of anecdotal fancy, in contrast to some of Reagan's favorites, were done in the name of uplift. So it was that Roosevelt, in his 1937 speech entitled "Quarantine the Aggressors," talked about how "there must be a recognition that national morality is as vital as private morality." And he went on to say:

> A bishop wrote to me the other day: "It seems to me that something greatly needs to be said in behalf of ordinary humanity against the present practice of carrying the horrors of war to helpless civilians, especially women and children. . . . Even though it may take twenty years, which God forbid, for civilization to make effective its corporate protest against this barbarism, surely strong voices may hasten the day."

And in a 1937 letter to a woman who said that a radio commentator had called him a warmonger, Roosevelt said that neither his administration nor the nation wanted "the kind of peace which means definite danger to us at home in the days to come." He continued:

> I happen to know a very nice Chinese family which lives quite far in the interior. For years they have said that China wanted peace at any price and that they felt no possible harm could come to them back from the seacoast. The other day most of the family was wiped out by some Japanese bombing planes which wrecked their community and killed one thousand people. I got a message from one of the survivors which read "we are no longer for peace at any price."

Historian William Stott, whose job it is to research such things, recounted the examples in his book *Documentary Expression and Thirties America*. He concluded that Franklin D. Roosevelt's pen pals—the bishop and the Chinese family—"are almost certainly imaginary."

PART TWO

FOUR

POSTMORTEM OF THE STARS, 1976

The stars of *The CBS Evening News* had come out in midmorning, and they were doing their best to shine beneath the chandeliers of the Plaza Hotel's choicest suite of meeting rooms. All the famous faces, and their executive bosses, were gathered around a large oval table to spend this November day taking a hard and critical look at the way they had just covered the 1976 presidential campaign.

It was the first—and it would be the last—such session CBS would hold.

Microphones had been strategically placed, the conferees noted, and the wheels of a tape recorder were turning. Just for the sake of in-house history, the president of CBS News, Richard Salant, was taping this session so a transcript could be made. "I detect that some of you are nervous about this," Salant said at one point. "This transcript will not go anywhere. I'm not even sure that you're going to get copies of it. . . . We will really do our best to keep security on this. It is not going to anybody . . . outside of CBS News."

The transcript provides a rare look at a network locked in the throes of introspection. At times the television-news elites erupted in gestures of self-congratulation, patting themselves and each other on their backs as their bosses looked on. Other times their gestures struck targets a bit lower, as they kicked themselves and each other with minimal regard for corporate civility and intramural sensitivity.

The transcript shows the CBS News celebrities making no attempt to conceal their contempt for the corporate heads who ruled their destiny from the dark-glassed Manhattan skyscraper they call "Black Rock." It shows them attacking the decisions of their CBS network bosses—and at times attacking each other's work as well.

There is Mike Wallace's jab at Walter Cronkite's campaign specials, Cronkite's confrontation with his executive bosses, Eric Sevareid's blast at Roger Mudd, Salant's embarrassment with a Dan Rather convention piece, a young Lesley Stahl's naïve first look at the realities of big-time politics, and, finally, Sevareid's rather poignant closing lament on the decline of his own role as a convention commentator and his loss of place and face on the broadcasts of CBS.

That long day in which CBS turned its practiced eye on itself provides a rare insight into just what moves a network's news elite—and a sharp reminder of just how little America's news networks have actually moved in the decade that followed in the way they cover presidents and campaigns.

And the CBS transcript of that long day provides outsiders with a rare opportunity to put their own eye to the keyhole of those closed doors of CBS's Plaza suite.

As Walter Cronkite sat surrounded by his fellow CBS Olympians, he seemed to feel that he was being cast in the role of the team javelin catcher. One after another, spears launched by his colleagues seemed aimed at the news presentation over which he publicly presided. After about an hour, Cronkite, clearly displeased by the pointed remarks and the tone of the day, interrupted to demand: "What is different about the criticism today? And why are we more obsessed with it today than we have been after '72, '68, '64, '60?"

And then, just a few minutes later, America's most revered television-news anchor flatly accused his bosses of having been "manipulated" by the politicians and the network critics into holding the very session that was commanding their daylong presence in the Plaza suite.

Cronkite's charge touched off the most tense moment of the day, those who attended recall. Quite clearly, one man's introspection seemed to be another's inquisition.

The moment had begun innocuously, with comments from a veteran producer and a fledgling star. The first speaker (who was apparently senior producer Sylvia Westerman, although the transcript is not precise in identifying her), observed:

"To me the most ironic thing about this meeting and this . . . uproar of criticism and critique . . . is that we all know what we did last fall.

We sat down and had a bunch of meetings, saying 'Okay, how do we cover this campaign better? We deal with the issues.' . . . We were proud of the fact that we were trying to do it that way. . . . And here we are at the end with everybody saying we didn't. Now there are only two possibilities to me. Either we don't know how to do what we set out to do; or the other explanation . . . [is] that there simply really were no issues, and it isn't our fault. . . ."

That prompted the network's youngest future star, Lesley Stahl, to speak up. She had just played her first major role in a presidential campaign, having earned the respect of her bosses with her coverage of the Senate Watergate hearings.

"Sylvia," Stahl said, "I think the truth is that the candidates have learned to manipulate us almost ninety-nine and a half percent—"

Stahl was interrupted by two voices. The first, unidentified, called out, "Here, here. Absolutely." The second was Cronkite, who seemed to be so upset, his remarks lacked their usual clarity of organization.

"Inclusing—including manipulating us into this meeting," said Cronkite. "I mean, they've manipulated us into this fact that—that it's not the—the message but the medium, again. That we—that we're responsible—"

"Walter—" (Senior vice-president for news William Small tried unsuccessfully to cut Cronkite off.)

"—for their having a dull campaign."

When one's corporate carpet is suddenly yanked without warning, the first priority is to regain one's balance; the second, to regain one's dignity; the third, to regain the floor. And so, the network executives fell all over themselves to explain, in a flurry of frantic footwork that was both instinctive and imperative.

SMALL: Walter, listen—listen to me.
SALANT: Bill, let—let's—this meeting—
SMALL: This meeting was not meant—

Amid the sputtering and stuttering, it was the stentorian tones of the network's star commentator, Eric Sevareid, that made themselves heard. The snow-crested, Brahman-casted Sevareid, whose nightly job was to put into proper context events large and small, dryly observed: "We've made it interesting."

Indeed they had. Two executives, William Small and news vice-president Robert Chandler, who had overseen much of the political coverage that year, went on to explain to Cronkite that the meeting was merely intended to discuss ways the network might have covered the campaign differently. Just a useful exercise, only an overview.

Finally, news president Salant dealt directly with Cronkite's barbed contention. "Let me for one minute address myself to that because this is my baby," Salant said. "Nobody manipulated me into this. I decided that we would have this long before the spate of criticism came out, from any source. I wasn't manipulated into it . . ."

"Knowingly," Cronkite interjected.

These were contentious, unsettled times. Watergate had claimed a president. Vietnam had claimed two nations. And Jimmy Carter had just reclaimed the presidency for the Democrats, with an appeal built upon the Pollyannish proposition that what America needed most was a government that is as kind and decent and *filled with love as the American people are.*

Times at CBS were equally unsettled. Mandatory retirement would soon claim Salant. Speculators were laying open claim to inside knowledge about who would inherit Cronkite's anchorship (the change was still one presidential campaign away). And the television networks were feeling, not without reason, that they were under heavy attack. It was coming especially from America's politically conservative right. It seemed aimed especially at CBS.

Consider the way Salant had chosen to open this day of introspection. "I just happened to pull out, in preparation for this, a series of articles that . . . are just typical of what we're going to see," he said amid the clatter of coffee cups and earnest munching of the Plaza Hotel's danish. "We get blamed for everything—trivialization in the campaign, apathy—from all sides, both left and right. I don't think any of you have yet seen probably the most bitter one of all." He told them about it: Conservative Kevin Phillips's column in the latest issue of *TV Guide* was urging a new law regulating and restraining television network news coverage of elections and campaigns.

Just a week before, the same magazine carried another lightning bolt that struck at the networks from the Republican right: Author Patrick Buchanan, an ex-Nixon White House hard-liner who would survive to launch his political salvos from the Reagan White House, had charged that CBS had blatantly ignored conservative military views and urged the government to retaliate by pulling the license of a CBS-owned station. In a rare admission, the *TV Guide* itself was moved to print an editorial apologizing for having published Buchanan's "unfairness"; the apology was carried on the page opposite the new Phillips thunderclap.

That was the way it was in November 1976.

The CBS transcript remains remarkable reading years later because it shows clearly that the concerns of the network personalities and executives after the campaign of 1976 remained the concerns of the network people after the campaign of 1984. The complaints of the critics in 1976 remained the complaints of the critics in 1984. (And if the campaign strategists have their way, these will be the same concerns and complaints that will be heard after the campaigns of 1988 and 1992 and 1996 as well.)

In 1976, Jimmy Carter had gotten great video mileage all spring and summer out of made-for-television events that were heavy on rural Americana and light on real issues. His celebrations of Plains, Georgia, ran the gamut from redneck chic to redneck shtick, as he appeared before backdrops of peanut farms and softball fields and that Tinkertoy train depot in the heart of his hometown that had been refurbished just for the sake of campaign television. Gerald Ford, meanwhile, was wrapping himself in the protective coloration of the White House Rose Garden in an effort to seem more presidential to a nation of television viewers that had come to doubt the abilities of their accidental president.

In 1984, Ronald Reagan rode the tube to new political heights, with prepackaged videos that took him to stockcar races and boyhood reminiscences and military fields of valor and sporting fields of celebration. He showed Ford and Carter how an incumbent president can avoid dealing with the issues that are his responsibility as long as he can create compelling picture events.

In 1976, the CBS summiteers discussed whether they had been had by the candidates and their strategists, whether they had paid too much attention to visuals and cosmetics, too little attention to issues and substance. There were grand resolves pronounced, but the campaign coverage of 1980 saw only modest changes made.

By 1984, CBS decision-makers had developed what they called a "plan"—really it was not a plan but a general agreement—that *The CBS Evening News with Dan Rather* would try to avoid the lure of those artificially created events that are low in news content and high in imagery. The news-program decision-makers vowed early in 1984 that they would try to make their decisions on which stories to air, and how prominently they should be played, based on the stories' news value, not their visual aesthetics. (The CBS plan, its successes and its shortcomings, is discussed in detail elsewhere in this book. For now, it should be noted that much of the time, CBS followed its plan—much to the consternation of its correspondents and producers in the field who wanted to get their stories on the air each evening. Other times the plan was not followed, much to the consternation of others at the network and critics outside.)

But even at that, in 1984, all three networks made news judgments that seemed to be based on goals of entertaining viewers—that traditional television goal of holding the regulars and attracting the dial spinners—rather than informing viewers. They did not delve deeply enough into the decisions and consequences of the president's policies and the challenger's alternatives. Too often in 1984 the networks lost sight of the fact that *news* is more than just what has happened on a given day that can be captured on videotape. *News* is also the story of what is *really* going on, the decisions and their consequences which the politicians would prefer not to see on the evening news (and which network officials are fond of saying are often hard for them to air because there are no good pictures of those pivotal policy decisions and debates that happen behind the closed doors of government).

But what happened behind the closed doors of the CBS summit of 1976 can be seen through the keyhole in the network transcript of the event. It paints a vivid picture of the in-house debates of one television network's best and brightest. It shows that television's most prominent newspeople were beginning to realize that at least some politicians were becoming adept at having their way with the networks that were attempting to cover them. It shows them first pinning the blame on their executive bosses, and finally pinning the blame on their colleagues.

THE SPIRIT OF '76

The morning's coffee and collegiality had been chilled by Cronkite's charge that his bosses had been manipulated by the politicians into holding this day of inhouse instrospection/inquisition. The meeting proceeded only after a network diplomat artfully suggested that instead of opening with criticism, perhaps everyone should first cite examples of CBS's "outstanding achievements of coverage" so the network figures could focus on some things they should emulate in the future.

That seemed a good way out of a tense situation. And Cronkite, in the spirit of corporate ecumenism, sought to smooth things with network-news president Salant. "Dick, since we are on the record here in a sense for posterity—our heirs at CBS News anyway—let me make clear I wasn't suggesting you were personally manipulated by somebody into calling this meeting," Cronkite said. "I was talking about our all philosophically being manipulated into the belief that we—that somehow we were the cause of a campaign that was basically issueless and basically dull. That's the manipulation I was talking about . . . not any personal manipulation."

And that said, CBS blinked and turned its eye on the good news of its campaign coverage of 1976, for the time being, at least.

Looking back on it all, it is easy to see how the distinguished CBS anchorman—a fellow who, after all, was admired more than presidents and potentates, according to public-opinion polls—had come to feel maligned by the turn the discussion had taken almost from the start. It was a case of a good intention gone bad. Salant had brought in Norman Isaacs, the well-known former editor of the *Louisville Courier-Journal*, to provide what was described as a print perspective of television's year of news coverage. Salant had hoped to thus get the network minds percolating; he got the network fuses smoldering instead. That was because Isaacs's perspective was to suggest that what CBS should have done that fall was to have an in-depth half-hour show each week that would have been a "campaign-and-issues thing."

The trouble was, CBS had done just that—with a series of campaign specials anchored by Cronkite. Cronkite's special reports ran that autumn on Fridays at seven-thirty P.M. But because that time slot traditionally belongs to the local stations, some 150 local CBS affiliate stations had not carried the special reports, much to the continued consternation of Cronkite and others. Thus Isaacs's comments served mainly to ignite a powder keg that had been primed for explosion months ago, as the network people were reminded just how many viewers there were who were like Norman Isaacs and had never even been aware that those CBS special campaign-report programs existed.

The famous names at the Plaza suite were quick to blame the faceless corporate executives at Black Rock for having dictated that poor time slot and for having a general disinterest in all things newsworthy. And that had touched off the first revealing exchange between the CBS news president and the CBS anchor extraordinaire.

SALANT: Whatever were the limitations, the constraints, whatever we did wrong . . . I think it's much too easy for us to take Black

Rock as the scapegoat. I didn't find any lack of support there, significant lack of support. Sure, it would be nice to have an hour of news [instead of the nightly half hour]. It isn't their fault that we don't have it. . . . It would have been nice to get better clearance for our half-hour [specials]. It isn't their fault.

CRONKITE: Why isn't it? . . . Why do they start us at seven-thirty on Friday night? Now isn't that their fault?

SALANT: No.

CRONKITE: We selected seven-thirty Friday night?

SALANT: Absolutely not. That isn't their fault, Walter. That's the fault of . . . the system.

CRONKITE: The what?

SALANT: Of the system. The nature of the beast.

CRONKITE: Well, they're the managers of the system.

After a brief side excursion, Salant moved once more to defend the powers of Black Rock. Someone—apparently veteran producer Don Hewitt (the guiding hand behind the *60 Minutes* show)—said: "I submit again that William S. Paley and Jack Schneider and Bub Wussler decided it. We don't decide it."

SALANT: Don, that's so easy. This simply is not true.

VOICE: A hundred fifty stations didn't take . . . [the special reports].

SALANT: That's not Paley's fault. That's not Schneider's fault.

And at that point, CBS's celebrated correspondent Mike Wallace fired a salvo at Cronkite's special reports. "Might be our fault because it wasn't very interesting," Wallace said.

The discussion had taken a new tack. Wallace went on in his criticism of the Cronkite specials to offer a suggestion:

"I would love to see . . . that seven-thirty half hour be devoted to nothing in the world but having four or five or six of our correspondents . . ." (Someone chimed in with a "Here, here!") "Why in the world don't we have a Mudd and a [Ed] Bradley and a Stahl and a [Bruce] Morton and so forth . . . sit down and just talk. . . . We know so much more than we have space to tell. And we're never given that damn space."

An unidentified voice added: "Those are the deadliest programs in the world."

ISSUES VERSUS PICTURES: 1976

The talk turned to whether the candidates' campaign of 1976 had been issueless or whether the networks' coverage had been issueless. It prompted two interesting revelations:

(1) The publicly restrained commentator, Sevareid, made no effort in private to conceal his clear disgust at the campaigns of the two candidates, America's thirty-eighth and thirty-ninth presidents.

(2) The news president, Salant, came out foursquare against the fact that television had begun airing campaign balloons and handshakes in place of campaign issues and news, and in the end he criticized his network's performance on the issues.

Neither man's views, it turned out, changed the course of video history.

This portion of the discussion began with Salant expressing the view that was most popular with television people then (and is now). He took the position that the low quality of the campaign coverage was due to the candidates, not the coverage.

SALANT: . . . We can't be called on to make a silk purse out of a sow's ear.

SEVAREID: That's it, exactly. . . . We made the candidates more interesting than they are. And the shortcomings of the candidates . . . has been visited upon us. . . . The candidates had no message.

SALANT: . . . The main change I would make if I had the courage, in the future—

SEVAREID: Change the candidates [that prompted general laughter].

SALANT: —is on these atrocious days . . . where people will pop in from city to city for photo opportunities [and] say nothing new —I would simply say if they did that . . . [we should] not bother with the pictures of the crowds and not bother with working the fences and not bother with the balloons and not bother with finding three sentences of the same old stuff. Simply report that they said nothing [again, laughter].

At that point, Salant's vice-president for news, William Small, noted that CBS had taken just such a position concerning the vice-presidential candidates that year. Ford's running mate, Senator Robert Dole of Kansas, had been the vanguard of the hard line, frequently on the attack and thus frequently on the evening news. Carter's running mate, Walter Mondale of Minnesota, had loyally roasted the same Democratic chestnuts each campaign day, saying little that was new or newsworthy.

SMALL: That's an example of how you can't win with your critics. We reported much more Dole than Mondale. And we started to get letters saying, "How come you never tell us about Mondale?"

CRONKITE: Our editors began to be concerned about that. I was the one who kept saying that there's no story in Mondale today. And some of my producers [kept] saying, "Well, we haven't had Mondale on all week."

SALANT: This is precisely one of the reasons here I would urge . . . that you report: "We don't have Mondale on today because he kept doing the same old stuff, saying nothing new." . . . That's important.

Meanwhile, at the White House, President Gerald Ford was doing new stuff while saying nothing new—and it seemed to have worked very well as he turned up night after night on the evening network news. It is worth a brief digression to recall how it happened, for this was the harbinger of video games to come.

DAYS OF WHINE AND ROSES

It had not taken the news media long to catch on to the video game in the fall of 1976, even though they never figured out whether to play or pass. While candidate Jimmy Carter spent September 6 campaigning in Georgia and South Carolina and Virginia, President Gerald Ford spent the day campaigning in the Oval Office. While Carter spent September 7 campaigning in New York and Connecticut and Pennsylvania, Ford was campaigning in the Rose Garden signing a disaster bill, and in the Rose Garden signing a child day-care bill as the cameras caught the moment for posterity or at least the evening news. While Carter spent September 8 campaigning through Pennsylvania and the District of Columbia and Ohio, Ford was campaigning in his own backyard, making himself available to cameras on the White House lawn.

The press had dubbed it the Rose Garden campaign. But Ford's September of 1976 actually had its origins in June, in a White House memo that proposed a "No Campaign" campaign. The memo, written to then–White House chief of staff Richard Cheney by two aides, Michael Duval and Foster Chanock (a bright young adviser who would die of cancer not long after the campaign), suggested a way of countering what the president's advisers had concluded was a public perception that Ford just was not presidential and not up to the job.

> Sensitive/No Distribution
>
> June 11, 1976
> MEMORANDUM FOR: Dick Cheney
> FROM: Mike Duval/Foster Chanock
> SUBJECT: "No Campaign" Strategy
>
> The best strategy for the President to win in November . . . may be for him to announce after the Republican Convention that he will not actively campaign for the Presidency. He would . . . go back to work as President with no campaign activities whatsoever. . . . An alternative is to announce a highly truncated campaign schedule.
>
> Reasons for Adopting This Strategy
> . . . The polls continue to show that issues are not a decisive campaign factor. The voters continue to react to personality traits and themes. . . .
>
> The Result of the Strategy
> . . . Although the press would be initially confused and very skeptical and distrusting of this decision, they would nevertheless have to report the President's actions as being Presidential. This could result in a very favorable contrast between Ford as President and his rival as a campaigner. . . .

The way this Rose Garden campaign (or No Campaign campaign) had appeared on the network-television news night after night was almost, but not quite, what the Ford strategists had planned. The networks carried Ford's frequent presentations and ceremonial cameos that used the White House as a backdrop; but every time one of these would-be "presidential" events appeared on CBS, a "Campaign '76" logo was superimposed on the screen. It was the same logo that was used for Jimmy Carter's campaign stump appearances.

Now, as the CBS dignitaries pondered their coverage in the summit at the Plaza, it turned out that the network's use of that Campaign '76 logo for White House events bothered some of them. This became apparent after William Small noted that "Carter complains that we tried to make Ford look presidential when he was in the Rose Garden," but, he added, White House correspondent Bob Schieffer, who is one of television's most able newspeople, had made a point of always putting the event in the context of how Ford was campaigning by trying to be presidential.

SALANT: Yeah, and we slapped on the Campaign '76 logo.
CRONKITE: As a matter of fact, that was so repetitious. I began to get a little worried about we were loading it the other way around—that maybe, you know, he's entitled to stay one day or so in the White House.
SEVAREID: He was entitled to be president once in a while [laughter].
SALANT: I'm glad you spoke up there, Eric.
SEVAREID: I got a little nervous, as Walter did, about that.

But while the CBS luminaries were worried about whether they had been unfair to characterize these events as the politics they in fact were, Ford's advisers were not at all troubled by the coverage they received. They were, in fact, elated. They didn't care about the flash of logo, they cared about the generous amount of video coverage. "Let's face it, we played to television's problems," said Ford's chief of staff, Richard Cheney, always a candid man. Cheney (who went on to become a prominent Republican congressman from Wyoming) was expressing his jubilation at the television coverage at just about the same time the CBS people were expressing their concerns in the Plaza suite in New York City. "We knew that their measurement of fair treatment was equal time. So we would go out in the Rose Garden and say nothing—just sign a bill—and we'd get the coverage. Issues did not dominate this campaign. Now, people can blame television for that, but we're no more virtuous than they are in that sense. We played it that way."

And Gerald Ford had gained almost twenty-five percentage points in the public-opinion polls that fall, coming within a whisker of winning the election.

Meanwhile, back at the Plaza:

Having spoken up on the subject of campaign logos, Sevareid continued speaking in defense of a class of Americans who were disadvantaged and defenseless at that oval table—maligned politicians. And this time he leveled criticism upon one of the network stars who was not there: Roger Mudd.

"I thought Mudd was terribly harsh from time to time in a very editorial way," said Sevareid, who often took a gentlemanly view of the candidates on that day at the Plaza. "Not all politicians are clowns and fools and full of clay. In fact, it's a pretty rough occupation. And I don't like that constant undertone that we've got to cut these guys down to size. It's [wrong to] presume they are worse than they appear and you must keep pointing that out."

An attack on Mudd in the presence of his bosses was no minor occurrence. Especially an attack questioning his fairness and balance. These were the days when Mudd and Dan Rather were the co-favorites in the speculation about who would succeed Cronkite as the CBS news anchor. Neither was at the Plaza that day. And according to the transcript, no one spoke in support of, or opposition to, Sevareid's view. The coming years would see Rather get the CBS anchorship and Mudd move on to NBC.

In print journalism, campaign coverage usually comes in two forms: articles about strategy (who is winning, who is losing, and how the race is being won or lost); and articles about issues (what the candidates say they will do about the various problems they will face as president or governor or senator or mayor or whatever). Unfortunately, far more stories are devoted to the former than the latter. Reporters like to call these strategy-type stories "horse-race" journalism; politicians often call it by a similar term, changing only the second syllable. The politicians have it about right; much of this sort of journalism has to be shoveled rapidly, for it contributes little to the national good and it often cannot stand the test of time without being remembered more for its aroma than its accuracy.

In television journalism, campaign coverage comes in three forms: pieces about strategy, pieces about issues, and pieces that are driven mainly by their compelling video footage (and which may have little to do with strategy and most surely have little to do with issues or things of such substance or importance).

For the purposes of the Plaza summit of '76, CBS News president Salant commissioned a quick little study that divided the network's stories into two categories: strategy stories and issue stories. And he shared them with his colleagues at the large oval table. The facts as he told them:

From February to November 1976, CBS spent twenty-two hours

on issue stories and forty-four hours on strategy stories on its morning news, evening news, and weekend news broadcasts.

He went on to provide a further breakdown, in figures rounded off to the nearest whole hour:

Morning news—11 hours on issues, 27 hours on nonissues campaign stories; evening news—8 hours on issues, 16 hours on nonissues; weekend news—2 hours on issues, less than an hour on nonissues.

And at that, the CBS officials gave themselves the benefit of the doubt. Salant noted that, explaining how they had categorized, for example, Jimmy Carter's controversial interview in the September 1976 issue of *Playboy* magazine (the one where he said, "I've looked on a lot of women with lust. I've committed adultery in my heart many times."). Said Salant: "We were very generous with ourselves by including that among 'issues.' "

The CBS summit discussion of the issues in 1976 showed much of the problem that the networks have in determining how to deal with the issues in any year. The way CBS approached the issues in 1976 was not unlike the way ABC, NBC, and CBS approached the issues in 1980 and 1984. And the comments of the CBS stars and executives about their coverage in 1976 were echoed by the stars and executives of all three networks as they were interviewed for this book following the 1984 campaign (their comments will be treated in a later chapter).

Discussion of coverage of the issues degenerated quickly into discussions of the way the issues were presented visually. There was little conceptual discussion around the CBS table at the Plaza of just what issues should have been covered and in what depth they should have been addressed.

In 1976 as in 1984, the network executives and talents were content to let the public-opinion polls drive their decisions of issue coverage. They contended that the polls should tell them what issues should be covered. Which means they confused adequate coverage of the issues with telling the public about the things people had told the poll takers they already knew. It becomes a nonvicious circle: People can tell pollsters what issues concern them often because those are the issues that have already been brought to their attention by television; and television then looks at the poll results and concludes that these are the issues that should be aired because they are on the minds of the people. People will usually not mention issues that have gotten scant attention on television, even though these topics might well have become matters of public concern if they had been more thoroughly aired.

Around the 1976 oval table, correspondent Bruce Morton, one of the network's most talented and generally insightful stars, brought up the matter of polls as they relate to issues. The concept of a network poll was a new thing in 1976, and Morton had high praise for the venture that was known on his network as the CBS/*New York Times* poll (and was known at the *Times* as the *New York Times*/CBS poll).

Morton made the transition by noting that after the 1972 campaign of Richard Nixon versus George McGovern, journalists said their biggest failure was that they had talked too much to the pols and not enough to the people. "I thought the [1976] poll was a really good step in that direction," Morton continued. ". . . I don't think it's up to us to say what's important and what the issues are. And that went some way towards finding out what was on the genuine voters' minds. . . . That was something we had not done before and I liked it."

Salant: "Yeah. . . . We got away from this dilemma that bothers me about [television] setting the agenda . . . by defining the issues. We let the people who are the voters find the issues, and then went after them. That, to me, is a very important thing."

When someone cut in to say, "We let the candidates determine the issues to their advantage," Salant responded: "No, no. No, no, that's just exactly what we didn't do by using the polls. We let the people define the issues." What they actually had done, of course, was to let the people define the issues *that they were aware of*—namely, the issues that the candidates were seen talking about on the evening news.

(There was one moment that was a refreshing departure from the sort of thinking that has become television tradition. It was injected by news vice-president Small, who has since made his own departure from network television. Small said that what he liked was that even though the polls showed little public interest in the issues of busing and abortion, CBS included those topics in the one series they did on the issues because the network people thought these were important topics that ought to be laid out before the public.)

But the mention of polls swung the focus of the oval table away from concerns about issues coverage and toward concerns of traditional television.

Someone—the transcript provides no identification—picked up on the mention of polls and went to work. "I came here determined not to play this role, but . . . I don't agree that the poll pieces as seen on the *Evening News* were very good. . . . I think they were badly produced . . . they tried to jam too much information into too brief packages."

That was greeted by a chorus of "Yeah!" "Right!" Among those chiming in, apparently, was polling guru Warren Mitofsky: "I'd like to agree with him."

"You—you agree with me?"

"Absolutely."

The television people were off on another television tack. Sevareid commented: "Once you get down to these questions—'But suppose Ford were running against a left-handed Lithuanian or something, how would you feel?'—you just lose people. You can't absorb all those nuances through the ear alone."

Mitofsky added: "I'm glad we got started with the polls, but I'm very unhappy with the way they were done." What was needed, he said, was a regular reporter and producer assigned to the polling, and the need to avoid "the tendency . . . to bury people in numbers, which I think are uninteresting and very confusing."

And soon others were injecting their video sense into the discussion: "Television's a visual medium . . . put the numbers up there in a graphic . . ." and so on.

The network executives and on-air newspeople would have benefitted significantly from a genuine, hard look at the issues that they covered, the manner and degree to which they were covered, the issues that were not covered sufficiently, and those that were not covered at all. And they would have benefitted from a long conceptual look at what television could and should be doing toward that end, regardless of the video grandstanding and Rose Garden puttering efforts of the candidates.

But the CBS dignitaries, in 1976, carried their summit toward other directions.

THE PRIMARIES

Salant's agenda called for a discussion of the primaries and the way CBS covered them. He opened with a series of provocative questions. Some were of special interest to television journalists, some deserved to be considered by all journalists. They are worth looking at because of the insightful and at times painful analysis they evoked, and because, for all their good intentions and acknowledged errors, the networks went on doing things pretty much the same way and making the same basic mistakes in the campaigns that followed.

Among Salant's questions:

"Most important, did our broadcasts and our hard news coverages . . . play a larger role than it should have in affecting the outcome of subsequent primaries?"

"Did we get roped into the Carter strategy of overemphasizing the importance of Iowa, and then New Hampshire?"

MORTON: We still go up there [to New Hampshire] and we live [there and we] . . . make it bigger than it ought to be.

SALANT: Why do we have a special? Why do we send up the army?

ROBERT CHANDLER (who directed the political coverage): You had ten Democratic candidates vying for the nomination. . . . The first test directly affecting the electorate was New Hampshire's. They all went into New Hampshire. . . . If indeed the primaries are part of that step in securing the nomination, and it involves appealing to the electorate . . . we damn well were right in covering it the way we did.

SEVAREID: Jesus, let's not do this overkill again in New Hampshire. And we had an army up there. I got awfully tired of it. I think . . . it's the Heisenberg principle in physics. A phenomenon observed alters in relation to other phenomena. And I think that's what we do. . . .

[Somebody asked what the alternative was to covering New Hampshire as it had been.]

SEVAREID: . . . This momentum business now . . . We were not as bad as the newspapers. But every day—Carter's got the momentum, now Ford's got the momentum—from some goddamn little [the rest of his reference to New Hampshire was, perhaps diplomatically, indistinct]. How the hell do they know what was happening with eighty million voters?

CRONKITE: . . . But the competitive factor is still there. And if we decided here that New Hampshire wasn't all that important, what can we really do about that if NBC and ABC and *The New York Times* and *The Washington Post*, AP and UP, *Time* magazine and *Newsweek* decide it is? Are we going to ignore the story and say, "Well, we will give it a few minutes on the *Evening News*" . . . ?

SALANT: Well, obviously you're not going to ignore it.
CRONKITE: I don't think we can do that.
SALANT: But I urge that kind of courage, if that's the conclusion.

That kind of courage was not to be found in the coverage of 1980 and 1984, not in the reporting armies of CBS, ABC, or NBC, not in the print-scaled commando units of *The New York Times, The Washington Post*, AP, UPI, *Time, Newsweek*, and *U.S. News and World Report*.

The CBS summiteers, meanwhile, launched into a lengthy discussion on the importance of *being there* on primary night—whether it was worth the expense of it all to truck the entire *Evening News* sets up to New Hampshire and the rest of the primary states just to have the news anchor sitting there on election night. This produced a chorus of "Absolutely!" and an "I do" from Cronkite—to which Chandler asked the question: "Why?"

CRONKITE: For one thing, it indicates the dedication of the news organization involved to covering the story. . . . [It] looks like you're really interested in getting out there and being on the scene and covering it.
MORTON: I agree with you that it's important to be in the state. I mean, you learn things—I do, Eric does—that you can't learn . . . sitting back home. But I don't think it makes any difference where you anchor the broadcast that night from. If everybody flies back to New York that day and does it, I don't see that it makes any difference. And you save a lot of money.
CRONKITE: It's a matter of appearances.

It is also a matter of money. Chandler told the group that CBS spent $1.6 million in 1976 to cover thirty primaries, anchoring on site in New Hampshire, Florida, and California; NBC anchored on site in eight primaries. To cover the 1980 primaries the same way, he estimated, would cost $1.9 million. And to anchor on site in 1980 would cost $2.9 million.

SALANT: . . . I want to record myself as saying it doesn't make any difference at all. . . . I don't think it makes any difference at all, either to the nature of the broadcast or the public perception of our seriousness of purpose.
CHANDLER: Take heart, Walter. Dick's not going to be here.

CRONKITE: But he's leaving such a legacy of strong words on this transcript.

SALANT: Legacy, hell!

ON BEING MANIPULATED

While news president Salant was making a point about how the networks really had not been the unthinking instruments of Jimmy Carter's success, Lesley Stahl was thinking about something that had been called to her attention just a week earlier.

"Yeah, but . . . it has, in fact, gotten to a point where everything . . . everything the candidates do is geared to how it will look on television," she said, adding with emphasis, "and I mean everything—and that was explained to me just a week ago. . . . I'm saying that every time Ford opened his mouth, or every time they planned to have him say or do anything . . . there was a paper written on how CBS would cover it." Sevareid and Salant explained that this was not a new development in the annals of political journalism. Sevareid told her all about Franklin D. Roosevelt's use of radio and the print press. Salant told her reporters should just report the story—"Get hold of that paper and show it."

"I think we've become so predictable that they can, in fact, predict what we're going to do," said Stahl. Around the table, others said they were not concerned that they were being had. Stahl went on to give them an example of why she had come to feel that she was being used by the politicos she covered.

"I remember being absolutely thrilled to get a glimpse at the Ford strategy book . . . someone showed me the first page and the size of it, and let me flip through and look at the charts, and I was just beside myself. And I got to see it for a Friday night issues piece on one of those specials, and reported it. And I was recently told that it was all quite deliberate, and the point was that Ford wanted people to know he had a strategy."

Around the table there was general laughter. Stahl went on: "And I was totally innocent. And then the person who finally confessed this to me just last week said, 'Everything we did was for the media. Everything we did.' "

Someone asked: "Did you doubt that?"

Stahl replied: "Yes. I thought this friend of mine was giving me this. . . . Well, am I being naïve to not to have recognized that . . . ?"

"You're being naïve," someone said.

Stahl: "Yes . . . I'm naïve."
Sevareid spoke: "It's still a story, Lesley. Why should you feel used?"
And Morton: "Don't they try to do that all the time?"
And Chandler: "Aren't you manipulated all week?"

The postmortem at the Plaza moved on to dissect other facets of the network's coverage of the body politic. They spent much of the afternoon on their performance at the Democratic and Republican national conventions and on election night (these are dealt with in the next chapter).

It was well into the afternoon when news president Salant refocused the table's attention on the network's coverage of the news of the presidential campaign.

And that led senior producer Chandler to raise a question: "Did we, in our coverage, by seizing on mistakes . . . did we indeed, as some people have charged, trivialize the campaign?" He specifically asked about television's coverage of Jimmy Carter's controversial *Playboy* magazine interview, Gerald Ford's debate statement that Eastern Europe was not dominated by the Soviets, and Carter's interview comment that he would raise taxes only for people above the median income level.

Salant was critical of CBS's coverage of the *Playboy* interview. "I thought it was an extraordinary interview," he said. "I got a flavor and a knowledge out of reading the whole thing that I didn't get by watching us."

Chandler pressed the same question in a different context. He asked about "Carter's charge: that every time he tried to talk about issues, I mean, his positions, the press wasn't terribly interested, but would start banging away at these [superficial] questions."

Salant responded that this was a "meaningless criticism." Others talked about how the whole campaign had, after all, been about the public's concerns, which were not about issues and specifics but about whether Ford understood the world well enough to be president, or whether Carter was susceptible to "latent bigotry" because he was a Southerner.

Sevareid went back to his view of why it was hard to deal with the specifics of an issue with these candidates. "Now Carter, almost everything he said on an issue you can find a caveat somewhere in his statement," Sevareid said.

Correspondent Bruce Morton agreed. He recalled that after Carter had said, off the cuff, that he would raise taxes above the median income level, a reporter told Carter that "the median income is $14,500—or whatever it is—and Carter said, 'Oh, my heavens, well, I don't know what income I'm talking about,' and just went waffling away, which is what he always does."

AND IN CONCLUSION

In daylong deliberations such as the CBS summit of '76, the most telling observations come not necessarily in formal summations at the end of the day, when everyone is too tired to think deep thoughts, but during the heat of the intramural debates, while opinions can be served fresh off the front burner.

And so it was that midway through one of the discussions of television and the issues, Salant offered this most candid assessment of his network's performance:

"There's one . . . question that runs through our entire coverage, and that is: Could we have done a better job than we did on the issues, of delineating the positions? . . . I continue to think this time around, yeah, we could have done a somewhat better job. It was very difficult, because if the candidates really wanted to talk about issues, we could have done maybe five or ten percent better.

"But it wasn't there and I'm not at all ashamed of—of—of what we did."

FIVE

MORE POSTMORTEM

The divergent voices of network television speak as one when the subject gets around to the quadrennial national conventions of the Democratic and Republican parties. Nobody really likes the way television covers them. Nobody really has a foolproof solution for turning them into good television news.

Part of the problem is that it is hard to make good television news out of something that often is not news at all. For decades now, America's national political conventions have produced no real presidential surprises and, in fact, only a smattering of real secondary-level news.

Still, the television networks wade into the Democratic and Republican conventions every four years with more commitment and battle plans than the United States had when it waded into Vietnam. And the networks then spend lavishly in self-promoting commercials designed to convince the masses that one of the truly worthwhile events of the history of the world is taking place, and only they are covering it in true depth.

So the CBS powers and personalities provided us with something of an eye-opener for the masses when they got around to talking in true candor with each other about what they really thought of the conventions in general and their coverage of them in particular.

The Knights of the Oval Table had returned from a brief respite for restroom and other relaxations when their leader, Salant, asked the group to focus on the way they had covered the conventions, and called for a volunteer to open the discussion.

"I would vote for limited coverage, doing an hour a night or something like that," said Bruce Morton, whose work at all things, from contested conventions to cakewalks, has always been distinguished by thoughtful and artful prose. This might have sounded like heresy, but it attracted some advocates—notably Mike Wallace. Others of prominence—notably Walter Cronkite—held the line in behalf of the unlimited, all-seeing eye.

MORTON: Seems to me we ought to try covering it on the . . . basis of how newsy it is, which means, for instance, that a 1964 Democratic Convention would be covered by, oh, maybe an hour a night or something like that, because it was just plain dull. And a genuinely contested convention, like the Republican one this year [where Ronald Reagan still had a chance of wresting the nomination from Gerald Ford] would be covered relatively freely.

CRONKITE: I think, aside from the story, that it's a great quadrennial exercise in our democratic procedures, a chance for us to deliver our once-every-so-often civics lesson on how this country runs and operates. . . . And therefore it has a value beyond the actual news story of each session. I also think there's god-awful problems in trying to plan coverage on the basis of whether or not a session is going to be interesting or not interesting.

WALLACE: Is this totally impractical? I know we can hardly get in cahoots with the two parties. . . . But is it possible to start now with a dialogue with the politicians which might persuade them to have the first two days of the convention during the daytime . . . say, from ten to five or ten to six, and in the hours of those two days, we cover everything and publish nothing, and do an eight to eleven [recap] on Monday and Tuesday? And then for . . . Wednesday and Thursday nights, they go nighttime and we give them gavel-to-gavel coverage?

SALANT: They prefer three hours of prime time than the whole day full of live coverage. [There is considerable cross talk and then Salant goes on to discuss the philosophic matter of the civics-lesson argument Cronkite had made.] . . . Are we journalists or are we teachers?

MORTON: The Watergate hearings were an important civics lesson, and they rotated [with each network televising one day's session], as I recall. It may be that there's a moral in that.

SALANT: . . . Oh, rotation! Rotation, of course. . . . Rotation is out of the question. . . . It's permissible legally only where your function is purely a transmission function, as it was in Watergate. We are at least partially, and I think more than that, fulfilling a journalistic role in convention coverage. Each of us have different judgments. Each of us have different things to say. We are not staying only on the rostrum, which would be the pure transmission function. So I think it would be a terrible thing from the whole point of view of a free, independent press and a variety of voices on which a free press is postured. . . . Rotation is simply unacceptable legally, I think, and journalistically.

[Salant offered a comment on the recent experience of ABC, which, as others had noted, tried a limited coverage concept that it has since abandoned.] . . . The ABC thing, I think we all agree, doesn't work, because they get stuck with recapping something at the very moment something important might happen. The going in and out live just by our pressing a button, having complete control, and which I dream about from time to time and proposed many, many years ago, will only work if the network devises a special program which is in effect a variety show, where you could move in and out. You can't move in and out on the regular schedule and chop up these damned things that, you know, the public gets absorbed in, and then jerk them out ten minutes before Kojak does whatever he does to resolve the story. It simply isn't practical. And they've never been able to devise a variety show —they don't know how to do it—that would allow us to give sixty-seconds notice to Ed Sullivan. . . . And I come to the conclusion that . . . it's like Churchill's democracy, you know: It's the worst system in the world, but consider the alternatives. . . .

CRONKITE: Also, the greatest function of television is being able to take people there. . . . This is good journalism to take them there, and let them be there and experience being there simultaneously with the event, not on tape.

The discussion went on for some time, rolling and rambling, bouncing from observation to observation, anecdote to anecdote, much like a silver pinball making its way from cushion to cushion, flipper to flipper, descending slowly through the agenda only to be thrust back to the top again by an old story or reminiscence, and then making its way through a new set of telling diversions, descending toward the inevitable bottom line that marks the way the game is played.

In a sense, the anecdotal diversions about conventions and television told as much about the magnetism that pulls and pushes the network powers and personalities as anything else. Because, as we have seen in the years of convention coverage that followed, the bottom line in this and all other such network discussions was that they would continue to cover conventions just about the way they had always done them, even though they did not really like what they were doing and did not necessarily approve of the way they were doing it.

So follow the bouncing ball:

One of those side discussions developed on the merits of recapping a day's worth of convention as opposed to televising it live.

SEVAREID: Why must we make the functioning of democracy, which is the most boring political system on earth, why should we try to make it unboring? One of the great fundamental civics lessons in the democratic society is to teach the discipline in enduring boredom. . . . When I started doing this little act I do on the evening news, it was the conviction of various of my superiors that nobody could sit still for two minutes listening to a talking head; TV was pictures. Well, they seem to have listened, whether to me or somebody else. They seem to have sat still. . . . We don't have to *Reader's Digest* everything in life, you know.

[After some side discussion Mike Wallace got back to that point.]

WALLACE: Did it ever occur to you that you drive people away from your civics lessons by overcoverage? . . . That you might give them a better civics lesson by doing [less].

Wallace went on to wonder whether there was any pressure from above for change. "I don't know what our betters in Black Rock think," he said. (To which Salant interjected: "Can we call them our associates?" Which prompted someone to add: "Our lessers over there.") Wallace went on: "Is there some appetite for change from over there?" Not so far as anyone outside Black Rock knew, he was told.

At another point, as they took issue with their own convention coverage, someone provoked much mirth in trying to note that much of what networks televise live at conventions are not matters of momentous proportion. "How do we justify interrupting some perfectly good quiz show or whatever it is for the arrival in Kansas City of

Ronald Reagan, an event that has no significance at the moment?" this unidentified speaker asked, amid laughter that was duly noted in the transcript.

Salant replied: "If we start weighing the importance of what's on the network—entertainment—and what we might do or could do, we'd wipe them out . . . because nothing they do is important."

And that prompted another telling side exchange. An unidentified participant recalled one of those immortal lines of in-house television—this one uttered by NBC's former news president Reuven Frank after he had been asked why the networks spend so much time and money on political conventions. The NBC executive's answer, as recalled by this CBS personage: "For the same reason that people used to dance the minuet—we know the steps."

Shortly, another bit of NBC lore was spilled out onto the CBS table. It came after Salant, responding to a question, said that CBS spent about 10 percent of its total 1976 news budget on the Democratic and Republican conventions, about $8–9 million out of an overall news budget of $82–83 million.

That prompted a fascinating comment that no doubt will have a nationful of network and local television corporation chief executive officers saying "I told you so." The speaker's identity was not listed in the transcript, but according to those who were at the 1976 session, it was the late George Murray, a senior producer of convention and campaign coverage who had come to CBS from NBC.

MURRAY: In 1972, at NBC, I cut the convention budget almost in half and accomplished virtually the same thing.

UNIDENTIFIED: You did?

MURRAY: Yeah. A year later I got fired, but— [He was interrupted by a roomful of laughter.]

SEVAREID: There's a valuable lesson. [More laughter.]

SALANT: Well, we'd like to think we hired you away.

MURRAY: The news division did not get the five million dollars that we saved. [He said the savings were achieved by making cuts in technical areas.] . . . I covered it pretty much on the concept that we cover a Super Bowl.

There was, as Salant saw it, a consensus of sorts. "The consensus is that we ought to keep on going with full coverage . . . with some important people disagreeing," the news president said. "Assuming that kind of complete coverage, are we doing it the right way? . . .

Are we making the right choices? Should we be on the rostrum longer? Are we emphasizing the right things?"

Cronkite had some criticism. He thought that the network spent too much time televising stories away from the rostrum, especially while the seconding speeches for the presidential nominees were being made. He didn't think that these stories away from the rostrum were being covered as deeply as they should have been.

"I think with some of the rostrum speeches . . . some we ought to carry that we don't carry," said Cronkite. . . . "I think that when we're not on the rostrum, we don't always do the best job of covering the convention off the floor, in putting into focus particularly the impact of local politics on the decisions that are made. . . . I think, in other words, our coverage is not deep enough when we're off the rostrum."

He went on. Talking about the seconding speeches, Cronkite said: "This is one of the places where I think we are wrong. Frequently, the parade of seconding speeches, which are not that long in themselves, are a rather interesting demonstration of where the candidate expects to get his support. . . . You're introducing a cast of characters that are presumably going to carry through for the next four years at least and play some role in the party's future. I think by passing these people, we're missing that opportunity to introduce them. . . ."

Salant pressed Cronkite for specifics on his other criticism, that floor reporting is not deep enough, good enough. Cronkite blamed unspecified decision-makers and not the reporters. "I'm sure that our reporters know these stories," he said. "Bruce knows them. Lesley knows them. They're there. But we get caught up in the excitement of floor reporting, kind of reacting to events of the moment, to the exclusion of these background stories—what's going on within the delegations and what their effect is on the politics of that state back home. . . . I think our reporters know those stories. We're not giving them the opportunity to go on with those stories . . ."

Salant pressed again.

SALANT: I'm trying to pinpoint this. Do they offer those stories and they get turned down? [Or] they just figure they're going to be turned down so they don't offer them? Or what do we do?

CRONKITE: I can't answer that. I don't know.

Later, an unidentified but clearly corporately concerned participant brought the discussion back to bottom-line basics. "I know that's a very mundane thing to bring into a conversation like this, but there are portions of the convention when we can't put commercials on," the speaker said. "Now, we can't put them on during ballots, which run for more than an hour; we can't put them on during keynote speeches and stuff; but we have to get some commercials in. And the only way to get them in during those nominating procedures is to get them into the seconding speeches. It's a practical problem, but it exists."

SALANT: Overwhelmed with reason, Walter. What's your response to that?

CRONKITE: Just that it seems to be terribly embarrassing when we have to say, you know, "There's one of the up-and-coming members of this party, selected for this—whoop!—we'll be right back after this word from our sponsor."

Salant moved on to a matter of embarrassment that seemed to be uniquely his. It was his professional embarrassment over the way CBS covered some breaking stories on the convention floor in general—and embarrassment over the way Dan Rather covered one such story in particular.

First he spoke of the generality: "It's probably the only situation where we put ourselves in the position of broadcasting to the public our pursuit of a story, where the story may fizzle out entirely. And so they watch us as we futilely pursue a story that doesn't pan out."

Then he got down to the particular: "I was talking about Dan Rather's story on . . . Rogers Morton. . . . I was embarrassed!"

A little background is in order. At the time of the 1976 Republican Convention, Dan Rather was a premier CBS correspondent, assigned to *60 Minutes* and major moments like the political conventions, a high-profile way station en route to succeeding Walter Cronkite as anchor of the evening news after the 1980 campaign. The late Rogers C. B. Morton, whose résumé was studded with high-level formers—former Republican congressman from Maryland, former secretary of the interior, former chairman of the Republican National Committee—was President Ford's campaign chairman.

At the convention, Ronald Reagan's challenge to Ford's presidential nomination was still alive, barely, and in the rules fight that would be the key test, the votes of Mississippi's delegation had become pivotal. In the face of that, Rogers Morton had breakfasted with a group of reporters and the result was a story in the *Birmingham News*, which ran under the headline FORD WOULD WRITE OFF COTTON SOUTH? and which quoted Morton to the effect that Ford would spend little effort in fighting Democratic nominee Jimmy Carter of Georgia in the Deep South.

Live from the convention floor, Dan Rather interviewed Morton, who denied he had ever said Ford would write off the South. And, cleverly seizing the moment, Rather—on the air—suggested that Morton ought to walk with him to the Mississippi delegation to clear up the whole matter once and for all. As the cameras rolled, Rather and Morton slowly made their way across the crowded convention floor toward Mississippi, with Morton stopping now and then to talk to pols, and the cameras and microphones of CBS staying with the correspondent and the campaign manager all the while. At Ford's headquarters the proceeding was being watched with all due horror, and finally someone got a call through to a state-delegation telephone as Morton was passing by; Morton was told to cease and desist, to free himself of Rather and find some safe sanctuary away from the convention-hall floor before he made Ford's political matters infinitely worse. And so Morton meandered off, with Rather and CBS still in tow, but he was clearly going nowhere near Mississippi, and Rather's story was clearly going nowhere.

That was the background. Now, as Salant proclaimed his embarrassment, Rather's handling of the story was defended by others around the table. And soon the network elites got themselves into a real donnybrook over whether CBS had been conned—live and in color—or had taken America to the very cutting edge of great video journalism.

It was Salant versus the rest of the table.

SALANT: . . . We kept the cameras on while he wended his way across the floor and Morton stopped and talked to this guy and that guy and the other guy, and never wound up to where he was going because he decided against it.

UNIDENTIFIED: Had lots of good moments in it.

UNIDENTIFIED: Listen, what's wrong with that?

SALANT: I think it's a waste of time!

SEVAREID: . . . How do you know how the hell a live event's going to turn out before it even starts to happen? Newspapers don't have that problem.

UNIDENTIFIED: Was the thing that bothered you that we followed the story, or that Morton was really following Rather?

SALANT: No, no. That didn't bother me. . . . But we spent all that time with him stopping along the floor and chatting with this guy and chatting with that guy—

UNIDENTIFIED: And one of those chats was a phone call where they said, "Get out of there! Don't do it!"

SALANT: We never recorded that, Bob.

CHORUS OF UNIDENTIFIED VOICES: We did! We did!

SALANT: No sir, we did not. We did not! [Indistinct] showed no phone call at all.

ROBERT CHANDLER *(senior producer)*: Of course we did. . . .

SALANT: We did not. You go back and look at the transcript. . . . We could have put that story together much better.

CHANDLER: I couldn't disagree more.

SALANT: You look up the transcript. We never said that he got a phone call telling him not to . . .

CHANDLER: We showed him on the phone, and then we—

SALANT: But [we] never explained what he was doing on the phone. And this is—this is not journalism.

CRONKITE: Yeah, I believe he did say [there was a] phone call. Didn't Dan say that was a phone call?

WILLIAM SMALL *(vice-president for news)*: Rather said he—he had been told that—he should not go to [the] Mississippi [delegation]. . . .

SALANT: No, he didn't. No, he didn't! And I'll bet you, anybody, any kind of meal, that he didn't.

They continued in that high standard of tone and content for some time before Salant offered his final word: "I—I think we've exhausted this. I'm in a minority of one. . . . Let's go on to another subject."

There was, it turned out, one other subject that would provoke discussion and discord. It was a subject of surprising nature, raised by what many would say was a most unlikely source. Consider this sentence:

"If I were running a political party, I'd ban television from the floor of the convention—from the aisles of the convention."

The speaker was not Spiro T. Agnew in his glory days or Jesse Helms on any day. It was Walter Cronkite, on this November day in 1976, tabling one last matter for his colleagues at the Plaza.

Cronkite spoke with seriousness and sobriety, offering the sort of critical examination and self-correction that is so often needed and so seldom tendered in all professions, including his.

"I would think that it would be a much more meaningful series of interviews that we got from the floor if we did them in the perimeter . . . in the back of the hall," he said, "rather than have the aisles clogged with electronic equipment, making a display and a show of what we're doing and what we're after, rather than . . . [we should attempt] to get a serious interview with these people. I think you'd get anybody off that floor that you wanted, with an occasional exception, obviously. But you'd get most of those people off of the floor, a thirty-second walk back to the back of the hall into the CBS booth at the end of each aisle. And you'd get something—you'd have a more orderly procedure."

Mike Wallace voiced reservations. He cited several recent convention stories that he felt would have been missed if there had been no floor interviews. Then network-news vice-president Small spoke. "This will surprise Dick [Salant], but I agree philosophically with Walter on this one," said Small. "I think that while indeed there have been important moments that we could not have gotten—remember, Mike, was it . . . eight years ago . . . when [John] Connally was still a Democrat and he was key to some issue . . . and you walked in the aisle with him, remember, and sat him down and finally got an interview?

". . . But we don't do this in any other event. If we cover a congressional hearing, it's unthinkable that we interview senators, for example, while it's going on, or walk up the aisle and interview a witness who's waiting to be heard or whatever. [Every time we have done it] it has always made me uncomfortable.

". . . The best argument, however, on the other side of that is that we are a participant in conventions in a rather strange way; and that is, when you have a contested issue, people who are delegates realize . . . that if they want to make a point, they can really make it more impressively frequently by getting interviewed on a network than by speaking from the floor. Look at the '68 [Democratic] convention with the Vietnam dissidents. They sought out those floor reporters to make known a point of view. And it was important, in that if you had had the kind of control that [then House Speaker and convention chairman] Carl Albert would have liked to exercise, they'd have never gotten to us.

"And the danger, of course, [of] our even suggesting to a party that we be kept off the floor is that then you take the next step, Walter, which is to keep us from having an area in the back."

* * *

In the years that have followed that meeting at the Plaza, Cronkite's idea to banish the networks from the convention floor has gathered no momentum, just dust. But it is an idea whose time will surely come. The impetus will not come from forward-thinking professionals seeking self-policing in the name of self-improvement; it will come from the simple fact that there is now a profusion of electronic news-gathering organizations covering conventions. There are new networks of cable and other varieties, and mainly there is the profusion of local stations from around the country who come with their satellite uplinks and expect the access that was once accorded just the big three. Convention-floor passes for print reporters have long been rationed—only a fixed number are given out, and they are good for only a half hour or so. As freedom of access is buried by fear of gridlock, television will be forced to face up to reform for reasons far less noble than those voiced by Cronkite (and backed by Small).

With television interviews conducted just off the floor, the result will be a style of television convention coverage that is a bit less dramatic and a bit less breathless, but also a bit more thorough.

It is perhaps endemic to the nature of television news that when the men and women of CBS turned their attention to that period of coverage that begins after the summer conventions and stretches all the way to the November election, two things happened: They went first to their election-night extravaganza, bypassing a truly in-depth look at their news coverage of September and October; and they began with a lengthy discussion of the style and shape of their election-night set. Fully two thirds of the entire afternoon session dealing with the fall campaign was taken up with a most-thorough discussion of these two points.

There was prolonged discussion of whether to use raw numbers or percentages, and what to flash on the screen when. Finally, Salant embarked on a diplomatic mission.

"This, then, leads us, if I may, to a very difficult issue and a very delicate one," Salant began.

Cronkite asked, "Do you want me to leave?" No, Salant said, but he understood that the veteran anchor had anticipated his agenda.

"We have such an enormous amount of information, which can be so confusing," said Salant, "that I think that we ought to find a better way of dividing it up between anchor and the other reporters. . . . We ought to find a better definition of what the anchor ought to do—not for any purposes other than clarity. We have been making Walter do so much that again you get this avalanche of figures and percentages and recaps and 'leadings' and House and Senate that it all comes tumbling pell-mell, and my ear, for one, is not fast enough to absorb that, and I don't know where I am."

"You know, Dick," Cronkite said, "I agree with that absolutely a hundred or a thousand percent. I'm a thousand percent behind you on that." The room erupted in laughter, for everyone understood this still-fresh reference to George McGovern's proclamation that he was 1,000 percent behind Thomas Eagleton just before he dropped Eagleton as his running mate on the 1972 Democratic presidential ticket.

Perhaps the most far-reaching observation to come out of the day of self-inquiry came in response to one of the more limited points that were discussed.

It came during the discussion on convention coverage, when Salant dealt directly with Mike Wallace's suggestion that perhaps the networks could talk America's political parties into holding their early convention sessions at more suitable times of the day. Salant's manner of response was to quote another CBS News executive, William Leonard.

"You know, Bill Leonard is the author of that immortal statement, 'They can hold their convention fifty miles off sea; we'll try to cover it,' " said Salant. "I think in news we ought to stick to that. We oughtn't to try to persuade them in any way to hold it in a particular place at a particular time, because then we really get into the business of encouraging them to do it for our benefit."

Leonard's line—and Salant's philosophic drawing of it—deserves to be framed as the blueprint that network-television-news journalists and decision-makers ought to follow as they seek to build a professional, working relationship with America's politicians and officeholders. It is a line that defines the limits for all journalists, including television journalists: Let the politicians conduct their own business and beware of symbiotic relationships. It applies equally to all journalists, whether they are covering political conventions once every four years or presidents and candidates every day, or zoning-board commissioners and county supervisers.

But it is a line that is crossed far too often by network television's decision-makers and mainly its workers in the fields of politics, especially when they are working in those places of high visibility and high competition, like the White House. And that is why William Henkel, the Reagan White House's impresario of video advance, speaks warmly and with appreciative affection about a "very unique relationship" that he feels exists between his office and the television producers and camera people and, to a lesser degree, with the television correspondents who are assigned by their networks to cover that beat.

The warning by CBS departing president Salant about the dangers of a journalist-political alliance is a video-news equivalent of departing President Dwight Eisenhower's warning about the dangers of the military-industrial complex. It is the sort of alliance that may be of immediate mutual convenience to the two parties, but is of long-term detriment to the country as a whole.

A BENEDICTION, OF SORTS

Dusk was starting to envelop the Plaza and the CBS powers elite had focused their network eye upon all they had done in the campaign of 1976. They were fresh out of bouquets and billy clubs, fresh out of energy and inquiry as well. In a final touch, the outgoing network-news president, Salant, turned to the outgoing network-news commentator, Sevareid, for what was to have been a benediction of sorts.

What Sevareid gave them that day started out sounding like a benediction, but it wound up more like a lament. It was a most remarkable soliloquy, more poignant than eloquent, and it was probably just a bit painful to listen to. For it soon became clear that this very proud man, who had been so much a part of the history of CBS radio and television, and, in fact, of the entire broadcast industry, was talking about how he had been eased and maybe elbowed out of the way as America's preeminent television commentator.

"I can speak, I think, very objectively, because I won't be around here to do this four years from now, or two years from now," he began. At the start of the day, his professional broadcast tones had made themselves heard above the din with commanding imperative; now his colleagues were urging the sixty-four-year-old commentator to speak louder, please. "I'm tired," Sevareid replied simply, and he went on.

"As to this little act I've been doing . . . [there's] been a great change in this over the years, and it's made it harder and harder. . . . The New York [Democratic] convention was almost impossible for us. It seemed to me we were asked simultaneously too much and too little. We got to the point where we have to persuade somebody in the control room ahead of time what we want to talk about—and we're not talking about hard news, we're talking about ideas, generalizations. Is it worth putting on the air now? You can't really do that, you know, unless you've written it all in advance or something.

"Over the years, everybody has become a commentator. Now, maybe that's good, but it made—it makes it very difficult for those of us in that slot. It was so bad a few years ago in one or two Chicago conventions that we would end up at midnight, and then we'd go around to all our guys on the floor [the CBS floor correspondents], all of whom became philosophers and historians. They'd come to Teddy White and me about one A.M. with audience and nothing to say. Finished. We sit there with difficulty [it was Bill Moyers and Sevareid doing the assigned commentary spots in this 1976 convention season] trying desperately to think: 'What can we talk about that hasn't really been dealt with here? Something a little deeper, or something—some perspective.' And then we would listen to what's going on. And suddenly Bruce [Morton] is on the rostrum, and he's dealing with this. Or Walter's doing a piece on it. Sometimes . . . a piece of Andy Rooney's. That sort of thing. And we got to scrap this, and we're in a desperate position. . . .

"Now, I don't know whether you need this function. And [the problem will remain] unless you very carefully set aside certain areas of talk . . . and say to the [CBS] people on the floor . . . 'Now, you're not going to do this'; or that Walter's going to be an anchorman, and he's not going to be chief philosopher, historian, and interviewer.

"A lot of interviews used to be done in the analysis booth—me and [Edward R.] Murrow, and a few, me and [Theodore H.] White. They're not anymore. It's all done in the anchor booth.

". . . If we weren't any good, it's our fault, my fault. . . ."

Sevareid's boss, Salant, sought to ease the moment with a gesture of praise. "There's—there's this great spate of facts. . . . Somebody must have the opportunity to put it in broadest— [Clearly, this wasn't working, and so Salant tactfully tacked, changing direction in midstream] —and that's, that's the trouble with conventions. . . ."

Sevareid got there first. "Even on election night we were asked ahead of time to sort of sell our piece in advance," he said.

Election-night boss Robert Chandler tried his hand: "I don't know that it was so much selling as letting us know so that it could be led into properly. . . . What about the primaries, Eric? We—I—I kind of made a deliberate decision to—"

Again, Sevareid got there first. "Well, we didn't do much—we didn't do anything."

CHANDLER: I know. I—I kind of made a deliberate decision not to incorporate analysis until the very end. Did you feel it was needed?

SEVAREID: Well, no. . . . You know, I had my little act in the evening news, quite a lot of it . . . and I didn't feel very good about it at all. . . .

CHANDLER: But I mean on those primary-night specials, did you feel that that was an element that was missing and that should have been there?

SEVAREID: I think everybody did analysis as they went along, because everybody's become very good at that. And, no, I didn't feel I should have been there.

Seconds later, a question led Sevareid into a heartfelt reminiscence about the halcyon days when he *was* there—the early days when radio was king and television a fledgling, when he was doing the conventions with Edward R. Murrow, and when a brash new NBC News team of Chet Huntley and David Brinkley captured the nation's fancy and the Nielson ratings and led us into a new era of television news. What Sevareid had to say stands today as a fascinating, fleeting one-man's-history, a sail down the stream of consciousness of his career, complete with recollections of those personal rocks that no one else would remember having been tossed his way long ago, but which of course remain etched in his own memory, larger than they ever were in real life.

It is a quick ride:

"In '52 and '56, the anchorman dealt with the hard news. Murrow and I were supposed to be talking [commentators]. Now, it was all right in '52. We got to '56 in both conventions . . . and [CBS] had set up a marvelous thing called simulcasts, simultaneous with radio. They had . . . assigned Murrow and me to a big round table with a mike out here. Had we sat up like normal human beings, [we] could not be heard. [*New York Times* TV critic] Jack Gould had a piece, a derogatory piece, talked about Murrow and Sevareid 'bent in solemnity' . . . [but we just couldn't] be heard unless we were bent over. And every time we would start to talk—we might go a minute or two at least—we'd get a cue, we had a radio commercial coming up, or something like that, you see. After one day of this, Murrow wrote out a telegram to Frank Stanton [the president of CBS then] and says, 'I'm quitting this convention.' I talked him out of sending it. We suffered through it. Then he was very sick [with the lung cancer that eventually took Murrow's life], so I had to fill for a long time. But that was the year, you see, when Brinkley came along with the two-man act with Chet.

"And we just got murdered by all those circumstances. And we couldn't call up [*Times* critic] Jack Gould then and bleed about it."

There was nothing else to say. It remained only for Salant to interject a note of contemporary reality. "Eric, we've run out of tape."

Which brought Sevareid to a quick summation on the role of the commentator on CBS: ". . . So what you ought to do with it, Dick . . ." (There was a burst of laughter, even in this poignant moment, from those who thought they could finish Sevareid's sentence for him.) "You clear an area, say that's his area . . . or forget it."

Salant made one last effort to restore a tone of uplift and dignity. ". . . You are underestimating your contributions," he told Sevareid.

"But I tell you it's changed, Dick," Sevareid persisted. "It's very tough now, you know. . . . There are only so many general ideas and historical analogies or what not, and if they get soaked up early . . ."

But he was just repeating himself now, and this proud and famous network pioneer mumbled a final phrase that the transcript says was indistinct, and then lapsed into silence.

PART THREE

AUTHOR'S NOTE

In May of 1985, Dennis Kauff sat in a cramped office off the WBZ-TV newsroom in Boston and shared with uncommon candor and insight his view of what it was like to be a local reporter covering the presidential primary campaign of 1984. Later that year, Kauff was killed at the age of thirty-two in an auto accident for which the other driver was eventually convicted of driving under the influence. The archives of WBZ are filled with videotapes containing the consistently high-quality reporting he did for that station, as are the archives of Atlanta's WSB-TV, where he won three Emmys for his previous work there. Part Three of this book, meanwhile, is filled with the candid and refreshing observations that were very much Dennis's style. And so it is gratefully dedicated to Dennis Kauff in the hope that his wife, Paula, will recall his comments fondly, and his daughter, Haley, who was just two when he died, will come to know her father just a little bit better from reading them and will appreciate his contributions to his profession, as his colleagues and this writer did.

SIX

A FEW PRELIMINARIES

A bit of a smile cracked the face of Martin Plissner as he sat at his desk in the CBS News offices in Washington and glanced at the cover of the latest issue of *Newsweek* in this, the very first week of the 1984 presidential campaign year. Martin Plissner is to the television-news industry what the microchip is to the computer industry: He is an exceedingly compact, exceedingly complete storehouse of the facts and stats and rules and regulations that govern the American political process, not to mention a valued repository of the myriad strategies and speculations that have both fueled and fouled the political process with regularity. Like the microchip, Martin Plissner works strictly from within; he doesn't appear on the screen, just his data does. Facts from Plissner's encyclopedic databank have been accessed at all hours by the CBS network's on-camera talents, and even by his personal network of politicos and pals, via interoffice memos or midnight repasts at the watering holes of the campaign trail.

And now here was Plissner, smiling back at that rather handsome photo of Walter Mondale that was grinning at him from the cover of the January 9, 1984, issue of *Newsweek,* the candidate's gray hair and blue eyes nicely complemented by the presidential-blue background, as the magazine's cover asked in bold white letters: "Can Anyone Stop Fritz?"

Plissner's smile was directed not at Mondale but at *Newsweek,* and for that matter at CBS, at himself, and at all of political journalism.

It was prompted by a wry remembrance. "I can't help thinking of that piece I helped put together for *60 Minutes* for the 1972 race," said Plissner, the CBS off-camera analyst. "We titled it: 'Can Anyone Here Beat Muskie?' "

The correct answers to those questions tell the story of what is wrong with the way America's political journalists, both print and television, practice their profession in the make-work years that precede the presidential-election years. *The way they practice their profession:* If political journalists were doctors, their practices would have been declared malpractice and they would have been sued right out of the business long ago (and yes, "they," as it is used here, could also be read as "we").

The answer to that *60 Minutes* question of 1972, about whether anyone could beat Muskie, was, of course, "Yes!"—as George McGovern won the Democratic presidential nomination months after the CBS network piece conveyed the impression that Muskie had the nomination all but wrapped.

And the answer to that *Newsweek* question of 1984 (the article inside carried a two-part headline, first asking CAN ANYONE BEAT FRITZ? and then salivating, MONDALE'S MACHINE IS SIMPLY THE BIGGEST AND BEST IN THE HISTORY OF U.S. POLITICS) proved to be another surprising "yes"—at least in the early primaries.

In their quest for the Democratic and Republican presidential nominations, America's most famous and not-so-famous politicians undergo a metamorphosis that takes them through several stages in their struggle to survive and thrive. And like the life cycle of the gypsy moth, the life cycle of the presidential aspirant is comprised of stages having distinct and clearly recognizable characteristics.

The first of these, the Preliminaries, begins soon after the inauguration of a sitting president and goes on for almost three years, until just a few weeks before the voting begins to pick the next one. It is a campaign in a cocoon, played out mainly for a handful of Americans who happen to be political activists, political bankrollers, or political journalists.

The second stage begins abruptly, just a few weeks before the first voting starts in the primaries and caucuses of the election year, under the harsh incubatory glare of television klieg lights. Only then does the public really begin to focus on what the candidates have been saying for the past couple of years. And only then, in this period of Primary Videos, does the message conveyed through television—especially local television in those early contest states—begin to dominate the presidential process. The candidates have only a few weeks in which to succeed or fail in this compressed second stage.

Then come the Waves, media waves which the survivors and their campaign messages can ride successfully or be swamped by. Those with skill and luck will see their message carried along by the currents of the television newscasts far more swiftly and powerfully than they could ever have accomplished with their own propulsion. Those lacking one or both will see their campaigns being swamped in a sea of trend seekers.

The Preliminaries are that familiar and seemingly interminable time of winks and nods and blushes and elbows when adult politicians feign coquettishness even as their glands are pumping pure jet fuel. It is that time when they form Exploratory Committees but then heed the counsel of their egos, which can see beyond the range of their telescopes and often well beyond their political horizons. It is that time when they say they are "testing the waters" even as they are plunging headlong into them, that time when they spout subtleties about being undecided and pretend to tiptoe to the brink of Sherman-like statements even as they are churning irreversibly forward with the full-thrust subtlety of a Sherman tank.

And mainly it is a time when the media carries all of this to a captive public that frankly just doesn't give a damn. People, after all, just are not focusing on an election that is still so distant. But that is all right with the candidates, because this long preliminary round is not aimed at influencing America's voters. It is aimed only at impressing a handful of Americans: those who write or broadcast about politicians and those who give money to politicians. The idea is for a politician to impress those journalists who cover politics so they will write favorably about the candidate, which will help the candidate make a dent in the public-opinion polls, which will impress the big contributors to donate money, which will impress the journalists and cause them to write still more favorable pieces. And so it goes.

All of this is what has the candidates grasping at straws. Those straw polls taken at various state party functions are the creation of two kinds of politicians: presidential candidates who are desperate to attract big media and big money in those uneventful out-years, and state party officials who know that if they contrive a straw poll, the presidential candidates and the media will show up at their trite little party affair. (There is, of course, a third category of politician, one who shows up at these straw polls only out of fear; it is a fear of failure, a fear that by not showing up and working the crowd, he or she could fail to get a respectable showing from this handful of activists, which could doom a candidate before his time.)

The history of the straw pollemics is a recent thing. Jimmy Carter caused most of this nonsense to happen because of the shrewd strategy employed by the manager of his fledgling 1976 campaign, Hamilton Jordan. The Carter people bought up batches of tickets to an Iowa Democratic party dinner in October 1975 because they knew a poll would be taken. Then they rounded up every supporter they could find and gave them free tickets—and so this relatively unknown ex-governor of Georgia won the poll and earned himself a prominent story in *The New York Times*, which reported that Carter "appears to have taken a surprising but solid lead" in Iowa. Jimmy Carter was on his way.

George Bush did the same as a prelude to the first caucus of 1980, at a time when he was registering less than 1 percent in the public-opinion surveys. Undaunted by the fact that he was listed in the polls with a cipher instead of a real number, Bush went into Iowa with only his asterisk—and came away a winner. His people set up a wholesale-clearinghouse–type operation in an Iowa motel, got their hands on every loose ticket to the local Republican party dinner, salted the crowd, won the poll, and later went on to defeat Ronald Reagan (who declined to debate) in that state's caucuses.

And so it was that by 1984, the candidates and the pols were up to their money belts in straw. They treated America to the Straw Poll Follies of 1984, and all they proved is that straw polls are a waste of the candidates' time and money and are now irrelevant to the process. Senator Gary Hart of Colorado went broke trying to compete in the straw-poll season and was almost forced to quit before the first votes were counted in 1984—yet once they let the public in on the process, it turned out that large numbers of those votes would be his.

And Senator Alan Cranston of California, who banked his entire roll on the proposition that the straw polls would bring him media attention and success, found only failure in success. He rented buses and bought hotel rooms to bring his people to the straw polls in his quixotic quest for media exposure; and he dyed his fringe of white hair a punk orange-brown and wolfed down waffles and sundaes to fill out his concave cheeks so he'd look good once he'd won his place in the sun. And lo, Cranston bested Walter Mondale in two straw polls and basked in the glow of television klieg lights. But when the real voting began the next year, Cranston found he had only a fringe of real support. He was the first candidate to withdraw, as he returned to his seat in the United States Senate and returned his hair to its dignified white.

The Preliminaries can be lonely times for the non–front-runners, what with their being so unknown and of course having not a prayer of a chance to be president. In the Preliminaries to Campaign '76, Jimmy Carter scheduled a press conference in Philadelphia—and the only two people who showed up in the room were the candidate and his press secretary, Jody Powell. Soon Powell learned the gentle art of campaign contrivance when he tried to get Carter on a talk show in Des Moines. The local TV people said they didn't want him on if he was going to talk about politics. So the next president of the United States got to go on the television show by agreeing to tell the viewers all about his famous Plains, Georgia, recipe for cooking catfish.

JIMMY CARTER'S PLAINS, GEORGIA, CATFISH RECIPE

INGREDIENTS: Catfish (or bass); Heinz 57 sauce; Bisquick or pancake mix; corn oil.

METHOD: Cut fish into strips like French fries. Marinate fish in Heinz 57 sauce for several hours. Coat fish with dry Bisquick. Fry in oil. May be served hot or cold.

These are times when this sort of nonrecognition puts a true strain on the egos of these politicians, who, after all, are so very big back in their home states, in the governors' mansions where they have presided or the U.S. Senate where they have served. So they cope the best they can. In New Hampshire, when a restaurant patron thought he recognized the importance of Senator Alan Cranston but could not quite place him, the tall, pale senator from California stuck out his hand and introduced himself as Senator Hayakawa of California, the former senator who was half as tall and twice as Japanese as Cranston. And Cranston beamed happily as the man said that yes indeed, he'd recognize the distinguished senator anywhere.

For months in the Preliminaries of Campaign '84, six Democratic candidates fumed in frustration that the television and print media had been covering the run for the Democratic presidential nomination as though it were a two-man race: Walter Mondale versus John Glenn, no others need apply.

And a check of the files of the major newspapers and logs of the major television networks shows that indeed that is what the media had done. Mondale and Glenn had received more newspaper-column inches and television air time than Reuben Askew, Alan Cranston, Gary Hart, Ernest Hollings, Jesse Jackson, and George McGovern combined in 1982 and 1983.

So when none other than Gary Hart, who had been written off by the experts as a fiscally and politically bankrupt cause, came suddenly Galluping out of the low single digits to win those early primaries of 1984, the experts of the press and politics were in their traditional, quadrennial posture of stupefaction.

In the newspapers and on TV it has always been a two-man race. That is because the media likes it that way: Who's the Front-runner? Who's the Spoiler? Where's the Action? Where's the Official Starter? Let the Race begin!

So it was that Campaign '84 was always portrayed as Mondale versus X. First it was Mondale or Kennedy: But Senator Edward M. Kennedy declared himself out of it before the race began.

Then it was Mondale or Glenn: The smart money said the Ohio Democrat was perfect on paper, an astronautic orbiter and a political centrist who came complete with built-in name recognition. But the whole thing came a cropper when Glenn was taken off paper and put on the trail, and then on television, and then back on the shelf.

So finally it became Mondale or Hart: The New Generation Coloradan with his New Ideas shtick was better on the trail, better on television, but uncharted on paper.

In 1982, the television networks talked sparingly about presidential politics, which was still two years away, but when they talked, they talked about Mondale and Kennedy and then Mondale and Glenn.

In 1983, it was more of Mondale and Glenn, only this time with thematics—the right organization versus the right stuff, those analyses of the AFL-CIO's endorsement of Mondale versus Glenn's celebrity status from the *Right Stuff*, the movie about his astronautic past. Newspapers and newsmagazines were just as guilty. *Newsweek* even celebrated Glenn's status by giving him a cover story—and using the actor who played him in the movie on the cover in full-space regalia. (It did for Glenn about what *Time* magazine's pre–Campaign '80 cover story on John Connally's candidacy did for his presidential campaign: nothing. Connally had a huge war chest of industrial-strength contributions and wound up with a total of one presidential delegate.)

About the only way for any of the other Democrats in the Campaign

'84 field to rate a mention on the 1983 network-news shows was to announce his candidacy officially, which he could do just once (and poor Askew, the former highly praised governor of Florida, got precious air time on only one network, CBS, for his official coming out). Or he could win a straw poll. Those straw polls! California, Massachusetts, Wisconsin, Alabama, Maine, Iowa, Florida. They were action, they were races, and they were covered in the media as if they mattered. Maine's October 1, 1983, straw poll—which unabashedly billed itself as "The Super Bowl of Straw Polls"—was won handily by Mondale after a sizable expenditure of energy and money. That was viewed as a major triumph because Maine is a caucus state and all experts know that caucuses are supposed to be won through organization; they know that television, news and ads, is supposed to mean very little to the outcome of caucus-state contests. But by the time the actual Maine caucuses of 1984 rolled around just five months later, Mondale wound up being swamped despite his all-out organization effort, as Hart caught a media wave just right and rode its free, nightly television newscast message to victory—which of course left the experts and pundits stupefied, one more time.

Perhaps the indoor record for straw-poll silliness was set on Saturday, June 18, 1983, as a handful of Young Democrats in Alabama decided to hold a straw poll and the well-aged Cranston went down there and worked the youth of the party. CBS, the only network with a news show that Saturday, gave the story a brief but breathless mention, in a report by the anchorman that day, Bob Schieffer.

SCHIEFFER: Senator Alan Cranston of California got his second major boost in a week tonight, winning a presidential straw poll of Alabama Young Democrats. Cranston overwhelmingly defeated South Carolina Senator Ernest Hollings. Both men had personally solicited the Young Democrats' support. Last week, Cranston won a straw poll in Wisconsin.

And *The Washington Post* went one better, dispatching a correspondent to Alabama to cover the event; the *Post* story, displayed on page four, was headlined CRANSTON IS FIRST IN STRAW POLL OF ALABAMA YOUNG DEMOCRATS, and devoted 618 words to explaining what happened in this meeting that turned out to be a mere 124 Young Democrats, out of which Cranston had amassed a grand total of 65 votes.

Two years later, Gary Hart still grinned broadly as he recalled those CBS and *Washington Post* stories. "The great hoodwink of the year!"

Hart said. "Cranston—I gave him great credit for pulling that one off."

The preliminary campaign year of 1983 ended with a resounding example of the sort of two-man coverage that drives the rest of the field to froth. For weeks, Mondale had waffled on whether the U.S. Marines should be in Lebanon, just as he had waffled on whether he supported Reagan's invasion of Grenada, which occurred just after the tragic bombing of the marine barracks on the outskirts of Beirut. Cranston, Hart, Jackson, and McGovern issued early calls for the withdrawal of the marines from Lebanon, but their statements received little or no attention from the nation's press.

On New Year's Eve, Mondale issued a hastily prepared statement calling for the withdrawal of the U.S. Marines still in Lebanon. He spoke out only after the political risk of such a statement had been erased. Conservative stalwarts William F. Buckley and Richard Viguerie had called for a pullout of the marines. CBS News's Lesley Stahl had reported on Dec. 20, "Recent polls show more and more people want the troops brought home, and there are signs Mr. Reagan is beginning to respond." The president, she said, was studying a plan to withdraw the troops by spring. Also, Jesse Jackson was on the verge of scoring his major diplomatic coup in Syria: the release of the American flier shot down while on a mission.

So, like a reluctant taxpayer rushing to beat the filing deadline, Mondale just got in under the wire with his New Year's Eve call for a withdrawal. And his statement was played as front-page news in *The New York Times* and *The Washington Post* (I was co-author of the *Post* article), and received prominent play by the television networks.

Meanwhile, the rest of the field could only fume from the sidelines. The media took note of Glenn's now-frequent attacks on Mondale policies—he called Carter-Mondale administration economic policies "failed" and called Mondale "weak" on defense, while Mondale countered that Glenn wanted to give the Pentagon "a blank check." As for the rest of them, their political trees fell unseen and unheard in the forests, as their stumping efforts received little notice.

Occasionally a network-news piece captured the fact that there were presidential candidates out there taking tough positions. NBC News's Bob Kur did one of the best of these, on November 15. He properly put the wood to Mondale and Glenn's indecision and still found a way to make it clear that in policy matters the rest of the field was doing the front-running.

KUR: In Iowa, seventeen days after the Grenada invasion, the first question Democrats asked John Glenn was whether he would have invaded.

GLENN: To rescue them was justified, and I support that.

KUR: For ten days, Glenn had vacillated. And sixteen days after the invasion, Walter Mondale still could not be pinned down.

MONDALE: And I have not tried to come to a conclusion till I'm sure I have seen all the facts.

KUR: It wasn't until today that Mondale said he knew enough to call the invasion legitimate.

HART: I think the more you look as if you're afraid or timid or waffling, the less of a leader you are.

KUR: Hart opposes the invasion. He and others running behind Glenn and Mondale are way out front on Grenada and the use of marines in Lebanon.

HOLLINGS: If they were put there [Lebanon] to fight, there were far too few; and if they were put there to be killed, there were far too many.

JACKSON: We need to get America out of Lebanon immediately. We have no purpose there.

CRANSTON: Ronald Reagan's trigger-happy recklessness has taken us to tragedy in Lebanon, to the invasion of Grenada, and to the brink of war in El Salvador and Nicaragua.

Next came anchor Tom Brokaw with a brief story about the latest Glenn-versus-Mondale charge and countercharge on defense spending.

The two-man race coverage occurs because political journalists take their campaign catechism from the public-opinion polls. They tell us all who the front-runner is and who the number-one challenger is—no matter if, at this early stage, it is only a measure of name recognition at the starting gate and does not reflect what the voters will be thinking once they finally focus on the campaign and take the true measure of the candidates.

There are differing views about just who is culpable for the fact that the coverage has long been weighted so toward the top two candidates, and even differing views about whether this really is the case. There are differences of opinion among politicians and journalists. And there are differences even in the views of some who have risen to prominence within a single network.

Consider the views of Edward M. Joyce and Dan Rather of CBS. Joyce was the president of CBS News throughout the 1984 campaign year (he has since resigned) and Rather was and is the anchor of the *Evening News*. Both were asked separately about the two-man-race coverage.

"My conscience is squeaky clean on this one," said Joyce while he was still the head of CBS News. He said he felt CBS News gave "a fair shake" to Hollings and McGovern *et al.* ". . . We wanted to make very sure that our conscience would be clean at the end of the campaign, that we hadn't made it impossible for someone other than the front-runner to stand a chance. And so to that extent perhaps we even bent over backwards to try to make room for others than the front-runner."

Dan Rather, however, sees it as a real problem. "I think all of that is legitimate criticism," he said when asked about the two-man-race tilt of the media coverage in 1983. ". . . It's true. No question. I think . . . we didn't do as much [campaign coverage as some media organizations]. But what we did, on a percentage basis, we were as guilty as anybody. . . . That's a legitimate and fair criticism demonstrated by the record. I mean, it's there for all to see. . . . If we had to do it over again, we would do more coverage in 1983, particularly from early summer to the end. . . . We particularly would have run more overview pieces. We would have been far less . . . convinced that it was basically a two-man race.

". . . We have nothing to be proud of in this area. I mean, we were just culpable."

Actually, it was Rather himself who did one of the year's few network-news stories that broke out of the two-man-race syndrome. In August 1983, Rather was struck by a *Wall Street Journal* story that seemed to read like a campaign obituary for Gary Hart. He went out to tour a New Jersey toxic-waste dump with Hart and did a piece that was far more upbeat, to say the least. Critics would say it bordered on fawning.

RATHER: Gary Hart does look like a presidential candidate—thinks like one too. . . . And he talks a good game; he sounds like presidential timber.

RATHER: As he works a factory gate in New Hampshire there are signs his campaign may be off the critical list.

RATHER: He's written a book that's just come out outlining his ideas. And his stand against the MX missile has helped too.

RATHER: Hart is a smart, good public speaker. Seldom gives exactly the same speech or answer twice. . . . And he has a sense of humor.

It ended with a factual statement on campaign finances that could also have doubled as a pitch straight from Hart's campaign treasurer.

RATHER: Ironically, Gary Hart's fate may not depend heavily on voters in Iowa or New Hampshire. It seems to depend much more right now on big-money backers here in New York City, Chicago, and Los Angeles. That's because, especially for 1984, the name of the game is early money. Without it, dark-horse candidates like Hart can't mount the kind of campaign that puts them on the map in all fifty states, the kind of campaign, in other words, that wins nominations.

After the campaign was over, when asked what he thought of Hart as a candidate in those early days, Rather talked in much different terms. It turns out he had seen in Hart the same genuinely puzzling and boring candidate that others had gotten to know on the stump. (Hart seemed to just be going through the motions in 1983, but somehow he transformed himself into a strong candidate at the outset of 1984, changing his entire stump presence.)

"We came back calling him Gary Sominex," Rather said, describing a candidate far different from the one he had reported to the nation about. "I mean it was sleep-inducing. Nothing. People came, small groups of people came expecting the most, and this guy was out of it. I mean he didn't touch any chords, even when he was talking about things they cared about."

Hart, meanwhile, cites the Rather piece as an example of one of the few journalistically worthy pieces done on television in 1983. "Well, you know, Dan Rather takes credit for, in effect, making me —because he did," Hart said. ". . . Dan Rather thinks that my campaign took off after that. And I think there's some doubts about it, but let's give him the benefit of the doubt. That [piece] is probably what television ought to be doing."

Hart's transformation from a lackluster campaigner and pedantic speaker in 1983 into a forceful and thematic and effective one in January 1984 has remained something of a mystery even to those advisers and confidants who know him best. One of his early major turning-point speeches came at Brandeis University in Boston on January 26. In an address that was heavy on theme and light on specifics, Hart spelled out his "New Generation of Leadership" and offered his candidacy as an alternative between "two discredited pasts: the outworn positions of the Reagan Republicans, who care only for a few, and the outmoded ideas of those Democrats who promise everything to everybody." Lest there be any doubt about whom he was talking, Hart went on to say, "We don't need a president—or even a presidential candidate—who dares to be cautious. We need a president who dares to be bold."

Hart's staff billed the speech as a "major" campaign address. And according to Hart's senior campaign advisers, it was was written for Hart not by his regular staff but by Sidney Blumenthal, who was working at the time with the title of national political correspondent of *The New Republic* magazine and was doing campaign analysis for NBC's *Today* show. (Blumenthal has since joined the national staff of *The Washington Post*, where he writes on politics.) Months later, when I asked Blumenthal if in fact he had written that speech for Hart, he replied, "No comment." And when told what the Hart advisers had said, he repeated several times that he would neither confirm nor deny authorship of the speech. He explained that he had studied at Brandeis and went on to talk at length about the speech and the rationale behind its message. He also talked about the propriety of an individual in his position writing a campaign speech for a candidate he was also covering for his publication. "I think it's certainly improper for anyone at *The Washington Post* or any daily paper to do that," Blumenthal said. "*The New Republic* is an opinion journal. . . . At *The New Republic* there's a long history of involvement in campaigns and issues." Blumenthal emphasized that his editor at *The New Republic* knew in advance of everything he had done during the campaign. "I had no vested interest in any campaign," Blumenthal said. "I expected nothing. I asked for nothing."

The week of the Brandeis speech was also the week *The New Republic* featured a cover story by Blumenthal which was titled "Gary Hart's Big Chill," and subtitled "Generational Politics in a Presidential Campaign." The six-page article, quite lengthy for that respected journal, talked in detail of Hart's intellectual development and the impact upon it of John F. Kennedy's politics. It made a passionate case for Hart's candidacy.

"Hart wants to lead not by appearances but by ideas," Blumenthal wrote. "His brand of liberalism, though anchored in enduring ideals, is experimental. . . . The split of vision and program is at the heart of liberalism's ideological crisis. Can they be reunited by the rediscovery of the experimental method that animated the New Deal? That is Hart's ultimate promise.

"If Hart could somehow awaken this excitement and win the nomination, he would be in a position to mount a general-election campaign unlike that of any other Democrat in the field. . . . Hart . . . may actually be highly electable. . . ."

The message of Hart's Brandeis speech was there in Blumenthal's *New Republic* article: "Just as Kennedy focused the scattered energies of his generation, Hart, if he is to succeed, must reassemble the younger generation for a new crusade. He must cast the election as a contest not between a Democrat and a Republican, but between the new generation and the old leaders, a continuum that runs from Mondale through Reagan. . . ."

And Blumenthal's conclusion, written with more emotion than Hart had mustered in all of 1983—seemed to be part passion and part prod, as it made the case in public that seemed crafted mainly to move one reader most of all: "Hart must do what he's resisted thus far: He must reveal his passion, demonstrating his politics are not bloodless and abstract. That may be a price he will refuse to pay, because, as he sees it, he has protected his authenticity by holding back. What he wants most may be what he's incapable of having. If he fails, he will have recapitulated the essential experience of the rebels of the 1950s: He will have become an isolated individual unable to make himself heard while older men drone on."

In all, it was a strong article of political opinion. As in the case of columnist/analyst George Will, who in 1980 coached Ronald Reagan for his debate with President Carter and then went on ABC and analyzed the debate for the nation as a resounding Reagan victory, there was no mistaking Blumenthal's own passions about the race of 1984. But the viewers of ABC News in 1980 deserved to know the added role their analyst had been playing, and the readers of the *The New Republic* and viewers of NBC's *Today* show deserved to know the same about their analyst of 1984. (Blumenthal's editor at *The New Republic* in that period, Hedrick Hertzberg, said initially he did not think that Blumenthal had written any speeches for Hart or any other candidate—and he would likely have remembered if he had known about it at the time; he said he did know that Blumenthal had offered advice to the Hart staff now and then. Later, after talking with Blumenthal, Hertzberg said Blumenthal told him he had given "language" for the speech to Hart advisers and that he had told Hertzberg about it at the time. That prompted Hertzberg to amend his recollection and say that he thinks he probably had been told in advance. In our earlier interview, Hertzberg had said that if he had been asked in advance if it was appropriate for Blumenthal to write or help write a speech of Hart's, "I think I would have said that's going too far. . . . I attacked George Will roundly for doing what he did in 1980. So I guess what's sauce for the goose must be sauce for the gander.")

ON POLLS

Political journalists come in two basic categories. There are those who swear by the public-opinion polls, and there are those who swear at them. Dan Rather is among the latter.

"Goddammit, I hate these fucking polls," said Rather. ". . . I hate polls. I've always hated polls. This is not a new development. I have never liked polls. I am famous or infamous inside our organization for hating polling."

Rather's concern, stated with some passion, is that these polls become the drivetrain that propels the journalistic coverage, especially when the journalistic organizations themselves get into the business of doing their own polling—which they then feel obliged to report at length with detail and importance. He remembers a meeting in Ed Joyce's office in which he urged that CBS get out of the polling business (CBS News and *The New York Times* do a joint poll, as does ABC News and *The Washington Post*; NBC News does its own poll). "I remember I had a meeting in Ed Joyce's office," said Rather, "and Ed said, 'Well, are you serious about closing it down?' And I said, 'I'm absolutely serious about closing it down.' . . . In retrospect, we didn't have the guts to do it."

Rather explained: "We said to ourselves time after time in early 1983, 'I'm not going to have our coverage dictated by polls. The tail is not going to wag the dog. Not this time.' Well, lo and behold, the tail did wag the dog. And I knew better, and had made ministump speeches in our newsroom . . . and everybody nodded sagely and said, 'Yes, yes, right. Too much of that in 1980. Won't do this again.' I got into a hellacious fight with our own polling organization, which is superb."

CBS News and *The New York Times* were especially embarrassed by a poll they came out with in late February that showed Mondale with overwhelming support nationwide—the problem was that it was released on the eve of the New Hampshire primary, where Mondale was about to be beaten by Hart by a sizable margin.

"We had a poll . . . the night before or the day of the New Hampshire primary that said never before in the course of human events has any candidate, any primary, anywhere on this and any other solar system ever had such overwhelming national support as Walter Mondale," said Rather, the pain of the memory apparently seared deep within. "And there it was. The problem with these polls is it comes out in black and white, and it all looks authoritative—and it isn't."

The problem of polls by news organizations becomes in part a question of what is news. Is it news that X is ahead of Y in a poll? Or is it only news if X is ahead of Y in your organization's poll and not the competition's? Advocates argue that the only way a news organization can vouch for the authenticity and controls of a poll is to do it themselves. Rather says he can't refute that. But he still wants CBS News out of the business as a matter of policy and principle. "I would much rather say we're out of the polling business," he said. "Let *The New York Times* have it. Terrific! And we'll report the *New York Times* polls if we think it's newsworthy, and we'll report the *Washington Post* polls."

But would CBS News report what might appear to be a genuine news development in an ABC News or NBC News poll? "That's a very good point—it's impossible," said Rather. "Not going to happen. And they aren't going to report ours." That is too bad, because in the name of truth in journalism, there is no reason at all why that could not be done. Major newspapers occasionally (but often far too grudgingly) report each other's poll results. Network-news organizations ought to do the same—it's time they start playing honest with their viewers and recognize that news is news; it is not just a public-relations ploy.

". . . We've got to learn," Rather concluded. ". . . As our coverage began gathering momentum [in] December, January, February, we were—CBS included, *CBS Evening News* included, Dan Rather included—worse than ever at reading the polls and saying 'Oh boy, that looks like it.' And it wasn't it."

INTERLUDE: THE VIEW FROM THE OTHER END OF THE FUNNEL

What the polls were saying in early 1984 was that the overwhelming front-runner for the Democratic presidential nomination was Mondale. But the view from the Other End of the Funnel in that same period made it clear that the front-runner was really a fellow named "Mondale-But."

Mondale-But, as in insurance-claims adjuster Tom Murphy's explanation, based on months of casually watching the campaign unfold on the television news and in the TV ads from his New Hampshire home: "I'm looking at Mondale—but I think Mondale is promising the moon and I don't see how he can live with it."

And retired district fire chief George Young's view: "I like Mondale. . . . But there's one thing that bothers me about Mondale. . . . He just doesn't look that solid. He doesn't seem to have that punch."

And New Hampshire civil servant Harold Jennings concern: "At this point I see Mondale—but I just think Mondale is promising too much, and Reagan will make mincemeat of him."

Each of them would have turned up on the pollsters' charts as a Mondale voter. But each of them was beginning to volunteer real doubts about the front-runner—even if they had not yet found an alternative. In one weekend in late January, comments like theirs were heard time and again during conversations with seventy-five New Hampshire Democrats at the Sweeney American Legion Post Saturday Night Dance in Manchester, and at the Veterans of Foreign Wars barroom in Portsmouth, and at the lively gatherings of the French-Canadian social clubs, and in the distinctly informal gathering in the back room of the Raphael Club in Manchester, where friendly bets have been known to be placed by folks enjoying their beer and TV sports. It was clear, when viewed from the Other End of the Funnel, that Mondale's future was not necessarily as rosy as the published polls were telling the media, and the media was passing all that along to the public.

What had happened was that for months television had carried John Glenn's charges in newscasts and in his ads that Mondale was promising too much, was courting the special interests, was a captive of the AFL-CIO, and was weak on defense. And by late January 1984, when Democrats and Independents were asked whom they favored for president, they were volunteering comments about Mondale that sounded like pages from John Glenn's scripts—even as they were saying they guessed they would vote for Mondale. He was, after all, the front-runner.

Glenn's television success was that he had made Mondale's "overpromising" a campaign coin of the realm, but he had not been able to cash in on it himself. For those American Legion dances and VFW bars and French-Canadian socials and back-room sports-and-beer joints were citadels of conservative Democrats, who should have been the core of Glenn's support. Yet these people made it plain that they had initially been interested in Glenn but had taken a long look at him and had come away singularly unimpressed.

So they contented themselves with a compromise called Mondale-But. They voiced soft support for Mondale but volunteered their doubts about him, doubts that were there to be exploited if only an alternative could be found.

It was then that the early televised debates, when viewed from the Other End of the Funnel, first indicated that indeed an alternative to Mondale-But might well be at hand.

In the family room of Dot LaValle's home on Bumblebee Circle in Shrewsbury, Massachusetts, Walter Mondale was clearly the pre-debate favorite on this, the first Friday in February 1984. The Democratic presidential candidates were in Boston for a debate on women's issues, and Dot and Armand LaValle had invited ten women from this middle- and upper-middle-class suburb to join them in watching the debate, which was being beamed by its sponsor, Boston's WBZ-TV, to New Hampshire, where the first presidential primary would be held in just three weeks.

One by one, most of the women had confided as they settled in to watch the debate that they probably were for Mondale. And one by one, at the end of the debate, a number of them said that they were switching to Hart. This was not a scientific poll, nor was it a debate that was watched by all of New Hampshire's voters—that is not what a look at the Other End of the Funnel is about. But the fact that there were changes of support—and all the switches were in the same direction—provided a strong indication of just what sort of problems lay ahead for Mondale and what sort of potential there was for Hart.

"I came here leaning toward Mondale," said Cathy Goodwin. "But tonight everything just went—poof! He just struck a negative note with me, very negative. His answers were too slick." Across the room, June Tomaiolo nodded. She is a town selectman in Shrewsbury—the only politician in the room—and before the debate she had confided that she leaned very strongly toward Mondale. But no more. "I was very disappointed in Mondale," she said. "He had too many pat answers. He was too general. I came away impressed with Gary Hart. When he was asked a question, he answered it. He was very specific."

These were women from a cross section of circumstances, some working inside their households, some working outside them, some members of a profession and some just reentering the workforce after raising their children. A few weeks earlier, at a Harvard forum on nuclear-arms control, Hart had gone all out to woo women voters with a blatant appeal, arguing that the world's leaders should listen to the women of the world because they were the ones who were talking sense on arms control. But that earlier Hart pitch bombed with women interviewed later; they saw it for the pandering that it was. So this time, on the advice of his strategists, he kept his appeal low key and specific, and wound up winning high praise from women.

"Up until tonight I would have said no to Hart," said Dot LaValle, who, after years of working as a personnel executive, works now at raising her young family. "But based on tonight, I'd go with Hart. He said the least, but impressed me the most."

One week later, in Clinton, Iowa, a Mississippi River town caught in the crosscurrents of economic hard times, a group of twenty-one middle- and upper-middle-class Democrats and Independents watched another televised debate starring the same cast of candidates—and came to the same conclusions as the women in Shrewsbury, Massachusetts. The candidates were debating halfway across this first caucus state, in Des Moines, on a wide range of issues. And twenty-one friends and neighbors of David and Arica Jansen had gathered around their television set to watch the event and discuss it. Arica is a schoolteacher; David is an ironworker who had been unemployed for more than a year; he also serves as the county Democratic chairman.

Once again, people entered mainly favoring Mondale; and once again, a number of them left Mondale and cast their support elsewhere. Some went to McGovern, who closed with a unique and impressive appeal, urging viewers to vote for him not because they think he can win but just because it will send a message to Mondale about which direction the party ought to go. Some support went to Hart, some said Cranston merited another look, and many pronounced themselves impressed with Jackson. (But as was so often the case among white voters, they stopped their statements of how impressive Jackson was just short of saying they would vote for him.)

Sue Eisenhower, a registered nurse, had come to the debate trying to make up her mind between Mondale, who was most likely, or perhaps Glenn. She, like the others, thought little of Glenn after the debate and found herself part of a sizable list of those who were turned off by Mondale. "I was really considering Mondale," she said. "But I still don't like the things about him that I didn't like before."

Her husband, John, a petrochemical-company executive, agreed. "That's the thing about Mondale. When he's put in a squeeze, he goes into his rhetoric. He ended up saying that promises—that's what America is all about." He thought Jackson had done well, and he was impressed by Hart: "Gary Hart seemed a little more definite than he was before. More mature."

This Clinton, Iowa, businessman then cited one moment that he felt was pivotal. He said he was especially displeased by Mondale's unresponsiveness when Hart asked him to name one union-backed position he disagreed with. "He never answered the question!" Eisenhower said. And around the Jensen's TV room, many others were nodding in agreement, blue-collar workers and union members included. They too said they were troubled by Mondale's ducking the union question, including two who had been staunchly for Mondale. "I came in here supporting Mondale, but now I think he's probably the last person I'd vote for," said Lewis Washington, a probation officer. And Norman Moon, a retired electrician, who had already signed up to work a phone bank for Mondale, now said he regretted his decision. "It seems to me like Mondale was just coasting along, saying 'I'm the front-runner,' " he said, shaking his head with disappointment. "It's bad—but I've committed myself."

The next day, in my motel room in Clinton, I telephoned Mondale's campaign chief, James Johnson, who was in Washington to collect the official line from the camp of the front-runner about the debate. People just are not really concerned about this whole matter of Mondale being too close to the special interests and labor unions, Johnson said. The special interest/labor union thing is strictly a creation of the press, he said. As Johnson was playing out his line, I noticed that just outside my window was none other than the front-runner himself. Mondale had flown in from Des Moines, and now, in the fine mist of a Midwest drizzle, he was holding a press conference in the motel parking lot. Shrewd, that Mondale; he must have sensed what his campaign chairman had not. Clearly, Mondale was going to take immediate action to cut his losses and his bad press by promptly citing a few harmless issues where he differed from his friends in the union leadership. I said good-bye to Johnson and joined his boss in the drizzle.

It was no surprise that Mondale was immediately asked the same question Hart had posed in the debate. It was quite a surprise, though, that Mondale's response was to refuse once again to draw any such distinction. He took his text from the Book of Johnson.

Repeatedly, Mondale was pressed to answer. And repeatedly, Mondale refused—which of course became the Mondale message on the television news that night, and the next day, and, for that matter, for weeks to come.

SEVEN

PRIMARY VIDEOS

It is the quadrennial boon and bane of Boston's television existence that the nation's first primary happens right in its own media-market backyard. Boston's stations profit grandly from candidates' purchases of campaign advertising aimed at New Hampshire voters; and the stations, in turn, invest grandly to bring their viewers the most technologically in-depth coverage money can buy.

A half million dollars was budgeted in 1984 by each of Boston's two leading commercial stations—WCVB and WBZ—for presidential campaign coverage that was designed mainly around an impressive array of satellite uplinks, mobile live-camera vans, and a movable feast of portable sets that enabled them to drop anchor at the blink of an eyewitness. And it was in that spirit of spending for depth that WCVB-TV, the ABC network affiliate, dispatched one of its finest young correspondents, Martha Bradlee, to the Iowa caucuses for a series of special reports and exclusive interviews—live, of course, via satellite—just a week before the crucial New Hampshire primary election.

Bradlee remembers how she prepared for this major assignment that would put her face to face, live nightly, with the Democratic candidates who sought to reshape the nation's policies, foreign and domestic.

"The day before I went to Iowa I was covering a fire in Chelsea," recalled Bradlee, a candid and conscientious journalist. "We had no time to prepare for that—we just went. . . . Did I find it woefully intimidating? Oh, absolutely."

* * *

Over at the competition, WBZ, Boston's NBC affiliate, Dennis Kauff, another young and talented and conscientious correspondent, recalled similar travails as he worked in New Hampshire to bring the essentials of that 1984 primary campaign to his viewers. (The next year, the thirty-two-year-old Kauff's life would come to a tragic end in an auto accident caused by an intoxicated driver.)

"There's no doubt about it, Walter Mondale knows a lot more about the issues that I'm asking him questions about than I do," said Kauff. "And obviously, if Walter Mondale says black is white, a lot of times I'm not able to say, 'Wait a minute, Mr. Mondale . . . is this what you really mean?' Or, 'Is that really the way it is?' Or something like that. There's no doubt about that. . . . I think that is a problem. . . . And the candidates know they can get away with some things with us that they wouldn't be able to get away with [with national reporters].

". . . The bottom line is maybe we should start each segment of the political reporting and say: 'Please bear in mind that the candidates may be putting one over on me because I have to admit that I don't know as much about it as [they do]. . . .' "

The New Hampshire Democratic presidential-primary campaign of 1984 stands as a testimonial to the power of television—especially local television—in the nomination process. The New Hampshire primary is the place where many presidential candidates have had their campaigns ended by the decision of just a fraction of America's voting public. Funds dry up and some campaigns are grounded while others sail on to further testings of the waters. And much of that happens as a result of the information and impressions New Hampshire voters get of the candidates from television's coverage, especially the local-television coverage of the Boston stations that feed so much of the state and devote so much more time to the primary than do the networks.

The New Hampshire Democratic presidential primary of 1984 also stands as a testimonial to just how much room for improvement there is in the way the local television stations go about their business of covering the candidates and shaping the way America selects its candidates for president and rejects the others.

For example: Not once in the last two weeks before the New Hampshire primary—that period when most people are really focusing on the race for the first time—did either of those local Boston stations devote any significant news coverage to a discussion of the issues (except for covering what the candidates said in debates).

The closest they came to covering the major policy matters occurred not in February but back in January, more than a month before the New Hampshire primary, when WBZ did a series that discussed the candidates' positions on several campaign issues. "January . . . was too early," conceded Gerry Chervinsky, who was the director of political coverage in 1984. But that period was selected deliberately, he said, so the station could do the issues early and "get that out of the way."

It has to do with good marketing, not good journalism. He explained: "Basically, the decision was that we would do these pieces earlier and let the people know . . . as a marketing thing: Here we are, we are going to cover the presidential race for you now; and the first thing we are going to do is tell you what the issues are. And we are going to get that out of the way, because the candidates are coming.

". . . Now, I really am sensitive to [the fact that] people really weren't paying attention in January. And while you are trying to get them to pay attention as a marketing vehicle to get them to watch your coverage, they aren't paying attention. . . . If you want to talk about why the issues weren't covered the two weeks before when people really were focusing, that's legitimate, I suppose."

Over at WCVB, assistant news director Emily Rooney was in complete sympathy with that view. "If in . . . the 1988 election, if we start doing things in depth and really looking at the issues and the subject matter at hand, day in and day out . . . we would end up in third place here at the end of that year."

Why?

"Because I just don't think people want to hear it. It's dull. It's dull television."

What with the issues out of the way early—or never really done at all—Boston's local stations did have time, night and day, to serve up a professional-looking package of what television people have themselves taken to calling here-he-comes-there-he-goes journalism. Their pieces took on a cadence as predictable as the snare drum's *rat-a-tat-tat-tat*, *rat-a-tat-tat-tat* in a drill team on parade:

Candidate X brought his presidential campaign to Y City today [as we see him alighting from his airplane or car and shaking hands]. . . .
And then he went to a rally at the high school gym [we see him entering the gym and shaking hands]. . . .

There he called for such-and-such [we see and hear him speaking one sentence from his speech, perhaps shaking his fist]. . . .
And then he went on to Z Town where he did the same thing.
But he faces an uphill fight in this primary. And the future remains to be seen. Live from the Old Gym, via Newscenter Satellite, this is Harry Spray, Eyewhittle News.

The local stations found ways to vary their political-coverage cadence mainly by falling for every media event and picture hokum that the candidates and their packagers could dream up to wheedle their way onto the evening news: hotdog-cooking, barbershop-singing, duckpin-bowling, ax-throwing—tromping in front of all manner of backdrops and fondling all manner of props.

"Maybe we just took the lazy way out," said WBZ correspondent Dennis Kauff. A sincere and thoughtful television journalist, he went on to talk about why it is that an issue rarely gets covered unless the candidate finds a way to contrive a photo opportunity that illustrates it. "Television has to show things as well as tell things. . . . If the candidate goes somewhere to stir up excitement, for instance, we can see that, we can show that, and we can talk about that [in our newscast]. If he goes somewhere to sit down and try to truly get his point across to the people about his belief on defense or the budget or the environment or anything like that . . . we end up falling back on kind of 'Let's show them what they're seeing' instead of 'Let's tell them what he's saying.'

". . . [We do that] unless the candidate has also taken it one step further and kind of set up his appearance to illustrate that issue. . . . I mean, if John Glenn is talking about acid rain and takes us on a trip to a forest that has been damaged by acid rain, it's a lot easier for us to do the story about acid rain and John Glenn's feeling about it than if he goes to a high school and stands up there in front of the kids, and says: '. . . I'm opposed to the current proposals on acid rain.' "

The one thing Boston's television stations always found time to do in their campaign coverage was to show off their latest in high technology, especially the hardware that enabled them to broadcast *live* from remote locations.

"The research . . . [shows] people want more live TV," said WCVB's Rooney. ". . . What they are singling out as the thing they really want is 'More live TV. We want more live TV.' "

So local television gave its viewers live TV—and when they couldn't actually get it live, they'd fake it live. "We do what is commonly called 'Revlons' in this business," explained Rooney. Revlons? Rooney explained that a Revlon is really just a "Sony Sandwich"—and, mercifully, she continued: "You are standing there in front of a state house or whatever, reporting on a decision that happened two hours ago. You're live for the beginning of it, and live for the end of it, but the story is on tape [the 'Sony']." She paused and added: "I contend . . . [the viewers] don't really know the difference."

WCVB's Bradlee conceded that greater emphasis was placed on getting candidates for live interviews than on the content of what those interviews would produce. "It was always a coup to get somebody live," said WCVB's Bradlee, who was willing to take a hard look at her craft and determined to learn from past mistakes (she is, after all, from a journalism family: her husband, Ben Bradlee, Jr., is a reporter with the *Boston Globe*, and others on his side of the family are known for their work on another newspaper farther down the Atlantic Coast).

"And I remember in Iowa I was happy to have a couple of people live—I think I had McGovern and Cranston one night. And WBZ didn't have anything and didn't go live at all out there. Now in effect you could say we did win because of that.

"After I got back from Iowa . . . it hit me when I looked at our coverage and the other stations' coverage. I remember sitting a few nights and thinking: 'Oh, John Glenn! You were using John Glenn for eight minutes just because we could get him live!'

"And it was a trap I think everyone in local television fell into early on. There was this fight for technology and if you had the candidate live, you won."

"NEW HAMPSHIRE VIDEOS OF 1984" A PLOT SUMMARY

Presidential-primary campaigns unfold on television in each state like a short story. And the New Hampshire Democratic presidential primary of 1984 proved a classic illustration of how the results on Election Day are often the natural climax of that short story that had been unfolding in television news and (to a lesser degree) in the television campaign ads in daily and nightly episodes. And the results of New Hampshire '84—which stunned the nation's pols and pundits—are more easily understood by those who have spent their evenings watching television than by those who traveled with the candidates and their entourage to the rallies and media events.

For what happens on Election Day is often a direct consequence of what happens to the candidates' messages as they are piped into the living rooms each night. And often these messages differ significantly from the messages the candidates are trying to sell.

The story of New Hampshire '84 is the story of the messages the candidates were trying to communicate—and what happened to them on their way through the television funnel to the voters in their living rooms. Walter Mondale and his strategists thought they were out there each day selling Mondale as the candidate of experience and competence and, therefore, leadership. "This president will know what he's doing"—that's the message the Mondale strategists tagged onto the end of their commercials; it's the one they wanted to leave the voters thinking about when they saw Mondale's television ads or when they saw Mondale on the television news. But the message that came across to viewers each night was quite different from the one Mondale sought to convey. The real message Mondale had transmitted by the end of the last week of the New Hampshire primary campaign was that he was the consummate Organization Man, a pol who surrounds himself with men in blue-gray suits, an anti-Populist who revels in endorsements from fellow pols and is proudest of his ability to rally America's suitable special interests and bring them together for the sake of his own. And, for good measure, Mondale was seen, live at five, film at eleven, taking victory in New Hampshire for granted.

Mondale's message was not that of a bold leader for the future. Rather, it was consistent with an offhand observation of Mondale's television-advertising specialist, Roy Spence, a Texan partial to lizard-skin cowboy boots and faded dungarees whom Mondale never really accepted as an insider in his world of worsted blue and never really allowed to get close enough to him to work truly effectively. In an interview before the first votes of 1984 were cast, Spence let loose a statement that was as painfully accurate as it was impolitic; he simply said of Mondale: "He dares to be cautious." It was a campaign slogan more memorable than any he was paid to produce.

"He dares to be cautious" *was* the Mondale message of early 1984—not because that was the one his strategists wanted to send, but because it was precisely what the television screens projected into the voters' living rooms nightly. Mondale ran a quintessential cautious campaign—and television caught him in the act. And while there is much that is wrong with the performance of television journalism in campaigns, it is also true that it performs a great public service and remains our greatest political hope. While television did poorly with matters of substance, it showed America the essential personal qualities of the candidates. It allowed people to know some essential truths—first about John Glenn, then about Walter Mondale and Gary Hart, and ultimately about Ronald Reagan. And it enabled them to make the choices they wanted.

While Mondale's message began misfiring nightly in the final days of the New Hampshire primary campaign, Gary Hart's was projecting exactly as it was scripted. He was trying to be the candidate of New Ideas—that was the message that was projected in his television ads, and, most important, that same message was projected in his nightly appearances on the television news.

As for John Glenn, if there ever had been a definable message to his cause, it was totally lost by the time the campaign came around to the final week of the New Hampshire primary. He had long since become the aero-adjective pol, as writers and newscasters sprinkled space-age adjectives through their Glenn reportage; and in that final week of New Hampshire, Glenn was introduced to voters nightly with adjectives representing everything bad that can happen to a rocketship—as in nosediving, plunging, tailspinning, plummeting, crashing, crash-landing, exploding on the launching pad.

Here then is the short story that was New Hampshire '84, the campaign messages as they were beamed into New Hampshire homes in that final week on WBZ and WCVB and the major television networks. The week began with Mondale holding a commanding lead in all the polls, his ratings just below 40 percent. Glenn was a solid second, around 20 percent; Hart was well behind him, buried with the rest of the field in single digits but perhaps gaining slightly while the others clearly were not.

"NEW HAMPSHIRE VIDEOS OF 1984" THE FULL SHORT STORY

As our week-long short story opens, Walter Mondale has just overwhelmed the field in Iowa. He has captured those February 20 caucuses in Iowa by winning 49 percent of the votes—more than three times the total of his nearest rival, Hart, who surprised the experts and even his own staff by finishing second with 16.5 percent. McGovern finished not far behind with 10 percent; "Uncommitted" received 9; Cranston, 7. Glenn, who had been campaigning as the only true alternative to Mondale, was sixth or seventh (depending on whether you like to consider "Uncommitted" as a candidate) with 3.5, barely ahead of Askew, who had 2.5; Jackson, 1.5; and Hollings, who openly ignored Iowa, less than 1 percent.

And although a political folklore has since evolved about how Hart came away with all of the greatest media glory and hoopla in the coverage and analysis of those caucus results, the truth is that it was indeed Mondale, not Hart, who got the greatest initial injection of media-hype as he went front-running out of Iowa and into New Hampshire.

What Hart got, though, was what he needed most—he got promoted to the rank of chief alternative in the two-man race. Some even began to drape him with "momentum." Suddenly, all of Hart's adjectives were good ones.

TUESDAY, FEBRUARY 21

WBZ-TV, 6 P.M.

The screen is alive with the ebullience of Walter Mondale and the cheers of his supporters.

MONDALE: Here in the state of New Hampshire, the first primary state of the union, we're going to take it the rest of the way and send Mr. Reagan packing to California!

JACK WILLIAMS (ANCHOR): Walter Mondale's flying high after Iowa! The story next, on *Eyewitness News*. . . .

LIZ WALKER: With the Iowa caucuses behind them, the first-in-the-nation presidential primary is the next big hurdle. Vice-President Walter Mondale campaigned this morning in Manchester—the joy of last night's victory in Iowa evident on his face. . . .

WCVB-TV, 6 P.M.

CHET CURTIS (ANCHOR): Good evening! Calling this "the beginning of the end of the Reagan administration," Walter Mondale brought his presidential campaign from Iowa to New Hampshire.

NAT JACOBSON: And with him Mondale brings the momentum created in last night's resounding victory in the Iowa caucuses.

MONDALE: I am ready to win this nomination! [The crowd cheers.] I am ready to defeat Mr. Reagan! [More cheers.] I am ready to be president of the United States!!

JACOBSON: And we get more now in this live report from Manchester

[New Hampshire], with *NewsCenter* 5's Mary Richardson. Mary?

MARY RICHARDSON: Walter Mondale looked in complete control today in New Hampshire. That impressive Iowa performance had a clear impact on the other candidates, the hordes of media, and the voters of New Hampshire. . . .

But it is the front-runner's burden that anyone who runs so far ahead for so long a time appears to be a stationary target—easy to hit (just fire when ready) and easy to cover (just toss in any old critic's attack and call it balance). And so, even on this day of his Iowa triumph, those old criticisms of Mondale got aired as well; even on his best days, Mondale's success on the television news would be mixed.

WBZ built an entire story around one of the daily diatribes of the *Manchester Union-Leader*, that neo-troglodyte newspaper that lets its conservative editorial views leak all over its news pages, and is to responsible journalism what connect the dots is to art. WBZ aired that newspaper's charge that a labor-backed "free lunch" Mondale rally was a bid to buy votes; then they interviewed rally-goers, who of course said they went there to see Mondale, not to get free food.

WCVB got in its dollop of balance when correspondent Kirby Perkins first took only whimsical note of the *Union-Leader*'s charge, but then went on to report: "Mr. Mondale's scent of victory in his own party apparently isn't shared by his most ardent ideological rivals—the National Conservative Political Action Committee." (What a newsworthy item it would have been if Mondale *had* miraculously converted NCPAC!) And he then played part of a NCPAC commercial the organization said it would be paying to have aired on TV; now the anti-Mondale ad gained its widest audience attention courtesy of WCVB's *NewsCenter* 5. In the ad, a mocking voice was heard saying, "Vote for Mondale—he doesn't owe anybody anything. Har, har, har . . ." That is the front-runner's burden.

Gary Hart was unburdened on the local news, carrying only his success wherever he went. He was pictured beaming at his good fortune and basking in his new status as the rising alternative. And if his notices were not quite as effusive as Mondale's, at least they were 100 percent positive, picking up where his New Ideas campaign ads left off.

WCVB-TV

ANNE MCGRATH: The man who bills himself as the candidate of New Ideas got a new lease on his political aspirations. With his surprise second-place showing in Iowa, Gary Hart was noticeably cheerful and optimistic today, fortified by the Iowa decision.

MCGRATH: How do you feel this morning, Gary Hart . . . ?

HART: I feel much younger. Maybe even thirty-nine [and he laughed].

MCGRATH: Hart has a new sense of confidence and purpose. His campaign has gained credibility and the candidate knows the money needed to finance that effort isn't far behind. . . . You couldn't say that Hart campaign workers are feeling smug today. But if pressed, they will say "I told you so." And then they will tell you that Gary Hart has the organization in New Hampshire to repeat the Iowa surprise.

The closest thing to a negative note for Hart on that WCVB newscast came only when Martha Bradlee sought to inject a note of numerical reality.

CHET CURTIS: Is it a two-way race between Mondale and Hart? I mean, Hart is making much about finishing second. It was a surprise, but yet, you can make an argument that nobody really finished second.

MARTHA BRADLEE: I think that's the argument that I would make. No one really finished second. I mean, Gary Hart was about thirty-five points behind Walter Mondale, if you look at the figures. . . . That's an enormous difference.

Over at WBZ, meanwhile, correspondent Andy Hiller, working with roughly the same figures, was explaining how it was Hart's distant second-place finish that was "the story of Iowa." He unwrapped that word—*momentum*—that others were tying to Mondale, and wrapped it around Hart instead.

ANDY HILLER: It's no surprise that Walter Mondale did so well in Iowa. His organization was always recognized as the best there. He was backed by labor and he's even been called Iowa's third senator, because when he represented neighboring Minnesota he was always sensitive to Iowa's issues. So, once again, the story of Iowa is the runner-up, Gary Hart, who now has that political magic called momentum. And the biggest story is John Glenn, Iowa's biggest loser, who now has a week to turn it around.

On the matter of John Glenn, all were agreed. All journalists—print and electronic, local and national—pegged it for the disaster that it was. And Glenn was left with no choice but to be seen, live and on tape, looking like General Custer striving to put some positive spin on the early returns from Little Big Horn.

WBZ-TV

DAN REA: John Glenn's presidential campaign . . . is in trouble. John Glenn now has to turn the disaster of Iowa into a solid showing here in New Hampshire. All of that in just seven days. . . . Senator, if you don't reverse things, and reverse them dramatically, here in New Hampshire, how much longer can you stay in?

GLENN: Well, and if Mr. Mondale comes in third up here, that'll change things too. So all these hypothetical questions—uh, we're looking forward to getting out a big vote up here.

REA: But it was not hypothetical last night. What do you have to do here in New Hampshire?

GLENN: Well, we plan to do a lot of work this week across New Hampshire and do just the best we very possibly can do.

THE NETWORKS

Network television left no doubt that Mondale would at least be off to a strong front-running start in that final week in New Hampshire. Not surprisingly, their reports were more pointed and polished than those of their local-television colleagues in Boston. They gave Mondale his due, used restraint in discussing Hart, and wore out the thesaurus in finding new ways to describe the disaster that had befallen Glenn.

Consider NBC's:

TOM BROKAW: Good evening. The results of the Iowa Democratic caucuses are being examined, explained, juggled, praised, and dismissed tonight. But however they turn up, they add up to a big victory for the front-runner—former Vice-President Walter Mondale. He was way ahead of all the others.

Then Brokaw gave way to chief political correspondent Roger Mudd, who offered assessments of what the results meant for each candidate.

Mudd on Mondale: "This victory makes his nomination seem inevitable."

Mudd on Hart: "He had a message: New Leadership. And it drew much of the anti-Mondale vote. He must now ripen and mature within six days, or wither on the vine in New Hampshire."

Mudd on McGovern: "Proof that a candidate with distinctive personality and a relaxed approach can score without big money."

Mudd on Cranston: "The campaign of this aging, gaunt, one-issue man failed to meet its own minimum."

Mudd on Glenn: "A virtual wipeout. He failed to prove his own theory—that he's the one to broaden the party base. He's become the victim of open contempt by his own staff."

Mudd on Askew: "He proved an organization of antiabortion Catholics and Amway distributors is not the way to victory."

Mudd on Jackson: "He will hang on at least until the Alabama, Georgia, and Mississippi primaries on Super Tuesday."

Mudd on Hollings: "He must live or die in New Hampshire."

NBC's top-of-the-line political correspondent Ken Bode, whose reports are always savvy and never routine, followed with a piece on Hart, noting: "In reality, Gary Hart is fighting the notion that this race is all but over, that neither he nor anyone else has enough money, time, or organization to overtake the front-runner."

And correspondent Mary Nissenson reported on Glenn: "Glenn tried to put on a brave front as he left Boston for New Hampshire this morning. But his aides know he can't win the primary, and some fear a weak showing will kill his candidacy."

At ABC, prophetic observations of caution were noted by two correspondents, Brit Hume, who in his first major campaign role would spend the year assigned to Mondale and would develop into a strong political reporter, and Sander Vanocur, the respected veteran of political wars.

First, Hume: "Walter Mondale stepped off his flight from Iowa today onto the more treacherous political ground of New Hampshire. Many a front-runner has come to grief in this state's first-in-the-nation primary now just a week off, and Mondale was careful not to overplay his Iowa triumph."

Then, Vanocur (asked by anchor Peter Jennings whether Mondale should be perturbed at his front-runner status and the expectations that come with it): "He shouldn't be perturbed, Peter, he should be concerned, because the voters of New Hampshire over the years have demonstrated a certain amiable quality. But it's a kind of amiable perversity when it comes to upsetting the well-laid plans of politicians."

* * *

If Wednesday, February 22, is to be remembered at all, it will be recalled as a day of campaign-message perversity, with John Glenn setting the standard for all to follow, or avoid. Mondale and Hart both had rather quiet television days, but Glenn dominated the political news—a bit more so than he had intended, in fact.

It was, for Glenn, a day of mixed messagery. First Glenn's managers paid ten thousand dollars for a special five-minute ad on WBZ that would not only air on prime time but would air during what was normally the last five minutes of the evening news (it is a decision whose profitability is undeniable, but professionalism is questionable, to put it charitably). But then the Glenn handlers topped their own message by closing down their Maine headquarters earlier in the day—an event that created a dire-straits, downcast Glenn story at the top of the newscast, after Glenn had just paid dearly to create his own upbeat finale.

WBZ-TV, 6 P.M.

A picture of John Glenn dominates the screen at the beginning of the day's political news, filling up all of the tube except for the part that contains three image-shattering words: "Campaign Closes Down."

LIZ WALKER (ANCHOR): With his back to the wall in the Democratic presidential race, John Glenn has closed down his Maine campaign headquarters. . . .

GLENN: We're not closing up shop completely in Maine. We still will be in Maine. But with the importance of New Hampshire coming up next Tuesday, we decided to reallocate some of our resources. . . .

JACK WILLIAMS (ANCHOR): We go now—live—to *Eyewitness* newsman John Henning. He's at our New Hampshire bureau. John?

HENNING: All right, Jack. Glenn was in New Hampshire today trying to bounce back from Iowa. . . . Glenn talked to [factory] workers, checked out products, and did his best to look like a winner rather than a candidate who may be on the ropes. . . . This newscast will be five minutes shorter tonight because we will be airing a John Glenn political ad. The ad is expected to be upbeat and not include any attacks on front-runner Walter Mondale.

(In the context of Glenn's campaign, that last sentence was indeed news—not in the sense that "Man Bites Dog" is news, but perhaps in the sense that "Dog Doesn't Bite Man" is news.)

In one of those occurrences that happened almost daily in local-television coverage, WBZ then decided to show its viewers its live-remote technology. They went live to a Jesse Jackson rally. It did not feature Jackson—he wasn't there yet; and in fact it was not really a rally—it had not even started.

HENNING: . . . Tonight Jackson will talk to students at the New Hampshire College in Hooksett. For more we go there to Dan Rea, who's standing there live. Dan, what's going on? Are they waiting for Jackson over there?

REA: Yes, we are waiting for Jesse Jackson, John. The Reverend Jackson is due here about six-thirty or so. The crowd is gathering here. . . .

What this was, it turned out, was one of those Revlons—a Sony sandwich—in which other brief videotaped bits from earlier in Jackson's day were shown. It was, like almost all other newsclips of Jackson in those days, a videotape he would just as soon not have had shown at all, because he was asked once again about anti-Semitic remarks that he was said to have made. Jackson had been short-circuiting his own message for more than a week, as he attempted to deny and dissemble his way out of an unpleasant situation created by an apparently accurate report; what happened, of course, was that he only made matters worse. A February 13 report in *The Washington Post* had said that Jackson had been known to refer to Jews in private conversations as "Hymies" and to New York City as "Hymietown."

Jackson's response, for days, was to say what he told Lesley Stahl on CBS's *Face the Nation:* "It simply is not true. And I think the accuser ought to come forth." But everywhere he went he was asked about it, and that issue and his denial would be the Jesse Jackson news of the day. The information had been supplied to the *Post* by one of its own reporters, who said he had been sitting with Jackson and had heard him make those remarks. Jackson's answer to that was, variously, that he did not remember saying such a thing, and so on. Eventually he would admit to having perhaps said it, but by not owning up to it in the beginning (with appropriate apologies and tributes for men and women of all persuasions and hues), he succeeded only in stifling his own "Rainbow" message while allowing the anti-Semitism controversy to rage as he repeatedly avoided facing up to the truth.

* * *

The *Eyewitness News* team closed up shop five minutes early and on came John Glenn in his videotaped commercial.

"Good evening," Glenn began, standing in front of bookshelves and putting his best face forward. "Tonight on the news you've probably been hearing what I have been hearing all week—that before even a single vote has been cast here in the nation's first primary in New Hampshire, the Democratic race for president is already over. . . . Well I don't believe that and I believe you still have the Yankee independence and judgment for which you've become famous.

"There are still only two candidates in this race—Fritz Mondale and myself—with the broad national support, resources, and ballot access to be nominated. . . ."

Problem was, the Glenn news item earlier in the show seemed to contradict the assertion of his paid ad.

WCVB-TV, 6 P.M.

CHET CURTIS: On *NewsCenter 5* at six, Mary Richardson will be live from New Hampshire with more on the presidential primary.

MARY RICHARDSON: Some conservative Democrats are ready to vote "none of the above" in next Tuesday's primary. They have a strategy of their own up their sleeves. We'll tell you all about it when we come back.

In an unusual news decision, WCVB opened its newscast with a long story about a relatively minor effort by a few conservative Democrats to urge New Hampshire Democrats to write in the name of Ronald Reagan in the party's primary election. The news decision gave the effort far more airtime than its sponsors could ever afford to buy. The write-in proved to be an event of little consequence.

Later in the newscast, WCVB passed up one more chance to deal with issues of regional or national importance, and instead devoted another long segment of campaign news to an interview with young schoolchildren about which candidate they favored for president.

WBZ-TV, 11 P.M.

In its late-night newscast, WBZ made a stab at covering issues, but it turned out to be only a superficial cut. After President Reagan's press conference, they had Alan Cranston in their studio to give his reaction—live—on the *Eyewitness News*. And that, in fact, was the first question from newscaster John Henning: "You heard what the president said on a number of issues. What did you react to most strongly?" Cranston took issue with Reagan's view that Americans feel safer since he became president.

HENNING: Let's get specific on defense spending. The president was slamming the Democrats tonight for not having a plan for cutting defense spending. [They showed a clip of the president saying he wants to see Democratic plans to study what they would do to "our national security."] . . . Some people think he has a point —that the Democrats haven't been meeting with him for those plan negotiations on cutting the defense budget.

CRANSTON: Well I have offered a plan for cutting the defense budget by thirty-eight billion dollars. Specifically, we can cut twenty-five billion dollars out of weapons systems we do not need, like the MX and the Midgetman and sea-launched cruise missiles. We can cut five billion dollars out of military construction and keep personnel at the level it presently holds to. And we can eliminate another eight billion dollars in research and development on absurd plans like Star Wars, for example. . . .

Cranston's answer cried out for follow-up questions aimed at pinning him down on the very point that Reagan was making: What would each of these cuts do to America's national security? Henning, however, beat a quick retreat to the security of the horse race.

HENNING: I want to talk about politics just for a minute. What about your campaign in Iowa on Monday. You came in fourth in the caucuses. . . . Now the vote in Iowa certainly has to impact here in New Hampshire, yet you spent more time in Iowa than you did here. How will Iowa affect your campaign here on the votes you'll get?

[Cranston of course said he thought he would do well; and Henning of course asked how well; and Cranston didn't answer but made one last campaign pitch; and so it went.]

The night's politics were not quite over. There was one late-breaking development, and Liz Walker had the story.

WALKER: Presidential candidate John Glenn is pressing ahead tonight with his campaign trying to keep everything upbeat—literally. [Glenn has joined with three other fellows in a barbershop quartet, and they are harmonizing, "Who cares what the 'morrow shall bring . . ."]

That photo opportunity was so hokey it worked. WBZ was perfectly willing to use this fresh but substanceless piece and scrap that politically disastrous story about the Glenn campaign's fold in Maine. It got him a new and decidedly more positive tone for his late-night coverage. That "Campaign Closes Down" graphic that had been the top of the six o'clock political report disappeared entirely, as the Glenn story was recast to match the videotape of the barbershop quartet singing. Glenn's fold in Maine now rated one sentence, delivered in passing, at the end of the piece.

THURSDAY, FEBRUARY 23

This was the day Gary Hart's video boom was born. It began with a poll vault.

Both WBZ and WCVB aired polls done after the Iowa caucus results and the media coverage of them. Both showed Hart gaining ground rapidly, Glenn losing ground just as rapidly, and Mondale merely holding his own. WBZ's survey, conducted and analyzed on the air by the respected Boston pollster Edward Reilly, showed Mondale with 32 percent and Hart tying Glenn for second with 15 percent of those interviewed. WCVB's poll had Hart still third, four points behind Glenn but clearly on the move.

Hart's strong television day had just begun. He next took the cameras on a tour of a hazardous-waste site, serving up a fine visual setting to help television solve its difficulty in finding a sufficiently sexy way to present his views on that issue (remember Dennis Kauff's explanation about how coverage of issues comes down to show-and-tell television?).

And there was more strong Hart video to come.

WBZ-TV, 6 P.M.

Mondale may hold a two-to-one lead in their poll, but the picture on the screen is Gary Hart. And the caption: "Moving Up."

LIZ WALKER: His campaign ignited in Iowa, now an exclusive *Eyewitness News* poll shows Gary Hart moving up in New Hampshire. The story next on the evening edition.

[The *Eyewitness* theme song is played and the *Eyewitness News* team is introduced.]

WALKER: Good evening. Here's what's happening. With New Hampshire's first-in-the-nation presidential primary just a few days away, some encouraging news tonight for the Hart campaign.

JACK WILLIAMS: An exclusive *Eyewitness News* poll shows Gary Hart tied for second among New Hampshire voters that we surveyed. . . . [Only then was front-runner Mondale and co–runner-up Glenn mentioned.]

The show then went to *Eyewitness* newsman Dan Rea, who, viewers were told, was "live" at the very spot where two hours later there would be a debate among the candidates. From that "live" setting, Rea introduced a videotape of Hollings kicking the right stuffing out of John Glenn.

HOLLINGS: We . . . thought all year long . . . that we had an alternative in John Glenn. . . . But he has flunked the course. He had every opportunity. He had the name recognition. He had the magazine cover articles. He had the movies made about him. He had the money, and everything else. And now he's struck out.

It is important to note that while Hollings's attacks could cut into Glenn's support (just as Glenn's attacks had done to Mondale), the support once again did not flow to the attacker. It shifted to the only Certified Political Alternative in the field: Gary Hart, C.P.A.

Mondale then appeared on the newscast, looking bored and sounding boring, as he droned his way through an attack on President Reagan's press-conference performance. "Last night, we were starkly reminded that the fundamental issue in this campaign is the question of presidential leadership, as all America saw . . ." What the viewers saw of Mondale throughout this last week of New Hampshire was precisely what Mondale was giving them, which was not much, given the cautious nature of the candidate and his campaign.

Pollster Ed Reilly came on next to report that most of the undecided voters had indeed already made one decision—they were looking for an alternative to Mondale.

* * *

The video short story of New Hampshire 1984 reached a new turn in plot development when—just as those undecideds were deciding to find an alternative—Hart was being clearly portrayed as just that. *NewsCenter* 5's Anne McGrath had nothing but positive adjectives and labels to paste on Hart's now-thriving alternative candidacy in this piece that aired on WCVB-TV at 6 P.M. The visual was Hart touring the hazardous-waste site. McGrath had just offered the view that Hart had displayed "a fresh sense of direction" at the site. In her report, Hart never got around to saying what he thought should be done about the mess, but he got a valuable testimonial in the form of image-building adjectives and labels.

MCGRATH: . . . Hart realized his high visibility is an opportunity to put across his New Ideas candidacy. And he is projecting himself as a Populist candidate, who listens to the . . . fears and concerns about groundwater contamination and death. . . . The Hart campaign is capitalizing on this difference in style to point out in a subtle way the separation between Gary Hart and Walter Mondale. And the candidate is complementing that with the single-minded view that Walter Mondale is now his only rival.

HART: As this race continues between myself and Vice-President Mondale, we will continue to contrast ourselves on policies and on issues. But that is not an attack. That is a debate over the direction of the future of this party and hopefully the country. . . .

It was about this time that Mondale got to make an appearance on the news—and again, he presented a stark contrast to Hart. Looking down at a piece of paper, he read for the cameras a brief attack on Reaganomics that he could have delivered with fire and conviction, if he had only cared to do so. Instead he spoke with all the enthusiasm of a guy reading his list of Saturday chores. He looked like he was taking New Hampshire for granted, and in her closing, McGrath seemed to be conveying just that.

MCGRATH: Walter Mondale knows he is well on his way to winning the Democratic nomination. . . .

The video short story rolled on. NBC's report about the cash flow that had gone from a trickle to a tidal wave was right on the money, but aside from its accuracy, it also added to the image-building look of a winner that was starting to envelop Hart.

NBC NIGHTLY NEWS

Gary Hart is beaming from the screen as correspondent Don Oliver reports about campaign money.

DON OLIVER: Until last Monday night, Gary Hart never got this kind of attention; and until last Monday night, Gary Hart's campaign was taking in contributions of just $2,000 a day. Now, the figure is about $12,000 a day. Some of that money is unsolicited. That's why the candidate is smiling.

HART: My candidacy is for those who still dream dreams . . .

Meanwhile, a subplot was being developed in the video storyline. Jesse Jackson's ill-chosen comments about Jews were being reexamined, and his efforts to dissemble his way out of trouble would only prolong and magnify his dilemma. NBC correspondent Bob Kur weighed in with a piece about Jesse Jackson and the Jews. And from the attention given the subject and Jackson's poor handling of it, it was clear that Jackson's candidacy was stalling of its own accord just as Hart's was being propelled.

KUR: This February thirteenth *Washington Post* report caused the latest trouble. It said that in private conversations, Jackson has referred to Jews as Hymies and to New York as Hymietown. At the time, no source for the quotes was reported.

JACKSON: It simply is not true. And I think that the accuser ought to come forth.

KUR: Now, *Post* reporter Milton Coleman, who has covered the Jackson campaign, has told NBC News that Jackson made those comments in a conversation with him last month. Jackson now wants to change the subject. . . . [Kur noted that an extremist Jewish fringe group had been picketing Jackson.]

JACKSON: It's clear that my campaign has been hounded by certain members of the Jewish community. We're being sued. We're being persecuted.

THE LAST DEBATE BEFORE THE FIRST PRIMARY: THE VIEW FROM THE OTHER END OF THE FUNNEL

On the television screen, eight Democratic candidates for president were putting themselves through their strategic paces in this, the final debate of the 1984 New Hampshire primary campaign. And in Loretta Carney's living room in Rye, fourteen Democrats and Independents reached a unanimous consensus on one point: It was hardly a grand finale.

All of that was not the fault of the moderator, ABC's Barbara Walters, who handled her task with sufficient skill and at times rhetorical force; it was just that the candidates had come to the event anxious to work their own strategic agendas, which at times meant they were more bent on making their points than answering her questions.

In the end, the debate proved to be but a cupful or two of campaign message units out of the flood of political news that was pouring out of television sets, inundating voters in this last week. But those watching in Loretta Carney's living room came to some clear opinions:

Mondale—low-keyed , cautious, and confident—was judged adequate but unmemorable; he didn't gain much support, but didn't lose any either.

Hart—aggressive and anxious to attack—was considered impressive enough by some, but not as impressive as his latest media notices led everyone to expect him to be; he didn't gain as much as he had in past debates.

Glenn—to the surprise of all who had been watching his candidacy being buried by the past week's television news—put in his strongest debate performance of the campaign. He was impressive enough to win the backing of three middle-of-the-road and Independent voters who had come to the Carneys' house undecided. He abandoned his tactics of accusing Mondale of uttering "gobbledygook" and wooing "barons and bosses"; at one point, the normally quasiarticulate Glenn was actually eloquent as he took exception to Jesse Jackson's reference to him as "Mister Right Stuff." Said Glenn: "I came from the day when Martin Luther King had the 'right stuff,' John F. Kennedy had the 'right stuff,' the time of moving ahead. I'm very proud to have had some of that 'right stuff.' " It was the first time he had come away from a debate gaining support in the group studies I conducted for *The Washington Post*. But it hardly seemed enough to counter the negative avalanche of nonstop television-news reports that were burying Glenn's candidacy even before the voters of New Hampshire had had a chance to do the job.

And viewers were at times puzzled by the byplay that occurred when Hart tried to spar with Mondale. For example, Barbara Walters asked what each candidate would do if Americans were taken hostage, as in the case of Iran. Mondale was quick to defend the way his former boss, President Carter, had handled the matter. "Every one of the hostages is home with his family tonight because we did not do anything wild and crazy," Mondale said. That in fact was not true; Carter had ordered a daring rescue attempt after receiving intelligence assessments that some hostages could well be killed in the effort and perhaps a considerable number of them would die. That military effort failed in a series of mishaps culminating in a fiery crash in the desert of Iran. Hart tried to make that point, saying: "If we had been prepared, if we had reformed our military institutions, if we were prepared for these contingencies, perhaps that effort to rescue those hostages would have worked. But it should only occur after every possible diplomatic and humane step has been taken."

Those in the group were unsure about whether the facts supported Mondale or Hart. And perhaps because of such exchanges, neither Mondale nor Hart gained or lost support in this group. That contrasted with Hart's more impressive gains among groups of voters watching the earlier debates in New England and Iowa.

There was one clear loser in the debate—it was Jesse Jackson. Walters determinedly pressed Jackson on those comments about Jews and Hymies. It was the first time any questioner had dared to press Jackson on any matter in the debates to date, the first time any questioner had dared to suggest that his response was, in fact, not responsive. Jackson said he had "no recollection" that he had used the term Hymies or Hymietown. Several times he added: "I am not anti-Semitic." When Walters asked about a 1979 statement in which Jackson said, "I'm sick and tired of hearing about the Holocaust. Jews don't have a monopoly on suffering," Jackson said the remarks were taken "out of context."

As all of that was going on, one guest in the Carneys' living room sat frowning, shaking her head, closing her eyes in frustration and disgust. Kay Dunfey, an elder member of New Hampshire's wealthy hotel-owning family and a volunteer in Jackson's campaign office, was clearly troubled. "I'm at the point of defection," she later told others in the room. "Jesse foundered on that first question—and if he can't answer that, there goes the Rainbow Coalition." The next day, Dunfey, who had been a Roman Catholic nun for thirty-four years, took off her Rainbow Coalition button.

Until he began stonewalling and caterwauling on that Hymie question ten days earlier, Jackson had been making significant gains among white liberals in New Hampshire. In the end, he succeeded in driving much of that support out of his own camp because of his decision to dissemble about something he would eventually have to admit was true.

FRIDAY, FEBRUARY 24

When future generations of campaign media-and-message strategists want to understand what *not* to have their candidates do, they will look back to February 24, 1984, and the three days that followed, and they will take their text from Walter Mondale. For this was the first of a series of campaign-windup days when Mondale and his advisers left for political posterity a generous catechism of commandments—all beginning with "Thou shalt not."

Consider what the voters saw of these two front-runners who were offering themselves as the next leader of the nation. Gary Hart was out there daily, selling himself on the stump and in his ads as the New Ideas candidate, offering a New Generation of Leadership, and building on the sort of John F. Kennedy idealism that is still remembered worshipfully, especially among the Democrats of New England.

Mondale, meanwhile, was offering as little of himself as possible. Unlike Hart, he was not providing New Hampshire voters with explanations of the kind of president he would be. He was not giving them a reason to vote *for* him for president.

WCVB's Clark Booth did a masterful job of giving viewers a sense of the tone and intent of the Mondale campaign that Friday evening. If television was doing poorly on the issues, at least it did well in conveying the vacuous nature of this video-game strategy of politics by media event.

The television screen showed Mondale shaking hands in a grocery store. Nothing more.

WCVB, 6 P.M.

CLARK BOOTH: If the candidate has nothing to do and no deep desire to say anything on a given day, he still must be seen, every day, in preferably as harmless a setting as possible. So it was that Walter

> Mondale was led to the produce section of a Concord grocery store at midday. The international board of media heavyweights who always attach themselves to the leader followed dutifully behind. There, Mr. Mondale held court with as many shoppers as were allowed to funnel past him by campaign aides and the Secret Service. He set up shop in front of the oranges, later moved next to the celery, and wound up being framed by bays containing carrots, broccoli, and artificial lemon juice. He got to meet perhaps fifty people. All of us, of course, were kept at a discreet distance. . . . At the end of the gig, Mr. Mondale chatted with a Scandinavian newsman. They spoke in English, but no one could hear him anyway. Then the entourage hustled back to Manchester for some rest, secure in the knowledge that they had claimed their fair share of television news time that will come out of here tonight. Mr. Mondale's appointment in the produce section took all of fifteen minutes and the world will little note —nor long remember—what happened there.

That evening's newscast on WCVB began, by the way, with Hart filling the screen speaking in behalf of his candidacy. It was an ad— WCVB is one of the many local stations around the country that sell ads immediately adjacent to news shows; many even sell ads to candidates for airing within the news hour. It is an abominable practice. The strategists want their ads there because people will confuse them with the news and the ads will be considered more believable. The stations want to sell political ads in that space because they care about making money more than they care about ethics, civic welfare, and commonweal.

Hart's ad at least features Hart doing the talking rather than a deep basso profundo.

HART (IN HIS AD): We've known other times when the past threatened our future. But we acted as a generation against racial hatred. To stop the war in Vietnam. To demand a halt in the pollution of our land. We acted and we did overcome. But now our promise is slipping away. The politicians of yesterday are trading our future by asking our price instead of challenging our idealism. My candidacy is for those who still dream dreams, who will stand together once more to build an American future.

It was right after Hart's call for idealism and a candidacy for those who still dream dreams that the viewer was confronted with the impressive spectacle of Mondale at the produce market. By that time, the week-long video short story seemed to be moving swiftly toward the more impressive-looking candidacy of Hart.

WBZ, 6 P.M.

Videotapes of the darkest hours of the Carter-Mondale administration—the frustration and even humiliation of the 1979–80 American hostage crisis in Iran—had somehow become part of the *Eyewitness* newscast of this day in 1984. The station, in one of the few moments of enterprise effort of the campaign, had decided to do an in-depth report on one of the controversies from the previous night's debate. And they picked the Mondale and Hart exchange on the hostage crisis as their point of departure. Mondale aides would later protest vehemently, and with understandable concern, that it had been unfair to rehash that most painful moment of the past administration at this sensitive juncture of the campaign. But, in fact, Mondale had brought it all upon himself in his answer that night by extending himself beyond the facts concerning the rescue mission that failed; and that had given Hart the debate-opening he had been looking for.

The Q-and-A of the debate was recycled, and then Hart was asked by correspondent Mike Macklin whether he had meant to say the Carter-Mondale administration had failed to take advantage of other options that had been available.

HART: I don't know whether there were other diplomatic avenues available to the administration, and I just brought the conversation back to point out that a rescue mission was attempted in which a number of Americans lost their lives, and I think was generally considered a fiasco. . . .

WBZ political editor Gerry Chervinsky remembers how Mondale's national and local aides reacted after the story aired. "They went crazy," he said. ". . . In the world of complaints about media coverage, the most complaints we got about anything we did was the story we did on Mondale and Iran. [They said:] 'How can you three days before a primary put pictures on the hostages on and do a story about us and Mondale's involvement with the hostages.' . . . I just remember them screaming. . . . It was showing the pictures. Hart could say what Hart wanted to say in the debate, but how could we show those pictures of the hostages being paraded around? . . . I understand . . . their point of view. . . . But I also understand that he [Mondale] was the vice-president when it was going on. That to me was the key. . . . I don't think they can expect us not to . . . pursue that."

Jesse Jackson also got himself some more television-news time, both on WBZ's local news and on the channel's NBC network-news show. Once again, his time was devoted to that issue he was keeping alive with his lack of candor. "Since 1979, I have been hounded and persecuted by some elements of the Jewish community," Jackson said in the local-news segment. And later: "I certainly do not intend to remain hounded and pushed and persecuted without standing up for my very basic civil rights and my very basic self-respect." At that point, remember, he still had not yet told the very basic truth about these remarks.

The short story continued to unwind. At eleven P.M., Mondale was not to be seen at a state employees' union forum, while Hart came by in time to speak up for the new generation in attacking Reaganomics.

WBZ-TV, 11 P.M.

DENNIS KAUFF: The candidates finally found themselves a union that hasn't endorsed Walter Mondale—the 6,300-member state employees' association of New Hampshire. And when Mondale passed up tonight's candidates' forum, it did not win him many votes.

WOMAN UNION MEMBER: I wish he would have felt it would have been important to come here. . . .

MAN UNION MEMBER: I don't think myself, as a union member . . . that I'm automatically going to vote for Walter Mondale. . . .

[*Enter Hart.*]

HART: And we cannot . . . tolerate a government that is willing to spend two hundred billion dollars a year that it does not have, from the future earnings—indeed from the very future—of our children and their children, to satisfy an election-year economy.

SATURDAY, FEBRUARY 25, 1984

Walter Mondale's video on Saturday picked up where his video on Friday left off. As seen on television, he was ever-cautious, ever-complacent, and—mainly—never giving New Hampshire Democrats a single reason why they should vote for him for president. Mondale's Saturday television began with an interview he had taped earlier in the day with WBZ correspondent Dennis Kauff. The Mondale officials had threatened to cancel the interview in their fury over the Iranian hostage piece of the day before. They agreed to permit the interview, but stipulated that Kauff could not ask anything more about the hostage issue, Chervinsky said. That, of course, only made it mandatory as a point of professional honor that Kauff ask about the hostage issue on camera—which he did, but that question and answer were not aired because, Chervinsky explained, there was nothing new in what Mondale said. What was interesting about the interview, actually, was that there was nothing interesting in anything else Mondale said, despite the best efforts of Kauff to draw him out of his protective shell. "That was about as much as Mondale wanted to talk about issues," Chervinsky recalled. "He was horrible; it was horrible."

WBZ-TV, 6 P.M.

DENNIS KAUFF: . . . With just two more full days of campaigning left before Tuesday's vote, Walter Mondale is a man who exudes confidence. He is calm. He is relaxed, almost serene. He considers his quest right on schedule and it is a schedule he has been following since leaving the vice-presidency four years ago. . . . [Mondale is sitting in a high-backed living-room chair in that guest cottage at the Wayfarer; the chair is so big it seems to engulf him, making this physically substantial man appear far smaller than he is in life.]

MONDALE: I'm convinced I'm ready now, and could be a good president, and I would hope a great president. But more than that, I'm very angry. I'm angry about these deep deficits and the cost of that policy to our future.

[He looked far from angry, however; he spoke very softly, seeming to lack conviction and force and looking indeed serene.]

KAUFF: Hollings, Glenn, Hart—they all say that you might be able to get the nomination but you won't be able to beat Ronald Reagan.

MONDALE: . . . I know how to campaign. I know what I'm doing. . . . I'm going to win this thing.

KAUFF: A poll that we just took where we asked people their attitudes towards various candidates . . . indicated that conservatives think you're conservative, moderates think you're moderate, liberals think you're liberal, people who want to cut the budget think you'll do that, and people who want to increase spending on various programs think you'll do that too. And then your opponents call you all things to all people. Aren't they being proven right?

MONDALE: No . . . I am a conservative in the sense that I want a tight budget; I want those deficits down. I am a moderate because I want things to work. . . . And I am a liberal in the sense that I want justice and fairness in American life. And that really defines what America is up to. And I'm proud of that.

At WCVB-TV, correspondent Kirby Perkins also had an exclusive interview with Mondale, which produced much the same as Kauff's on WBZ. Perkins, however, tried another tack, hoping to see if Mondale was willing to take a stand in the growing controversy between Jesse Jackson and the Jews. Mondale wanted nothing to do with that, and he responded with a classic combo of duck and dodge, with a fillip of filibuster thrown in.

KIRBY PERKINS: Your views, sir, on the current dispute between Jesse Jackson and some elements of the Jewish community.

MONDALE: You know, I have difficulty knowing exactly what was said. Or what wasn't said. And I don't wish to pass judgment on things when I don't know. You know, it's my personal opinion on the Middle East, for example, that we should not deal with the PLO. . . .

PERKINS: The Democratic party has some traditional coalitions . . . central elements to it being Jewish voters and black voters. And do you think that there is a chance that this fight is divisive?

MONDALE: First of all, if I'm the nominee, one of my strengths is that I can bring everybody together. I am very strong in minority America because of my lifetime commitment. . . . [et cetera, duckus, dodgis et al.]

The networks, meanwhile, had begun to celebrate Hart's genuine increase in public support. CBS that evening presented a special report by its accomplished correspondent Bruce Morton that was a sort of it's-time-to-get-to-know-Gary-Hart story. The piece went through the litany of Hart's early political involvement with the John F. Kennedy campaign of 1960, his campaign-manager era with George Mc-

Govern's presidential race in 1972, and how his positions have evolved into less liberal stances over the years.

And NBC's Don Oliver did a piece on how the candidates had been attacking each other—which really means they had mainly been attacking Mondale. Among the examples used was a clip of Hart's stinger: "When Ronald Reagan invaded Grenada, it took the front-runner in the Democratic race, who dares to be cautious, eighteen days before he decided where he stood on that invasion. . . ."

WBZ-TV, 11 P.M.

Mondale's exclusive interview with Dennis Kauff, the one where he is sitting engulfed in the huge chair, dispensing political placebos for the electorate, is playing one more time. It's a different slice this time; he is saying "I never made a promise that I can't keep," and that sort of thing.

Hart's segment on the nighttime news is everything Mondale's isn't. He is dressed casually but correctly in sport shirt and jacket, and he is addressing a gathering, standing tall and talking like a leader—the index finger of his right hand jabs the air in that practiced way that makes it unmistakable which leader he is trying to look like and talk like. He still speaks in that flat-accented Mid-America voice, but he has gotten his Kennedyesque stance perfected to the point where he is beginning to look from a distance less like Gary Hart imitating JFK, and more like John F. Kennedy lip-syncing Gary Hart recordings.

HART: I have confidence in this—that you not only reject the politics of Ronald Reagan, but the politics of the Democratic past which will not lead this country into the 1980s and '90s!

SUNDAY, FEBRUARY 26, 1984

Suddenly the images of Campaign '84 crystallized on the nonstop television news for all to see. They were impossible to miss, impossible to forget. And their impact on the voting public, in retrospect, should have been obvious to all, even though at the time strategists and pundits alike were not quite attuned to experiencing the campaign as New Hampshire's voters were experiencing it in their homes.

IMAGES/HART:

He is the man on the move, the man of the hour. The ABC News/ *Washington Post* poll has shown Mondale clearly the front-runner, with 38 percent. But the news and excitement was Gary Hart's surge to second, with 24 percent, while Glenn was down to 14 and falling.

WCVB-TV, 6 P.M.

ANNE MC GRATH: . . . *NewsCenter* 5's Kirby Perkins found an *EXUBERANT* Hart on the campaign trail this morning!

[The theme from *Rocky* blares from the loudspeaker.]

KIRBY PERKINS: That's right—the theme from *Rocky*, that anthem of underdogs everywhere, is still with us. Senator Gary Hart. All of a sudden he has become New Hampshire's hot ticket, and crowds like this one in Nashua today are standing room only. Enthusiasm, excitement, and the self-proclaiming message of something new.

HART (looking strong and confident and ever-Kennedy, and trying to steer that same "Ask not" higher calling): The issue for the American people is our future or our past. . . . This campaign represents an opportunity for the seventy-five million Americans who did not vote in 1980 to come back to public service and concern about their country. . . .

PERKINS: . . . And to his credit, he has never used the phrase "You gotta have Hart." From Nashua, New Hampshire, Kirby Perkins, *NewsCenter* 5.

CBS NETWORK

It is the visual, not the dialogue or commentary, that carries the political impact. Gary Hart has gone to a lumberjacks' jamboree, and he is wearing blue jeans, a checkered shirt, and bold, bright-red suspenders. He is wielding a huge, long-handled woodsman's ax, and now he is poised with it over his head, gripping the handle with two hands and flinging it toward a tree-stump target of the woodsmen's competition. BULL'S-EYE! Hart hits the stump dead center, beating the loggers at their own game. They are stunned; he spreads his hands as if he had known all along what he was doing, and takes an exaggerated bow. The scene will be replayed many times on many channels in the next two days, as though a metaphor for what is happening in the campaign. Not to put too fine a point on it, but that was actually Hart's second throw of the ax. NBC originally used the footage of Hart's first throw, which missed; that tape apparently was not recycled.

IMAGES/MONDALE:

He is so confident, he is not even bothering to campaign anymore in New Hampshire. He is out in front of his own bandwagon, but he is marching to a lullaby.

WCVB-TV, 6 P.M.

ANNE MC GRATH: Front-runner Walter Mondale is confident he is doing well. He didn't even campaign in New Hampshire today. Mondale was working Maine and Vermont. [That is all Mondale rated on the six P.M. news.]

WBZ-TV, 6 P.M.

KATHERYN KIEFER (ANCHOR): All the polls seem to indicate that Walter Mondale will win the Democratic primary easily.
[Of course, the polls showed nothing of the kind; they merely showed Mondale with a lead as of the date the survey interviews stopped.]

MIKE MACKLIN: Front-runner Walter Mondale started this last Sunday of campaign . . . with churchgoers in Concord. . . . Outside the church, Mondale spoke with the calm assurance of a front-runner.

MONDALE (greeting churchgoers): It feels good, but it's too soon to know. Now isn't that a good story? You can take that. Use it any way you want.

IMAGES/GLENN

It is his gimmicks, not his views, that are shaping his last hours of video respectability. CBS News shows Glenn playing the role of a chef at a hotdog cookout as correspondent Bob Schieffer says: "the question is whether he can make a decent enough showing here to keep his campaign alive." NBC News has Glenn saying: "I wouldn't want to get skunked in New Hampshire and come in dead last in New Hampshire. That would not be a good omen for the future, I think." ABC News is quoting Glenn as saying it more succinctly: "Polls shmolls!"

WBZ-TV, 11 P.M.

DAN REA: A Sunday evening at the Portsmouth Bowlerama, the sort of place New Hampshirites can generally go to escape the candidates and cameras. But on this Sunday night, Ohio, Senator

John Glenn and entourage dropped by for a string of candlepins. [Glenn is pictured bowling with little success and a man is quoted about how tough candlepins is.]

REA: Senator Glenn bills himself as a candidate of the sensible center, an area of the alley that for the most part eluded him in Portsmouth. After a string of bowling, some handshaking with voters, many of whom weren't bowled over by the senator.

FIRST MAN: I think he's all right.

REA: Gonna vote for him?

FIRST MAN: He stands a good chance.

REA: You gonna vote for him?

FIRST MAN: Just say it that way. He stands a good chance.

REA: Of winning or getting your vote?

FIRST MAN: Of winning.

SECOND MAN: Somebody told me the TV cameras were here for a new bowling show that was going to go on TV, but I don't know.

REA: You think he'd be a better bowler or a better president?

SECOND MAN: I don't know.

REA: You gonna vote for him?

SECOND MAN: I'm gonna vote. I haven't decided really. I'm not committing myself. [All of the above represented John Glenn's last and longest chance to have his views aired on television in New Hampshire.]

IMAGES/JACKSON:

After more than a week of denials, a period in which he succeeded only in burying his own Rainbow message, Jackson finally admitted that he had indeed used the words *Hymies* and *Hymietown* in what he said were "private talks." He made that admission in a synagogue in New Hampshire.

IMAGES/ASKEW

On WBZ-TV, John Henning interviewed Reuben Askew—live, of course—for the six P.M. news. It is worth looking at to consider just what it is that local television officials choose to produce while saying there just is not enough time to look at the issues. These are the questions Henning asked. The answers are immaterial here; they were just what one might expect from a candidate in Askew's dire position (except that they were also unfailingly polite, given what surely must have been his temptation to make them otherwise).

HENNING: . . . No one has campaigned harder or longer than you have up here, yet the polls continue to show that you're down on the bottom of the pack. You've got to be a little disappointed.

HENNING: Can you change anything between now and then?

HENNING: Do you think you've been covered fairly by the media?

HENNING: What if you don't come in in the top four or five? What happens to the Askew campaign?

HENNING: Where would you like to come in on Tuesday?

HENNING: But if you don't?

HENNING: But the polls keep saying that you're not in the top five or six. Realistically, can you continue your campaign if you don't make it?

HENNING: All right . . . what else can you do to change this around? It looks like Mondale, Hart, and Glenn right now.

HENNING: Okay, Governor, thank you very much.

ASKEW: My pleasure to be with you.

HENNING: Dan, David, Katheryn? That's about it up here in New Hampshire. . . .

MONDAY, FEBRUARY 27, 1984

MORE IMAGES/MONDALE:

Walter Mondale's bizarre lack of awareness of the campaign messages he was sending continued on the television news. The front-runner —who hoped to win the approval of those independent-minded, Populist-oriented New Hampshire Democrats and Independents—called out another corporal's guard of blue-worsted suits. And he surrounded himself not with New Hampshire voters but with a new cadre of pols and endorsers—in Boston, no less. On the television news, Mondale continued to have nothing to say to the people of New Hampshire. All Mondale gave the voters in the nation's first primary state was the knowledge that he had collected the endorsement of the mayor of Boston. That, of course, is something these very unmachine, nonorganization New Hampshire Democrats and Independents would view in one of two ways: Either they would have no opinion about it, or they would view it with scorn and derision.

That was how Walter Mondale chose to conclude on the television news this New Hampshire campaign he had been waging for three years.

The local anchors all talked of it in terms of political reverence: Mondale made *an important stop* in Boston to pick up *a key endorsement*. They showed ample footage of Mondale and Mayor Ray Flynn of Boston touring Boston Harbor by boat, and they showed Mondale very concerned, asking questions about Boston's harbor development and so on—all of which was a great prelude for the next primary in Massachusetts, one of the Super Tuesday contests of March 13. But up in New Hampshire, it would of course be viewed only as a sign of supreme confidence or overconfidence, and clearly not indicating even the slightest concern for the views of New Hampshirites.

WCVB's Martha Bradlee concluded with a nice touch of added information about how the Boston Harbor–tour media event came to be, which revealed the true, misguided nature of Mondale's own message instincts.

WCVB-TV, 6 P.M.

MARTHA BRADLEE: Blue sky, chilly wind, and a brisk boat ride in Boston Harbor. Not the kind of setting you'd expect to find a presidential contender in this day before the New Hampshire primary. But most will agree Walter Mondale doesn't have to worry about tomorrow. . . . The Boston Harbor tour was not Mayor Flynn's idea. It was Walter Mondale's. In fact, he said he stayed up till two o'clock this morning reading up on Boston Harbor. . . . Mondale also insisted that he's taking nothing for granted—even though he is in Washington tonight and will not return to New Hampshire until long after the polls have closed.

ABC NEWS

The ABC News/*Washington Post* poll, which is doing nightly tracking of the candidates' standings, shows Hart gaining and Mondale slipping. Mondale is at 32 percent, Hart is at 25 percent. On the screen, Mondale looks unsure and sounds the same when he is asked to assess his New Hampshire prospects. "I think we're doing very fine, er, very well," he says.

IMAGES/HART:

Meanwhile, in the short story of New Hampshire 1984, Gary Hart was bringing his campaign to a very different crescendo. Hart was finishing in New Hampshire by surrounding himself with the people

PHOTO COURTESY OF CBS NEWS

CBS News 1984 election team on set (clockwise from left on platform): Dan Rather, Bill Moyers, Lesley Stahl, Bruce Morton, Bob Schieffer

PHOTO COURTESY OF CBS NEWS

CBS Evening News anchor Dan Rather conferring with producers off-camera on the election-unit set, 1984

PHOTO COURTESY OF CBS NEWS

CBS News White House correspondent Lesley Stahl interviewing Vice-President George Bush at the GOP Convention, 1984

PHOTO COURTESY OF CBS NEWS.

CBS News senior political correspondent Bob Schieffer covering the Democratic Convention, 1984

PHOTO COURTESY OF CBS NEWS

Dan Rather and vice-president for special events Joan Richman on CBS Election Headquarters set, 1984

EDDIE TAPP

Dennis Kauff (1953–1985), reporter for WBZ-TV in Boston

Tom Brokaw at the
New Hampshire primary,
1984

Roger Mudd at the
New Hampshire primary,
election night 1984

John Chancellor at the New Hampshire primary,
election night 1984

DONNA SVENNEVIK/ABC NEWS

William E. Lord, executive producer of *World News Tonight with Peter Jennings*

Brit Hume, ABC's Senate correspondent, covered Walter Mondale's campaign

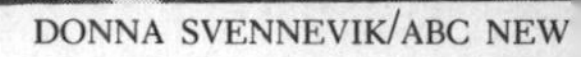

KEN REGAN/CAMERA FIVE

Roone Arledge, president of ABC News, oversaw all of the political coverage.

Ted Koppel in the ABC newsroom, Washington, D.C.

DONNA SVENNEVIK/ABC NEWS

TERESA ZABALA

Sam Donaldson reporting from the first 1984 presidential debate, in Louisville, Kentucky

DONNA SVENNEVIK/ABC NEWS

In New York City, Peter Jennings and David Brinkley co-anchored ABC News's 1984 political coverage, including primaries, conventions, and election.

of New Hampshire. There he was—the new matinee star of live at five, film at eleven—jabbing his finger into the air, giving them his New Ideas/New Generation message, and basking in their cheers. Polls had shown that most of the undecided voters were women, so Hart was standing in Concord at a rally his people had created as a television play for New Hampshire's women voters.

WCVB-TV, 6 P.M.

MARY RICHARDSON: But while the confident number-one man could afford to spend his day scooping up support for the Massachusetts primary, the others were digging in here. Gary Hart, the pollsters' favorite number-two man, was after the women's vote today. *NewsCenter* 5's Anne McGrath reports.

ANNE MC GRATH: The long days of campaigning began to show today in the face of the man looking for second place in New Hampshire. But Gary Hart recognized the importance of this moment when he would make the crucial pitch to women voters. So it was at this women's rally for Gary Hart that the candidate introduced his wife, Lee, and his daughter, Andrea. Hart's campaign in New Hampshire is managed by a woman, his pollster is a woman, and a woman handles the media. . . . Hart supports the Equal Rights Amendment and economic equality for women and he's urging women to use their power tomorrow.

[On the makeshift stage in Concord, Hart is doing his JFK and scoring against the absent front-runner, who of course holds precisely the same views and would have expressed them in just as forceful words, had he only thought to do it.]

HART: You literally have the chance and have the power to change the course of American history. We ask you to join with us. We ask you to help this campaign go from New Hampshire forward to offer to the American people an opportunity for hope and promise in the next decade and the next century. And with your help, I intend to be the nominee of the Democratic party and the next president of the United States.

[The correspondent came on to close the piece, and Hart himself could not have said it any better than she did.]

MC GRATH: Gary Hart hopes his strong appeal to women today will be discussed in homes across New Hampshire tonight. But more than that, Hart wants the voters to know that a vote for Gary Hart tomorrow is a vote for equality in America. Anne McGrath, *NewsCenter* 5, Manchester.

IMAGES/GLENN:

For John Glenn, things had reached the point where he cast no positive image at all on the television news. And so, in the hopes of being able to put forth one final bit of positive message for himself, he agreed to go live on WCVB's six o'clock news. There, at least, he could be sure that whatever he had to say would be aired.

It was, for Glenn, one final disaster. He found himself under a more relentless attack than any that had come from his opponents in their debates.

MARY RICHARDSON: Welcome, Senator. Senator, you finished fifth place in Iowa after your campaign predicted a strong second-place showing. I know you have said you will continue in the Southern primaries. How can you possibly go on if you don't at least finish second here tomorrow?

GLENN: All of these surmises about things . . . we're talking about a very small number of people. . . . But to think that I'm out here for some ego kick is ridiculous. I'm in this for the long haul. I got in it for principle . . . arms control . . . education on research . . . the future . . . our destiny . . .

RICHARDSON: But let's talk about here in New Hampshire.

GLENN: No, the answer in advance is no. Period. I'm not getting out. Period.

RICHARDSON: All right. . . . If you don't come in at least second, what does that tell you?

GLENN: I refuse to answer that. I went through that with you just a moment ago. I am in this thing because I believe in some principles . . . the long haul. . . . Let's put it the other way around. Let's say I win this tomorrow. Is Walter Mondale going to get out? I doubt it. . . .

RICHARDSON: . . . Is there a point at which a U.S. senator does the country better by withdrawing from a race that isn't going anywhere?

GLENN: . . . I'm going to stay in this because I believe in what I can do for the future of this country. . . . Big spenders . . . weak on defense . . . overpromising . . . I'm in it on principle. . . .

RICHARDSON: Senator Glenn, thank you for joining us here tonight.

AND IN CONCLUSION . . .

ABC NEWS

PETER JENNINGS: And finally, tonight, David Brinkley. David, there is a lot of frenzy up here, as we noted. . . . It makes me wonder whether New Hampshire voters don't . . . decide to really get pernicious and not tell us what is on their mind—period.

DAVID BRINKLEY: Well, I hope so. . . . Over the years, numerous candidates in New Hampshire have been sent away limping, staggering, white, pale, wondering if they're still alive, and in some cases they were not. Adlai Stevenson is one I happen to remember. . . . So if there are any surprises tomorrow, they will have to be at the expense of Walter Mondale. The only surprise would be if he won by less than, say, ten points, or something like that.

THE RESULTS

The short story of New Hampshire 1984 gave the pols and the pundits a surprise ending far grander than that. It turned out that this was a short story that had played itself out on the television nightly news so fast in the final week that the public-opinion polls just couldn't keep up. For those campaign players and aficionados who monitor politics by consulting the polls (or by consulting each other into the early-morning hours at the Sheraton Wayfarer Hotel watering hole outside Manchester), the results were a bit of a shock. But for those who had watched television with an eye toward the only messages the undecided voters of New Hampshire were getting in that last week, the line score on election night read like the logical conclusion to this videoplay. They voted for the only candidate who was featured each night giving them a convincing reason to vote for him for president, a sense of theme and direction—and a sense of the sort of leader he would be.

The margin of victory in New Hampshire proved to be not ten points for Mondale but eleven points—for Hart. The hero of the nonstop newscasts had 40 percent of the vote, Mondale 29, and Glenn 12.

EIGHT

REFLECTIONS FROM BEHIND THE EYE

Phil Balboni and Stan Hopkins, two executives for competing firms on the outskirts of Boston, were in agreement on one thing: They said they really could not have decided who to vote for in the 1984 Democratic presidential primary on the basis of the information provided by local television's final weeks of campaign coverage.

Their view is worth noting because they are the news directors of WCVB and WBZ, Boston's two most influential television stations.

Months after the New Hampshire voters had spoken in 1984, Phil Balboni sat in his office and put himself in their place. He considered the question that had just been put to him: Had his station's campaign coverage given him enough information to enable him to make a responsible choice for president in the last weeks of the primary campaign—that time period when many, and perhaps even most, voters make their final choices based on what they have seen on television?

"I think the answer would have to be no—I think it would be totally dishonest to say anything other than that," said Balboni, glancing around the office that is decorated with a few of the plaques and scrolls WCVB has won for news excellence. "All you're going to get in that period of time, for the most part, is a snippet of the candidate's ideas, his demeanor and attitudes in a very short form, probably within the context of a few minutes a day. And as I said, I think it would be totally dishonest to suggest that that was sufficient."

Balboni, who has risen through the ranks to command the news operations of his television station, is a most thoughtful and candid news chief. He is one of those local-television news executives who recognizes what is good about the product his organization produces and what is not; and when his admissions fall into that latter category, they are invariably accompanied by a resolve to improve next time around.

"I don't think it is fair to put such a total burden on us—but your postulate is probably accurate," he finally replied. "They [the voters] may not turn their attention to this business until that close [to Election Day], and therefore what they see at that point may be what determines their judgment.

"And that is most unfortunate. . . ."

Over at the opposition, WBZ's Stan Hopkins sat in a similar office, surrounded by similar plaques and scrolls for broadcast-news excellence, and voiced similar concerns about those areas in which local-television coverage—including his own station's—was not adequate for a voter seeking to make an informed decision.

"A lot of people are continually dismayed by the fact that the media covers the surface, the candidate as opposed to the issues," said Hopkins, who, like his counterpart across town, is a thoughtful news executive. "I think that is a valid criticism. But one of those things that television can do is it can be very revealing in terms of a person's character—characteristics of strength and leadership.

". . . I'm saying that's television. You have Walter Mondale. Here he comes, there he goes. Here he is laughing, cheering on his supporters. 'How do you feel, Walter?' 'I feel great. I'm going to have a big win in New Hampshire.' I think it's an important part of coverage of the campaign. Is it a valid criticism that television does not go beyond the surface? Absolutely! And does not get into issues? Yes! . . . I think certainly in local-broadcast journalism, and in the case of our national networks, it is a criticism that we should certainly take to heart, and find new ways to get at those issues."

Hopkins hesitated, dropped his voice, and added: "But if it is at the expense of showing some of those events and showing that personality and those characteristics . . . I think that would be a sad thing."

While the network-television news stars have the big nationwide reputations, it is the local-television news shows that have the big clout in America's major media markets. In Boston, for example, the Nielsen Station Index reports make it clear just how dominant the local-news viewership is. In the six to seven P.M. local-news hour in February 1984, WBZ news was watched by 432,000 adults (over the age of eighteen); the NBC News show that aired immediately afterward, from seven to seven-thirty P.M. was seen by 312,000 adults. WCVB news was watched by 424,000 adults in the six to seven P.M. time slot; the ABC News show that followed was seen by 329,000 adults. The third station, WNEV, the local CBS affiliate, was considered one of that network's weakest local affiliates; the local news was seen by 189,000 viewers, while the CBS News that followed drew 240,000 adult viewers, one of the few times when the network news outpolled the local affiliate, a circumstance that still left CBS far behind in the Boston market.

Not only do the local stations have more viewers, they also have many more hours of news each week. Local stations have anywhere from three to four hours of news a day—and some do even more. There is at least a half hour in the morning, at least a half hour at noon, at least an hour in the evening, and at least a half hour at night. Networks, of course, have a half hour of prime-time news in the evenings and have their morning shows, portions of which are given to news but most to entertainment and so on in the waking hours of most of America.

Moreover, the news pieces done by reporters at local stations are longer than those done by their network counterparts—often two and three times longer. WCVB's Martha Bradlee, for example, estimated that her pieces "were never shorter than two and a half minutes" and would generally be three to four minutes long. Network reporters on the same story would generally get one minute and twenty seconds to two minutes of precious network airtime.

Looking back, news directors Balboni and Hopkins both conceded, it is easy to see some of the things that their television stations—which are among the nation's very best at covering politics—failed to do and in fact have never done before. For example: planning.

"To be honest, we didn't have an early game plan," said Hopkins. There was some early planning, of course, but it dealt only with budgeting and technology, not with any concept of what the content of the news reports should be, or what sort of information the station wanted to convey to its viewers during the course of the year.

"Interestingly enough, in this business of television news, we more often than not sit down and determine operating expenses and determine project costs well before we decide in terms of actual coverage plans," said WBZ's Hopkins. "So early, by the spring of '83, we were looking at the extent of coverage that would be required in February of the following year. And in New Hampshire and Massachusetts and Iowa and Illinois on Super Tuesday. And that includes . . . what is it going to cost us . . . ? And, naturally, you say: 'To what extent are we going to cover it—are we going to be live out of Washington? Are we going to be in Atlanta? Are we going to be here and there and elsewhere?' . . . So all of those plans were developed very early without any real clear sense at the time of exactly what we were going to be doing with what candidates or what angles."

Local television takes its cues from the nationally based news organizations, Hopkins said. "We are, on our coverage, influenced by the national coverage in the media . . . what we've read, what we've seen . . . which front-runners have been pointed to in the press." He cited all three television networks, *Newsweek* and *Time* magazines, *The Washington Post*, *The New York Times*, and, of course, the *Boston Globe*. "The one thing that was really interesting in this year's primary is that no one was giving Mr. Hart the time of day . . . nationally prior to the [New Hampshire] primary," said Hopkins. And WBZ took its cues from the national journalists who are supposed to be the experts at divining which candidates in a large field are worthy of greater attention and lengthier coverage.

The two news directors budgeted grandly for their coverage of the 1984 presidential campaign. Hopkins estimated he spent about half a million dollars and Balboni said his station spent about the same.

What the viewers got for their money, they conceded, was technology. Both news directors said that their early planning focused only on technology and logistics. Neither station attempted any conceptual planning to decide just what sort of coverage they would be providing viewers, what issues would be explored in depth, how their station could best inform the viewers. Instead, they thought about hardware and personnel, and contented themselves with just covering the scheduled events.

"I would say our planning in 1984 was event-oriented," said Balboni. "It was built around the known milestones on the race to the White House, and we wanted to ensure that we would be there, that we would have good people there, that we would be technologically able to bring our report back to our viewers in a timely and competitive way."

In the end, all the money spent to outdazzle the competition did not result in a significant advantage for either WCVB or WBZ. The results, the news directors conceded, left them about even. "In 1984, I think basically we were two fighters of equal weight with equal armorage," said WCVB's Balboni. ". . . We [both] invested heavily in our ability to be live at candidate headquarters and so on and so forth. We both did polling. . . .

"That's not to say that there wouldn't be [planning] discussions about the kinds of stories we wanted to see. . . . But in terms of conceptualizing the kind of election coverage in 1984 and how we might distinguish ourselves—no."

Why not? The news director shrugged. "It's very simple. Not enough time. And too many other things to do. Not enough time to sit back and to think creatively about what you're going to do, and your back's too much against the wall in a competitive major local-television market." There was a silence, as Balboni considered what he had just said, then he shook his head and added: "But I guess, like anybody else, you learn as you go along, and hopefully you grow, and sometimes you get a chance to do things better, having learned from your mistakes."

In that spirit, local television would do well to rethink the manner in which it spends its money. For in fact, it is not at all certain that the benefits derived from the expenditures outweigh the detriments to overall coverage that are created by them. Consider the stations' penchants for live remote broadcasting and for polls.

The compulsion for filling the air with live remote coverage is most often an abdication of the sort of advance planning and constructive editing that produces pieces that are clear and to the point—or at least make a point. In live broadcasting there can be no editing—and often there is not much more thought and planning—to the reports that are aired. Many are, at best, a waste of precious airtime; and at worst, they can be misleading and just plain wrong.

Polls are costly for local stations—and once the stations spend to have them done, the polls often tend to dominate a given day's coverage, regardless of whether that is the most important or even relevant information of the day for viewers to be told. Certainly, far more airtime was given to "exclusive" polls than was given to a discussion of issues.

The news executives and many of their employees are more aware of these problems than their 1984 coverage would indicate. But they will probably continue to saturate their campaign coverage with live remote reports and polls—just out of fear of looking less lavish than the competition.

Still the doubts persist. Consider their concerns about their own use of polls. WBZ's Hopkins has concerns about all polls—and especially polls done well in advance of an election. Early polls, he said, can't measure anything more than the fact that people have heard of some candidate and have not really heard much or anything about the others. And they bear little relation to the way the contest will actually turn out months later. "I don't think the viewing public understands a lot about polling, because we don't understand a lot about polling," said Hopkins. ". . . What is the value of doing it? I'm not sure there is any great value."

WCVB's Balboni also has doubts about the journalistic value of polling done by news organizations. But he concedes his station will probably continue polling—fearing that a decision to stop polling would be considered by viewers as a sign of less-than-complete coverage. "I'm kind of torn, and nothing in our business can be evaluated unless you include competitive considerations. And I don't know, had we not done polling, that all the viewers would not have noticed it. Certainly our competition would have made them aware of it through promotion and advertising that would have emphasized the fact that they were doing more."

One of the greatest dangers of the reliance on polls is the subtle ways they cause journalists to reshape their own reporting. WBZ's Dennis Kauff conceded that as a reporter, he found polls often tended to lead correspondents to tailor their presentation of facts and choice of adjectives to suit the figures of the polls. "The problem . . . [was] often what you found yourself doing is that no matter how well a candidate's appearance seemed to go over at a particular event . . . it was always—yes, but this doesn't change the fact that the polls show that he is falling behind. So if John Glenn goes to a factory, for instance, and is met with enthusiasm by the workers . . . and the event seems to go well, that is still overshadowed by the [poll figures] . . . that we all had in the back of our mind that said John Glenn is going down the tubes. . . .

"And even though these people might seem to say, 'I like John Glenn,' we almost were reacting to that poll— What do these individuals know? The polls say that John Glenn is not doing well."

Generally, when television executives and producers are asked why they do not devote more time to the issues, they will reply with an explanation about time constraints; and then they will add that it is difficult to get sufficient access to the candidates. Indeed, some of those interviewed at the Boston stations made precisely those arguments. But, in fact, the station had ample time and access to have done thoughtful coverage of the major issues and to have made it interesting too—if only they had taken the time to plan and package and edit their news product well. And others candidly conceded this was so.

"We definitely have the time," said WBZ news director Hopkins. And correspondent Dennis Kauff added in a separate interview what was obvious to any correspondent traveling New Hampshire during the many weeks of that interminable primary season. He spoke with a bit of wonderment still remaining from his first campaign of encountering candidates hungry for local-television coverage and adept at having their way with local-television interviewers:

"They [the candidates] couldn't do enough for you when we were up there. We had an office set up in Manchester . . . they would come in if we wanted them. The candidates would come in, they'd stay for as long as we wanted them. They'd make arrangements so that . . . if two newscasts wanted their guy, they'd adjust their whole schedule to just get you live on the six or eleven o'clock newscast.

"They loved live because we couldn't edit. . . . It was amazing—you'd ask them a question about one thing and they'd give you an answer about something totally different. You could tell what the decision had been that morning on what issue, or what proposal or whatever to emphasize. 'Let me say I'm for that, but on the other hand, let's talk about this kind of stuff.' "

The pressure to do "live" TV led the local stations to avoid precisely the sort of detailed conceptual planning and editing that they were in a most ideal position to do. Given the candidates' salivation at the prospect of local-television exposure, it would have been possible for the stations to package a series of nightly reports on issues that were of special interest to their viewers—national issues, perhaps, but especially regional issues, such as positions on shoe imports and so on. The stations could have put together a list of questions, and then asked those questions to each candidate, individually—on videotape, not live. Then those interviews could have been packaged so that each night's piece would have been devoted to a single issue. In that piece, the views of each candidate could have been aired on one issue of regional interest, perhaps with a little background material presented by a reporter who had done a bit of homework on it; and each candidate could have been pressed for specifics if she or he had merely sought cover in the bomb fog of generalities or platitudes.

But that was not the priority of either WBZ or WCVB. Television either presented viewers with a grab bag of whatever the various candidates were choosing to speak about that day—a hodgepodge from which no viewer could keep track of where every candidate stood on this issue or that. And most often, the reports were just a few snappy visual images from the campaign that day with a story about the horse race: Who's ahead? How well do you have to do? When will you drop out?

The reporters who were out there daily spoke candidly about what motivates local television to show what it shows and ignore all the rest.

WCVB's Martha Bradlee said that fear of having good pictures show up on the competitor's show leads the local stations to get suckered into doing those stories about Glenn bowling for votes or singing with a barbershop quartet. It is a case of consenting adults who know well the games they are playing. The candidates know that going bowling and singing barbershop is just a trick to get the television stations to put them on the air; and the stations know that too, but they do it just the same; and then all of them wonder why it is that the public says political stories on television are boring.

And as Bradlee explained the whole sordid affair, the pols and the TVs seemed akin to the birds and the bees: "We know why they [the candidates] did it—I mean we *know* why they did it. . . . And because you think the other stations are going to do it, you do it. Why did we do it? Because you think the competition's going to do it.

"What do you think the voters think when they look at a bowling piece? Nothing? Something? . . . Sometimes, I suppose, what's frightening is that I think people do make up their minds just by watching television and seeing the candidates like that."

Along with coveting silly pictures, local stations inevitably fall victim to the standard journalistic trap of judging what is news solely in terms of what is new. WBZ's Dennis Kauff believed that was why his station and the competition covered New Hampshire by slighting the substance and sweeping up after the horse race instead.

"I think one of the things we feel out there is when you have to do a story every day, and when you're basically covering a person's daily activity—[you tell yourself] let's search for something new," said Dennis Kauff. ". . . As important as issues are, I think there is a feeling that we've done that, or he's said that—even if it's just *us* who heard it, if we've heard the same campaign speech day after day after day, maybe four or five times a day.

"There is a feeling that, gee, he hasn't said anything new. Let's try to get him to say something new. And since his issue positions are not going to change hourly or daily, his reaction to the horse race. . . is the thing. . . . We find things that interest us as reporters. And we forget that we are not out there reporting for each other. . . . We are supposed to be finding things that are going to be interesting and helpful to the people who are just watching the show."

In every look back at their work in 1984, Bradlee and Kauff and a number of other people of talent at these Boston stations were both candid in assessing their product and determined to serve their viewers better. That stands as good news for those in the media market who look to these stations for real news. And perhaps even more encouraging for these people is the fact that the executives at the top say they too recognize the need to raise the quality of the product.

"Television being in its adolescence and local-television news being very young indeed in terms of our expertise and sophistication . . . and knowing better . . . we've made mistakes," said WBZ news director Hopkins. "It is a matter, first of all, of mastering this medium of technology. . . . I thought as a news organization we missed a lot in the campaign of 1980. . . . In 1984, again . . . I guess what I'm trying to say is that we did that here-he-comes-there-he-goes handshake coverage better in a lot of different ways. But . . . I think the next step for the news media to take is to explore issues in a much greater detail than we've ever done before. And certainly television is at the forefront when it comes to a responsibility for that maturing process."

And WCVB news director Balboni is even more emphatic in voicing determination to change the way his station covers presidential primaries. "Somehow we have to de-emphasize the spot news of the day, since the spot news has become almost a . . . charade," he said. "It's a meaningless exercise in garnering television time, structured to get us on the Tarmac live at six or eleven or whatever."

"We've got to use the limited airtime we have to better purpose."

Even the television industry itself is populated by many who do not think that local television will make the sort of commitment that is needed to reshape the way it covers campaign news. But Balboni spoke with rare and unmistakable determination when he vowed to change the way his station informs the voters in the nation's first primary. He said:

"If it's always going to be this way, then somebody else will be doing it, but it won't be me. I can't speak for my colleagues, but the one thing that keeps you going is the belief that you're going to be able to make it better. Because if television is important . . . if it's fifty-seven to sixty-five percent [the] primary news source for people, then we don't have any choice but to struggle to make it better.

". . . And so if I didn't think that we had a chance to make it better, if I didn't think that I had the ability to make improvements, fuck it —I mean . . . if this is the best it's ever going to be then I want to do something else.

". . . But I think that there is a chance at a good station with good ownership to do things better. And I just hope we're smart enough to be able to do it."

NINE

WAVES

Viewed from safe sanctuary, hurricanes and typhoons and tidal waves and twisters can be fascinating—even riveting—things to watch. Their sheer power and turbulence are an adventure unto themselves as they strike with fury, run their course, and leave nothing but stillness and debris in their wake. So it is with Video Waves.

Video waves are, in a sense, like any other wave. You know them when you see them, and you know at a glance that they pack the power to sweep heavyweight objects along with inexplicable ease as they roll unchecked through all manner of seas. It is hard at a glance to know just where they come from, or just what has caused them, or how long they will last. The fact is that video waves, like all waves, are caused by forces of nature: human nature, political nature, journalistic nature.

The 1984 campaign provided a classic example in the study of the making and breaking of video waves. Buoyed by his 1984 New Hampshire victory, Gary Hart caught a video wave just right and rode it for a couple of weeks of unmitigated triumph and glory. He experienced the sensation of feeling the wave carry his campaign message with greater speed and impact than he could have ever provided under his own political power. All he had to do was keep his balance and enjoy the ride.

And Walter Mondale, meanwhile, experienced the sensation of Video Undertow, as he was pulled down and nearly out by forces beyond his control and beyond his capacity to overcome. He could only hope his machine would continue to churn sufficiently beneath the surface to keep his candidacy from being swamped until Hart's wave had run its course.

On the morning after the stunning New Hampshire primary, Hart was considered by the experts to be organizationally and financially incapable of fully capitalizing on his success in the upcoming Super Tuesday primaries and caucuses just two weeks away. It was, after all, a day of nine contests, five of them primaries in the Northeast and the South.

Consider Florida, the largest of the Super Tuesday states. Even after New Hampshire, the experts saw Hart's chances there as somewhere between slim and none. Hart had no real organization, no delegates in many of the districts, and no comfort from the polls—he had been listed at just 4 percent in the latest public-opinion survey.

All he had was the wave.

The nature of the television medium is that it cannot cover the passing of the torch without fanning the flames in the process. And that is precisely what happened for Hart in the wake of New Hampshire.

Night after night, Hart arrived in Florida's living rooms via local and network television being celebrated as a conquering hero, basking in new-found adulation and the discovery (mainly by local-television reporters) that he seemed rather like JFK—*All hail the knight of the New Generation of Camelot*. And night after night, Mondale arrived in those same living rooms to a funereal drumbeat, a cadence of downside adjectives and questions about why he looked like a loser and seemed so dull. Suddenly everything negative was a metaphor for a campaign on the rocks—a door shutting in Mondale's face as he is leaving a building, a computer graphic on a terminal that plunges downward as Mondale is watching it—and every metaphor was suddenly worth airing to illustrate a point.

It was possible to understand what was happening in Florida before Election Day without commissioning a private poll. All one had to do was watch the television news and note how Hart's message was successfully being carried on the crest of the video wave while Mondale's message was delivered down and damp.

And so, *The Washington Post* was able to report from Miami two days before the election:

"As network and local television cameras brought the presidential candidates into voters' living rooms this week, the images seemed to do for Sen. Gary Hart's momentum what the wind does for the windmill, and for Walter F. Mondale's what gravity does for even a well-thrown rock."*

MAKING WAVES

Gary Hart was coming! And the television crews and correspondents for Miami's local television stations were lined up, having drawn their straws, and they were waiting their respective turns for their respective exclusive live interviews with the latest celebrity of presidential politics. Lacking the organization and funds to put together huge rallies, and pressed for time to be in all states at once, Hart was bouncing from airport to airport in the Deep South and New England, working the five primary states by giving live runway interviews to grateful local stations who, of course, were airing his message unfettered and unedited. If Mondale was the front-runner, Hart was the runway runner as he hopped through Florida, Georgia, and Alabama in the South, Massachusetts and Rhode Island in the North.

It was Thursday, March 8, and both Hart and Mondale would be in South Florida this day. At Miami's Channel 10, WPLG, the ABC affiliate, Cheryl Stopnick, the special-projects producer and election coordinator, was unhappy because Walter Mondale's staff had turned down their request for a live interview—he inexplicably turned down all the stations, even though it would have been his one chance of getting his message out precisely the way he wanted it. "We never got that opportunity with Mondale," said Stopnick. "Believe me, the requests went in every time, and it went in on several different levels. I mean, I worked the local, I worked the national, I worked the advance team." What if Mondale had said yes—maybe even consented to a sit-down interview? "We would have jumped on that, believe me," she said. "We would have run that over several nights and we would have done a big deal on that."

Instead they all went with Hart. The exclusive live interviews are all cut from similar cloth. There is a pattern to them that is very much a part of the making of the video wave. Nobody seemed to have done any homework for this, not the interviewers or the interviewee. At no time was Hart challenged on any of the issues of his campaign that might have been of special interest to South Florida.

* * *

*Schram story, *The Washington Post*, March 11, 1984, p. 1.

At Miami's Channel 7, WSNV, the NBC affiliate, as in many other interviews, the questioning began with a peon of praise for his campaign success—and Hart got a free chance to comment on why he was so successful.

WSVN'S STEVE RONDINARO: Senator Hart joins us live now from Miami International Airport. . . . You're managing to pull off what many are calling one of the most dramatic political turnabouts in our history. I'm interested in your view of how and why.

HART: . . . I think there was a buildup and latent desire there for new hope and promise for this country. I think my campaign just happened to represent what people were looking for.

Then there was the ritual observation that he was a lot like John F. Kennedy—Hart let that quasi-question speak for him, and so he struck a modest pose about his newfound charisma.

RONDINARO: Many say that you're capturing that old Kennedy charisma . . .

HART: Well, I said throughout 1983 that charisma came when you started winning primaries. And I think that's what usually happens.

Then there was an observation that he was wearing a Florida-seal necktie (which he wore so that he would be asked about it on television), and Hart got to talk about his Florida supporters and about how close he was to Florida's former Governor Reuben Askew, a refrain that Americans had not heard from Hart in all those months when Askew was running for president. For good measure, he went on to offer Askew a job once he became president.

RONDINARO: I see that Florida emblem on your tie. Obviously, this is a very important state to you. I know that you picked up the endorsement of our secretary of state, George Firestone.

HART: Secretary of State Firestone gave me this necktie.

RONDINARO: Ah! Okay! He was an Askew delegate.

HART: A lot of Governor Askew's support has come our way and I'm very very grateful for it. Governor Askew made a profound contribution to the debate this presidential year, particularly on the issues of trade and economic growth and expansion. And I believe I have inherited a lot of that support because he and I fundamentally agree on those policies. . . . I think he has a role to play in a future Hart administration.

And finally there was the requisite bow to the horse race.

RONDINARO: Have you set a goal for your finish in Florida next Tuesday?
HART: We want to do the very best we can down here. Demonstrate a broad base of support . . . including retired and elderly people who have as much at stake in this election as any other group. . . .
RONDINARO: Senator, thank you for joining us. Senator Gary Hart joining us live from Miami International Airport.

Mondale had two brief blips on the local newscasts that day. The first came when he tried to match Hart's media skills by conducting a photo opportunity of his own. In northern Florida, he went out to a lake where he posed for the cameras with some bass fishermen; he wore a fine dark business suit and a crisp white shirt and tie. One of the fishermen, Kenneth Metcalfe, who said he was a Reagan Republican, talked to the cameras. "Once upon a time I shook hands with Calvin Coolidge and now I've seen Mondale," he said on WPLG's newscast. "I've completed my life."

Later Mondale was seen on WPLG touring a Miami senior citizens' apartment complex with Republican Claude Pepper, who was a New Dealer back before Hart had any of his New Ideas. Reporter Susan Candiotti got close enough to him to ask a question about House Speaker Thomas P. O'Neill's fresh criticism of Mondale's problems communicating to the public—and that became part of her newscast, which meant it became part of Mondale's message for the day whether he liked it or not.

CANDIOTTI: Afterwards I asked Mondale if he plans to change his image as House Speaker Tip O'Neill suggests to overtake Hart.
MONDALE: It's the issues that count. With me, it's "What you see is what you get."

The way the week had been going, though, this was about as good as it got for Mondale. For the last week of the Super Tuesday primary campaign was an unmitigated message disaster. It began with Hart and Mondale as back-to-back guests on ABC News's *This Week with David Brinkley*.

Hart went first. Brinkley, quite appropriately, asked him just what new ideas he was offering; Hart, quite appropriately, had anticipated this and had come clearly armed for the occasion. And so, like a gunslinger picking off bottles lined up atop a fence, Hart began ticking off his new ideas—boom, boom, boom.

Then came Mondale. While Hart had been sitting with his questioners in their Washington studio, Mondale had elected to remain in Maine so he could do some last-minute politicking for the caucus voting that would take place later in the day. So there was none of the easy face-to-face conversation and rapport that had characterized the Hart segment; Mondale was seen sitting alone in a room, with only a camera to talk to and a plug stuck in his ear.

The first question dealt not with his ideas for the future but his explanations for the disaster just past, the one in New Hampshire. "Well, I lost bad—that's what happened," Mondale began. His delivery was slow, there were circles under his eyes, and his voice was flatter than the plains of his Midwest. His voice had none of the animation and wit that make him so likable in private. He was just a face pasted on a wall in a remote studio.

That was the last message that most of Maine's caucusers got from Mondale that day. And when they voted in that state, where all the smart money had said organization was everything, it turned out that Hart—who had been beaten so soundly by so many in that meaningless straw poll that was so widely publicized in 1983—won the Maine caucuses. He won without organization—but with his wave.

On Monday the news began carrying Hart's message better than his ads ever could. ABC News opened its nightly campaign-news segment with a woman-on-the-street comment from a Bostonian who had shaken Hart's hand at a subway stop: "I think his momentum is going; it looks like the Democrats are voting their own way instead of being pushed around by labor interests or other interests. They're doing what they want to do."

Correspondent Steve Shepard explained that Hart could do well in Massachusetts on Super Tuesday, but he was not expected to win in Florida, Georgia, or Alabama.

Brit Hume, whose skills as a political correspondent grew during the campaign year and who was well respected for his work, began his piece with still a new metaphorical twist. It has become cliché for television to use inclement weather as a metaphor for a floundering campaign; Hume found a way to do it with good weather.

ABC NEWS, MONDAY, MARCH 5, 1984

HUME: It wasn't raining when the Mondale campaign got to Boston this morning, but in political terms, it was pouring. He had lost in Maine and a new poll showed Mondale suddenly twelve points behind in Massachusetts. For the first time in months, he appeared on the morning news shows.

[A clip was shown from *Good Morning America*.]

DAVID HARTMAN: You want to explain your new availability?

MONDALE: Yes. I'm in trouble. I need help.

Then came those visual metaphors—a Secret Service agent let a door close in Mondale's face as he left a building—and now this sort of thing that happened frequently during the rosy days in the campaign was a part of the big news. So was the computer graphic that dipped on the screen as the candidate watched it at a nearby campus.

HUME: But even the little things seemed to go against Mondale today. There was the door that shut in his face as he left for his first campaign event. Later at a small college he got a demonstration of computer graphics that might have been tracing the recent course of his campaign.

On NBC, correspondent Lisa Myers used the closing-door photo metaphor as well.

After the campaign, Hume talked about that period of the Mondale campaign as an especially trying one for the press corps as well as the candidate. He said he felt it was fine to use those visual metaphorical examples. "They're kind of amusing," he said. "You can do it harsh and savage or you can do it light and not unsympathetic. So I felt comfortable using them." Mondale's inability to use the medium effectively and crisply troubled Hume throughout the campaign, as he felt it affected the quality—and thus the appeal—of the pieces. "A lot of times you'd do a Mondale piece and the opening would be crisp," Hume said. "The shots would be good. And then he'd speak and the piece would come to a standstill. . . . Watching Mondale talk about issues continuously is like watching grass grow."

It bothered Hume that it was so seldom that he was able to convey even a glimpse of the real Mondale—"a funny, fun-loving, likable man," he said. And it bothered him that he always found himself seeking to humanize a politician who at least in one sense seemed to belong right up there with America's immortals. This was all due to the Mondale look: "Mondale sprayed his hair—hard—to the point it was firm. Every day. He had a pompadour like Mount Rushmore."

So when Mondale's television self was at its most downtrodden, Hume suggested something to the Mondale aides. He wanted to interview Mondale—and he wanted to do it with just the two of them sitting around in their shirtsleeves. It produced a more informal-looking piece, and it presented a more human side of Mondale. The candidate talked about how he had accepted the notion that he could be defeated. He said he could handle that, because anyone who runs for president "better be pretty well wired inside." But he said: "The thing I'm worried about is my kids getting hurt" (a reference to his younger aides).

That was a decent piece for Mondale, coming as it did in the midst of the video wave that Hart was riding. An even better one for Mondale perhaps was one that did not even mention him: It ran on Thursday night, as CBS News took a hard look at Hart.

"Who is this man, this Gary Hart . . . ?" Dan Rather asked in his introduction. And Bruce Morton, the correspondent on the story, said, "Gary Hart is the hottest political property around—this week." It was a piece that depicted Hart as an outsider within the Senate. It noted Hart's criticism of Mondale on education issues and then quoted an official of the National Education Association (which had endorsed Mondale) who said, "I wouldn't say hypocritical, but it's interesting" (because both Mondale and Hart had the same basic positions on education issues).

When Morton asked, "What new ideas?" the piece had George McGovern answer. He said of Hart's new ideas: "Those are rather attractive slogans, but they really have no intellectual content."

And finally, Rather came back to note that Hart had been given a Naval Reserve commission in 1980—even though he had never served in the military before and was six years older than the maximum age at the time he received his commission. And Rather noted the puzzling discrepancy about Hart's age; George Lardner of *The Washington Post*, a consummate professional who applies an investigative instinct to seemingly innocuous assignments, had written a profile of Hart weeks earlier, and in the course of his reporting he had discovered (and printed midway in his story) that birth records show Hart was born in 1936, although he had been listing 1937 on his biography and other documents for some time. Rather noted: "Senator Hart recently blamed the age discrepancy in his official Senate biography on mistakes by staff aides."

* * *

But this was no time for Mondale to catch his breath. For just as it seemed that Hart's video wave might be losing some of its force, along came a piece by NBC's Roger Mudd that same night that made it painfully clear to the Mondale forces that the wave was rolling still.

NBC NEWS, THURSDAY, MARCH 8, 1984

ROGER MUDD: . . . Ten days ago, the Mondale machine hit a stone wall in New Hampshire. Mondale's confidence was shaken. And now, with his campaign hanging by a thread, his response to the Hart phenomenon seems to be one of resentment, bewilderment, and stubbornness. What's your problem? Is it Gary Hart or is it Walter Mondale?

MONDALE: I believe that it was my failure for some weeks to respond to Senator Hart. In other words, I was hoping to win this nomination, in a way, without getting into a fight with Senator Hart, and I took several shots and didn't return them. . . .

MUDD: How do you think you come across on TV?

MONDALE: I don't know.

MUDD: But what do you—I mean, you see yourself, what do you think when you see yourself?

MONDALE: You know, I'm telling—I'm saying what I believe. I'm not a PR type. I'm not going to be different than I am. One of the things that irritates me about politics, they say, "If only you're somebody you weren't, you'd really be hot."

MUDD: Who says that?

MONDALE: Well, you hear it all the time from PR types. "If you'd only somehow emphasize things that you don't really believe in but some poll tells you it's hot, that'll sell." I don't believe in that. I am who I am. And that's the way I'm doing it. That's the way I'm gonna do it.

MUDD: So Mondale will not change. He is putting his faith in the pulling power of his message and his experience—no matter how out-of-date the polls say they are. His problem, of course, is that faith may not be enough.

It wasn't; Mondale's polls told him Florida was rushing toward Hart. Even Jimmy Carter's Georgia could be close now. Mondale and his aides were ready to withdraw if Georgia went for Hart. Mondale, anxious to squeeze every drop of prestige out of his past tenancy at the vice-president's mansion, stopped in to talk with his former boss in

Plains. And NBC's Lisa Myers noted the event like this:

"After months of emphasizing his differences with Carter, Mondale made a pilgrimage to Plains to try to save his collapsing candidacy. . . . Some observers believe that the appearance of Carter may be a mistake because it reinforces Mondale's ties to the less-than-glorious past. But Mondale's advisers decided they have to chance that Carter help. As one aide put it, at this point we have almost nothing left to lose."

The Great Debate of the Super Tuesday primaries reached Florida voters mainly in snippets. It was carried out of Atlanta on Sunday by Cable News Network. For the few in Florida who have cable television, the debate was live at five—but for most of the rest it was film at eleven or highlights the morning after. The League of Women Voters despaired that few commercial stations bothered to carry the debate live or even on a delayed basis, though it was offered to them.

Those who saw it live were there in time to witness the birth of a comeback slogan, voiced by Mondale, aimed at Hart. Mondale campaign manager Robert Beckel had thought it up—a way of ridiculing Hart's New Ideas based on the hamburger-chain ad that all America had been watching on television for months. Mondale had been reluctant to use it because he had no idea what it was about, having never seen the commercial.

Finally, he agreed to try it. And he turned to Gary Hart and said: "Where's the beef?"

The results: Hart had ridden the wave out of nowhere—no organization, no delegates, no base in the polls—and swept Florida's primary decisively, along with big wins in Massachusetts and Rhode Island. Mondale got his expected easy win in Alabama—and saved his candidacy for at least one more Tuesday by finishing one eyelash ahead of Hart in Georgia. Jesse Jackson would carry his unique campaign ever onward; John Glenn and George McGovern would concede the obvious and withdraw.

A view from within the wave: The campaign coverage by Miami's television stations did not measure up to the modest standards of Boston's two largest stations, not in effort expended nor results achieved. And no one is more aware of that than Steve Wasserman.

As vice-president for news at WPLG (Channel 10), Wasserman operated under no illusions. He said he recognized the deficiencies in the coverage by his station and that of his Miami competition. "I think one of the big problems that happens for us when we try to gear up for the big elections [is that] there is probably a certain amount of well-intentioned groping," he said. "Groping for how to do it, how to do it well, how to do it better than the other guys.

"For better or worse, there is not what I consider to be at this station and other stations in the market an ongoing political-reporting process. . . . There is not a sterling tradition of long-term reporting. . . . [We are] without the kind of depth and background and expertise that either network can bring to bear, or a WBBM [in Chicago] or a WBZ [in Boston], where they're reporting politics all the time, because politics is so much a fabric of those cities."

"Can we do better?" Wasserman asked. ". . . Sure, sure. I'm not sensitive about it." One of the big problems of bringing experienced political reporting to stations such as those in Miami is the staff turnover. "I would say every four years somewhere between seventy and eighty percent of the local TV stations' reporting staff is different," he said. "Seventy to eighty percent of the reporters I had here in 1984 won't be here in 1988."

Much of their coverage was geared toward the prospect of making a long race with former Florida Governor Reuben Askew, said Cheryl Stopnick, who coordinated campaign coverage under difficult circumstances. "Askew campaigned so hard in Iowa we were sure he was going to at least do a third place," she said. When Askew's candidacy collapsed, the station collapsed its coverage plans. Covering its own state primary became something of a fallback position for this disappointed station that had geared for the great race and now found itself confined to its own backyard. Thin resources hampered Stopnick—but one resource they did have, of course, was the capability of doing live coverage from remote locations.

"For a while it was done just for the sake of doing it, so you could show everybody you had the right kind of truck," said Wasserman. "I think all of us in the business are groping for ways to be different. . . . While live TV is frequently a device, it does not necessarily enhance the journalism. Sometimes it detracts from the journalism.

". . . Now, the candidates are not stupid. They know that even if . . . you're a news director who cannot stand live, if Walter Mondale is going to be smart enough to come into town at 6:08 and be there only for four minutes, you have two choices, either cover him on tape—and watch the other guys have him live—or you go live. And so you're going to choose going live. And Walter Mondale knows that and you know that. And so Walter Mondale is going to get four minutes or whatever . . . of unedited television time. And it's going to be such a gang-bang kind of mode, the chances are slim of anybody asking anything really significant."

Wasserman smiled at his own choice of example. Of course, he added, Mondale never actually found the time to avail himself of all this live, unedited television.

Hart did.

In the high councils of the Reagan command, the president's top campaign strategists had become very worried about Gary Hart, for Hart was riding a wave that showed no indication of dying or drying. After months—years, really—of preparing to face Walter Mondale, they were not enthralled with the prospect of having to run against a phenomenon. Let alone a New Generational phenomenon who was appealing to all generations of Independents.

In their strategy meetings, the Reagan operatives decided that perhaps one good way to stop a wave was to throw garbage at it. This time-tested tradition of politics by pollution is not considered evil within the confines of the trade. It has been used by the operatives of most of America's greatest political heroes, and even by most of the heroes themselves.

In this case, the Reagan officials decided it was time to help the media find the story. And so, shortly before that vote in Florida, the top-level Reagan agents began several days of intensive fellowship with friends in prominent media places. Roger Stone was one of the operatives, and, he says, so were Reagan campaign manager Edward Rollins, press secretary James Lake, and strategists Lee Atwater and Charles Black. The idea was to get the major news-media organizations to start looking into and reporting the series of very minor but nevertheless unusual things about Hart's background. And so they fanned out and began finding good excuses to call their media pals for a round of pump-priming.

"We'd hit the talking points casually—not to make a big thing of it, but just to plant the seed, stir things up," said Stone, who is one of Washington's biggest of the big-money political consultants. "I'd call reporters I know and I'd call the munchkins—you know, researchers—just to get them interested in doing a little checking. I'd say something like, 'What about this name change thing—isn't it strange?' Or, 'Have you seen those four different signatures of his—aren't they weird?' Or, 'What do you think that age thing means?'

"The country, having been burned by one dark horse—Jimmy Carter—would be a bit more careful about rushing to another."

But the Reagan rainmakers could have saved creative energies and political dry ice. Other forces were at work that would make their efforts irrelevant.

For one, the media was itself swinging belatedly into the business of discovering what it should have long ago known, since all the information had been published some time back as nuggets in other stories. At various times in the days just before and after Super Tuesday, all three networks had opened stories on Gary Hart by asking: "Who *is* Gary Hart?" (It is interesting to wonder just what would have happened if *The Washington Post*'s George Lardner had taken a different approach to the story he wrote well before the New Hampshire primary, if he had converted his assigned Hart profile piece into a modest little Hart exposé. Would television have been lured by headlines in *The Washington Post* reporting the news that Hart had given out conflicting dates for his birth and that there were conflicting explanations of why his last name was changed from Hartpence? And would that have damaged Hart's drive in the first primary race? Or would television have ignored the story until Hart had proven he could defeat Mondale and Glenn? There is no way of knowing.)

The other force at play was that Hart himself was about to halt his own momentum quicker than the Republicans could ever have done. If this were one of those television adventure shows, Hart would have been seen derailing his own swift bandwagon by unscrewing the wheels at high speed.

Hart could have survived the new media fellowship drive of the Reagan operatives, and could have ridden out that "Who is Hart?" phase on the networks, if it had not been for the fact that he was about to drown out his own New Ideas/New Generation message in the Illinois primary just when he seemed to be one victory away from wrapping up the nomination.

BREAKING WAVES

There comes a time, when Man is performing such unnatural acts as riding a wave atop a piece of board or running for president atop a platform, when he can no longer rely on the forces of nature to do all his work for him. All waves eventually begin to run their course and lose their force; you can see it happening on the beach and on the trail. But there is still plenty of good riding to be done—if the performer is prepared to do a little creative tacking.

One of the givens, when a campaign reaches the point of classic confrontation and the field is winnowed to a precious few, is that the candidate will get a chunk of time on the television newscasts. The only variable is how he or she decides to fill it. With a little creative movement and tactics, the candidate can serve up ample amounts of news that wiggles—enough to satisfy the television planners and amplify his or her message for the masses. Absent that creative tacking and tactical planning, the candidate will still get that same chunk of time on the nightly news—but how it is filled will be left to the local and network television people to determine for themselves. There is, of course, a third possibility. It is that the news-that-wiggles that the candidate provides will be in the form of a political pratfall, the sort of maxiflub that happens in full spotlight and fills up all of that airtime, much to the candidate's political consternation. What is certain is that the candidate who creatively survives that test of wills and waves will have surged to a commanding and quite possibly irreversible lead in the race for a presidential nomination. Failure to ride the wave skillfully could leave a candidate's prospects permanently dampened.

Illinois voters trying to make up their minds between Hart and Mondale in the final days of the campaign there turned on their television sets and saw a week that opened with several good and tough reports delving into matters of Hart's substance and style.

The week's television began on Monday with a memorable, tough piece on *The CBS Evening News* by the network's senior political correspondent Bruce Morton. He went after two inconsistent statements Hart had made in the previous day's debate in Atlanta.

"For the first time, tough questions are being raised about Gary Hart—not just where he stands on the issues, but whether he remembers where he stands," said Morton. A clip showed Mondale saying that Hart had once been asked whether Cuba is a totalitarian state, "and he said no. That is wrong." Then Morton showed Hart explaining that "in the incident involved, I refused to say whether it was totalitarian or authoritarian—and it wasn't because I didn't know."

And then Morton showed and quoted from a transcript of the incident (a 1982 luncheon with *Washington Post* editors) that showed just the opposite was true. In it, Hart said: "Well, Cuba is not totalitarian and it's not democratic." And asked just what Cuba was if it was not totalitarian, Hart replied: "I don't know."

Added Morton: "So Mondale's memory was better than Hart's."

A second issue—whether Hart had said he would as president withhold projects from states opposed to the Equal Rights Amendment:

Hart had denied to Glenn that he had ever said that. Morton quoted from a transcript that showed he had.

Just three hours later, Chicago viewers heard Hart attacked again—not by a politician but by a journalist. The influential anchorman and commentator of WBBM-TV, Chicago's CBS affiliate, was in his commentary mode.

JACOBSON: Gary Hart has been saying it over and over again—and the media repeat it: "Mondale is the candidate of labor and Democratic bosses; I am not running a campaign based on special-interest endorsements." Gary Hart's advantage is that he gets away with whatever he says because nobody's had the time to doubt what he says and collect the facts on things like the special-interest endorsements he's had in the past. In his very last campaign for the U.S. Senate, Gary Hart received more than a quarter of a million dollars in contributions from special interests. [Jacobson then listed the contributions from interests, including a company that produces asbestos and oil and gas companies.]

On Tuesday, NBC's Roger Mudd weighed in after Hart's Super Tuesday victories with an interview in which he was clearly minimizing Hart's accomplishments for the night. Mudd's celebrated pre-1980 interview with Senator Edward Kennedy had done more to undo Kennedy's challenge to President Carter than any other single event—because he had kept his questions low key and basic, while Kennedy showed the unfocused nature of his own mind by phumphing and flubbing such questions as the one about why he wanted to be president. But in this 1984 interview, Mudd took a combative tack.

MUDD: Apparently he [Mondale] has won in Georgia and Alabama. So you have not got rid of him. When are you going to get rid of him?

HART: Well I don't—It's, first of all—it's not my task . . .

MUDD: But you didn't win in Georgia and you didn't win in Alabama. So really, all you won was Florida, which isn't a true Southern state. So you're really not a national candidate yet, are you?

HART: Well, Mr. Mudd, please—we won two New England primaries. We won the two largest Southern states. You may think Florida is not a Southern state, but Floridians may quarrel with that.

Then, for good measure, Mudd began to probe Hart about his Kennedy ways.

MUDD: A lot of people want to know, Senator, why do you imitate John Kennedy so much?
HART: I don't.
MUDD: What do you do?
HART: I'm Gary Hart.
MUDD: But I mean all the motions, with the necktie, and the chopping of the air, and the hand in the pocket . . . people all over the country say, "All he's doing is imitating John Kennedy."
HART: No, reporters say that. People around the country say we like this candidate and we want to support him. I've spoken the way I've spoken all my life. And I think there are plenty of people that'll verify that. I'm not imitating anyone. The American people can spot a phony. . . .

There was more:

MUDD: One more question about John Kennedy. You were quoted as saying that if you used the phrase "Ask not what your country can do for you," you'd be dead. But you went down to Alabama and used that very phrase before the legislature. Why did you do that?
HART: Well, what I intended to say was that we used to have presidents that asked us what we could do for our country and now we have too many candidates that only promise what they're going to do for us. . . .

And more:

MUDD: And a final question. Would you do your Teddy Kennedy imitation for me now?
HART: No.
MUDD: I've heard that it's hilarious.
HART: I don't think it is.

Mondale, meanwhile, was off on his solid but unspectacular way. He spoke to the Chicago Council on Foreign Relations, and after that, WBBM's political correspondent Mike Flannery conducted a live interview that should be a campaign-year model for local newscasters around the country. For Flannery had done his homework, listened to Mondale's speech, and pressed the candidate successfully to elaborate on what he had said in his speech.

For example: "What do you mean that Senator Hart has introduced a 'strange new vision of the world'?" That got Mondale to present his charge about Hart and Cuba, and to talk about their differing views on the Persian Gulf.

Mondale's normally video-blind staff had also served him very well this week as it created for him precisely the sort of visual version of his own campaign message that translated into strong and memorable television. Mondale was seen driving a new car off the assembly line of a Chrysler plant on the outskirts of Chicago.

WMAQ-TV, MARCH 16, 4:30 P.M.

REPORTER: This was the setting and the people the Mondale faithful have been waiting for—labor's rank and file. . . . Walter Mondale took a walking tour of Chrysler's Belvedere assembly plant this afternoon. . . . Mr. Mondale told his supporters he was largely responsible for the plant being in the position it is in today. Mondale seemed to take pride in driving the plant's one-billionth front-wheel-drive four-door sedan off the line this afternoon, knowing that the Chrysler rescue plan which he helped push through saved 600,000 jobs.

MONDALE: If Gary Hart had had his way, this plant would be idle today. Our country would have 600,000 more unemployed. This microphone wouldn't be here the way it is, and that's the difference.

REPORTER: Those workers I talked with working the line this afternoon say they plan to support the presidential candidate one hundred percent.

For the first time in a long time, Mondale had put Hart in the position of having to react in his own television-news segment to Mondale's message. It was, for Hart, a no-win position, because this was not the subject he wanted to be using his television time to talk about.

WMAQ-TV, MARCH 17, 5 P.M.

REPORTER: At a town meeting in Rockford, Hart was asked about his opposition to the Chrysler bailout loan. Yesterday Mondale underscored his support of the bailout with an appearance at the nearby Belvedere plant.

HART: My complaint with the loan was that it had to do only with one mostly mismanaged company and that it did not put the entire automobile industry back on its feet.

ILLINOIS: THE MOMENT OF TRUTH

The Illinois primary of 1984 was one of those classic moments of campaign truth; it should serve as a standard of sorts for those who practice politics, cover politics, study politics, or simply endure the consequences of politics.

What happened was that Gary Hart drowned out his own New Ideas/New Generation message, which had been the making of his candidacy, and doomed his own 1984 presidential prospects in the process. He did it in two inexplicable, made-for-television blunders that became the only major Hart campaign stories in the final week of television news before the Illinois primary.

In the first—call it The Mondale Ad That Didn't Exist—Hart falsely accused Mondale of running an unfair ad that belittled Hart's change of name, age, and signature; and then he had to apologize because there had never been any such Mondale ad.

In the second—call it The Hart Ad That Wouldn't Die—Hart bizarrely attacked one of his own ads as unfair, even though all it did was point out the fact that the Chicago Democratic political machine run by Cook County Democratic Party Chairman Edward Vrdolyak had endorsed Mondale and was working to elect him. Hart promised to yank his "Vrdolyak ad" off the air, and then watched for days as the ad continued to run anyway, throughout the weekend, because it was already locked into the local-television-station computers. Hart's inability to control even his own commercials became a source of daily and nightly media reports and ridicule.

Once again, the fate that awaited this new front-runner on Election Day could be understood in advance just by watching a week's worth of television in Illinois, which revealed reality faster than the polls could grasp and report it. Thus, two days before the Illinois primary, *The Washington Post* could report:

> Chicago—This was the week when the fate that befalls all surfers caught up with Gary Hart.

> The media wave that Hart had caught just right and ridden to instant stardom crested and inevitably crashed over him, as nationally and locally he was swamped by critical television coverage while he campaigned for the important Illinois primary Tuesday.
>
> As he struggled to regain his form in the swirl of political tides, Hart wound up clobbering himself in a frantic performance of accusation and apology that at least may have provided a much-needed lesson to his live-at-5, film-at-11 candidacy.*

All Hart had needed that week was a couple of creative visual news events to keep pushing his New Ideas/New Generation message, which had been serving him so well. All he got on the nightly news, however, were his two made-for-television mistakes: "The Mondale Ad That Didn't Exist" and "The Hart Ad That Wouldn't Die."

INCIDENT NUMBER ONE: "THE MONDALE AD THAT DIDN'T EXIST"

"The Mondale Ad That Didn't Exist" opened before the Illinois television-viewing audience on Thursday, March 15, with Hart appearing in livid color, crying foul and making the accusation Mondale had sunk to a new low by running an ad that made personal attacks upon him. Then Hart was seen having to apologize—because it turned out that there never had been any such Mondale campaign ad. The candidate and his staff had just gone off half-cocked, igniting their own short fuses on the basis of rumors, speaking without checking their facts.

It was an amateur-hour sort of screw-up brought on by an inexperienced and unsavvy staff that fed the frayed feelings of a candidate who was getting his first round of the sort of fire that front-runners routinely come under and which Mondale had endured for months.

The episode began back at Hart headquarters in Washington, where aides in a large meeting had been talking loosely about strategy. One of their number talked about how he had information that Mondale forces had prepared a new ad that was attacking Hart's name and age controversies. The aide talked about it as if it were fact—and soon it was accepted as fact. At no time did campaign manager Oliver "Pudge" Henkel even suggest that the matter be verified. Nor did his deputy, David Landau, as he passed along suggested attack lines to the traveling

*Schram story, March 18, 1984.

Hart staff even though not one of them had bothered to check the authenticity of the alleged ad. Nor did the candidate. It struck a receptive chord with Hart, who by this time was feeling very put upon.

Months after the campaign of 1984, even as he was planning for his presidential campaign of 1988, Hart's eyes flashed with hurt and anger as he spoke about the way it was for him back then.

"I had been hammered by Fritz since February twenty-ninth (the day after the New Hampshire primary)," Hart said. "So for two or three weeks I had been relatively silent, or had treated semihumorously the 'Where's the Beef?' the 'Red Phone,' or whatever. 'Hart's weak on civil rights.' 'Hart's weak on the environment.' 'Hart's weak on women's rights.' Whatever was going on. 'Hart's incompetent.' 'Hart doesn't know what he's talking about.' And that had been virtually the whole Mondale campaign for three weeks."

Hart had been preparing a high-road-attack response. "The essence of the statement was that there's something more important than winning. It's retaining your integrity, retaining your sense that you're telling the truth, and that you're running an honorable campaign. And I had come to the conclusion that my opponent and his staff were purposely and consciously misstating my record. And I felt that they had gone beyond the bounds of what was legitimate to win."

That was the state of Hart's mind as his press secretary Kathy Bushkin brought him the word from the headquarters about this new Mondale ad. "And so I wrote another couple of paragraphs at the end of [my statement]," Hart said, "and that was it."

Hart had mainly succeeded in doing to his own campaign what the Reagan rainmakers had tried surreptitiously to do to it: He had focused the attention of the public on those very minor irrelevancies that they had wanted to exploit. And he had been wrong. He had shown himself capable of the sort of intemperate, ill-considered acts that Mondale was saying was the danger of having an untested president such as Hart.

(A brief look backstage: The controversy could have been worse for Hart—it could have dragged on for days of charge and denial and journalistic recap. For Hart learned less than an hour after he'd made his charge that he'd made a major mistake, and he reacted quickly to cut his losses. In Springfield after Hart had read his statement for the cameras, I asked his press secretary, Kathy Bushkin, just what Hart had been referring to. She said there were new Mondale ads that made these petty charges. I then telephoned the Mondale headquarters in

Washington and reached senior adviser Paul Tully, who denied that there were any such ads.

(Bushkin was walking on the runway toward Hart's plane when I caught up to her and told her of the Mondale camp's denial. She just shook her head, as though fearing the worst, returned to the airport terminal, and called her headquarters in Washington. She was told that no one there had actually seen or could cite any such Mondale ad. At that point Bushkin went to Hart and together they reacted smartly. They decided to do a prompt rollback and apologize in time to make the network-news deadlines, so at least the crisis would not become a two-day story—or more!)

The episode was limited to a one-day disaster. For example:

ABC NEWS, MARCH 15

PETER JENNINGS: Well, things are getting a little more tense between the two front-runners. Today Gary Hart accused Walter Mondale of running a negative campaign. Today, at least, the accusation was based on less than conclusive evidence. ABC's Steve Shepard explains.

SHEPARD: This morning at a campaign stop in Springfield, Illinois, Gary Hart accused the Mondale organization of preparing ads that amounted to personal attacks on his integrity, attacks based on Hart's change of name, change of signature style, and some confusion about his age.

HART: I've spoken about new ideas for the future, for some reason former Vice-President Walter Mondale wants to talk about my handwriting. I've spoken about a new generation of leadership for this country, and for some reason Vice-President Mondale wants to talk about my family name.

SHEPARD: But later, in Galesburg, Illinois, Hart said he was wrong, that his staff in Washington was mistaken, that there was no such Mondale advertising campaign.

HART: We were incorrectly informed that they had reduced some of their personal references that do go on and had been going on fairly systematically for the past number of days to some paid advertising. That seems, apparently at least at this time, not to be the case. And I have said that was a mistake on our part and I apologize for that.

INCIDENT NUMBER TWO: "THE HART AD THAT WOULDN'T DIE"

The map of Illinois hurtles toward the television viewer. A photo of Edward Vrdolyak appears on the left, Walter Mondale appears on the right. The announcer explains what it is all about:

Eddie Vrdolyak has decided that Walter Mondale will be your candidate for president. Gary Hart and a lot of people who think for themselves stand in the way. [Hart's photo appears, shoving the other two off to the side.] This election is a choice between the past and the future. Between special interests and new directions. Between bosses and a new generation of leadership. It's your choice and America watches. Let the future begin.

That was tame and rather run-of-the-mill stuff by the measure of Chicago politics, a branch of the profession that draws its tactical lessons not from the political science texts of colleges but from the guerrilla-warfare manuals of the War College.

Cook County Democratic Central Committee chairman Edward Vrdolyak, who has always been known by the regulars as Fast Eddie, had endorsed Mondale and had swung his machine into high gear in his behalf. Back in Washington, Hart strategist and pollster Patrick Caddell had concluded that Hart ought to be able to use that fact to invigorate his natural constituency, the independent-thinkers and the baby-boom Democrats. And he could cut into Mondale's substantial black support by reminding black voters that Mondale's main man in Chicago is Vrdolyak—who is the main enemy of the city's first black mayor, Harold Washington. If the blacks were not anxious to vote for Hart (and not many were in 1984), then perhaps they might switch to hometowner Jesse Jackson, which of course would also help Hart.

So Caddell and Hart media adviser Raymond Strother prepared their modest ad.

Meanwhile, out on the trail, Hart was insisting that he personally approve all ads before they are aired. The deadline for getting the ad on the air was just hours away when Hart's friend, Senator Chris Dodd of Connecticut, went to Chicago Thursday night with a copy of the ad script in his briefcase.

Actor Robert Redford was also there to lend campaign support and fellowship, and it was late at night when Dodd caught up with Hart in Redford's suite. They had a late supper, and as Hart recalled: "At the end of the dinner Chris says, 'Look,' and he gestures down at his briefcase. 'I got some ads that the people in Washington want you to look at. Do you want to do it now?' And it was eleven-thirty P.M. or a quarter to twelve or whatever. And I had to be up at six A.M., or whatever, and I said, 'No, I'll look at them tomorrow.' And I left."

Early the next morning, Caddell spoke to Dodd by phone, and although the line was clear, the versions of what they said to each other are not. Caddell remembers that when he asked if Hart had approved the ad, Dodd said Hart had had no objection. Dodd remembers saying something like "not yet."

Caddell then told Strother that Hart had approved the ad; Strother made a call and the ad went immediately on the air.

In Chicago, the ad was news.

On WBBM-TV on Friday, the Hart ad was played as news. Correspondent Mike Flannery had the story:

FLANNERY: Hart is also launching a new offensive, $340,000 worth of television and radio commercials. One of them tries to turn chairman Edward Vrdolyak's Cook County Democratic Central Committee endorsement of Mondale into a big liability for Mondale.

The Hart ad was played as part of the story. Next Flannery reported that Hart was getting just 4 percent of the black vote in the latest Channel 2 poll, and he recounted the Hart strategy behind the ad.

But the strategy was not Hart's. And Hart was of a mind to take that personally, since he was once again in the mode of operating as his own campaign manager. When reporters first asked Hart about the ad, he said he hadn't seen it but defended the propriety of it. "People have a right to know who is supporting which candidate and make their decisions based on that," the *Chicago Tribune* quoted him as saying. But then he went to a phone and had campaign manager Oliver Henkel read him the text of the ad. He then ordered his campaign manager to yank the ad off the air. Then Hart went out and told *Chicago Sun-Times* reporter Robert Hillman that the Vrdolyak ads were not going to run again.

Like a book banned in Boston, Hart's denouncement of his own ad was the big Hart campaign news of that day and the few days remaining until the primary election.

And Hart was seen as testy, petulant, and everything that you don't want a president to be when the going gets tough.

WBBM-TV, MARCH 17, 5 P.M.

MIKE PARKER (*anchor*): . . . The latest controversy is over a television campaign commercial that Gary Hart has cancelled on at least two Chicago television stations because of heavy criticism.

CAROL KRAUSE: This is the television ad Gary Hart says was a mistake. An ad linking Walter Mondale to Edward Vrdolyak.

[The banned Hart ad was shown as a news item.]

KRAUSE: It is the second time this week that Hart has been thrown on the defensive. Thursday he retracted statements he made about statements attributed to Walter Mondale that turned out to have never been made. . . . Today, Hart was reluctant to answer questions about the Vrdolyak ad.

HART: Why should I have to? They're not my ads. I didn't want them produced and I didn't want them on the air. So I don't have to say what's wrong with them.

Behind the scenes, the Hart headquarters was in a turmoil, and on the television screen, it seemed, so was Hart. The candidate—trying to decide strategy on the run and perform in the spotlight at the same time—was seen morning, noon, and night making statements that were at times contradictory, at times intemperate, and most often ill-advised. Back in Washington, Caddell and Strother were fuming that it is impossible to yank ads on weekends—and it was awful strategy to be seen condemning and yanking your own ad under any circumstances. Caddell is known to have been volatile and trip-wire–tempered on many controversies in his career, but on this issue he was certainly right. Campaign manager Henkel, middled and muddled, was in tears.

The candidates gave a debate in Chicago on Sunday, but it didn't seem to count much as news. The newspapers and the newscasts played it well, and WBBM's Flannery did an especially impressive final round of issue-oriented interviews with the candidates. But "The Hart Ad That Wouldn't Die" was the focus of the campaign's closing messages. It looked like the sort of visual leadership test that was made for television.

And all the while, in the background, the red phone was ringing. The "Red Phone" was a new Mondale ad—a most clever invention of media strategist Roy Spence in conjunction with campaign manager Robert Beckel. The ad went right to the core of the public concerns that were being formed about Hart—fomented mainly by Hart himself.

MONDALE'S "RED PHONE" AD

[A red telephone fills the television screen. The red light on the phone begins blinking ominously.]

ANNOUNCER: The most awesome powerful responsibility in the world lies in the hand that picks up this phone. The idea of an unsure, unsteady, untested hand is something to really think about. This is the issue of our times. On March twentieth, vote as if the future of the world is at stake. Mondale—this president will know what he is doing. And that's the difference between Gary Hart and Walter Mondale.

Strategists like to recite to their clients and their associates a basic political theorem: It is crucial that a candidate's message in his television ads be reinforced by his message on the television news. Illinois added a corollary to that. For night after night, the message of Mondale's "Red Phone" ad was being reinforced by the message of Hart's performance on the nightly news. Mondale's Red Phone warned of an *unsure, unsteady, untested* president. Hart's news demonstrated just that.

WBBM-TV, MARCH 19, 5 P.M.

[This is the news hour and Mondale's red phone is ringing again. In a journalistically obscene policy practiced by so many local stations because they make money doing it, the Chicago stations permit candidates to buy time so close to the news that their ads blend as one with the news in the voters' minds. Now Mondale's ad warns about a president who is "unsure, unsteady, untested . . . And that's the difference between Gary Hart and Walter Mondale." Then comes the real news, reinforcing that message.]

WALTER JACOBSON: The last full day of campaigning before the Illinois primary . . . Mondale demanded to know why some Hart TV commercials that have linked Mondale to the political organization of Ed Vrdolyak kept running forty-eight hours after Hart promised to take them off.

MONDALE: Here's a person who wants to be president of the United States because he said he'd run the federal government. He can't get an ad off TV that he's paying for in forty-eight hours.

JACOBSON: . . . As for those TV commercials, Hart's people are saying the orders were given to the TV stations to pull them off the air.

But the Hart people say the TV stations were slow to respond because the change was made during the weekend. Meanwhile, the race is tight.

WBBM-TV, 6 P.M.

[Reporter Carol Krause is interviewing Hart live at O'Hare Airport on this last day of the campaign.]

KRAUSE: This thing that keeps haunting you, this business about the Vrdolyak ad which was supposedly pulled. I have to tell you, when I was driving to the airport, I heard one on the radio.

HART: I know. Well, it's maddening to me and it's maddening to our campaign. . . . I am just totally disgusted with the thing, I really am.

In the end, the Mondale and Hart messages that reached people through television's newscasts proved to be one and the same. Gary Hart became the issue and Walter Mondale became the nominee.

The wave had broken and the dark horse of 1984 had been left floundering in white water, much of his own making. In the last hours of the Illinois campaign, Hart reflected for just a few moments on the wave of message politics he had mastered for so long, only to see it finally wash out from under him.

"Very little surprises me now," Hart said softly. ". . . There have been two campaigns now—the one where I talk about my message and the one that the media presents to the public." He is asked if he resented those questions about his private life. "That's all right," he said. "But I don't know why everyone has to do it. I would have thought after ten reporters did it, that one hundred others wouldn't have to. . . .

"I am once again impressed by the difference between what the press wants to talk about and what the people want to hear.

"But I'm pretty stoical about it."

FINISHING TOUCHES: AN UNVARNISHED VIEW

The Illinois primary was painful history and New York clearly was going the same way when, on April 1, 1984, Patrick Caddell put the finishing touches to a blunt memo to his candidate that outlined his view of what had gone wrong. Polling in New York was showing that people were favoring the New Ideas/New Generation positions and themes of Hart's campaign, but were rejecting Hart's candidacy. Caddell began by analyzing the data, but eventually offered the sort of candid, sharp criticism that is the sort of thing most candidates need to hear from a senior insider at one time or another, but which most advisers never provide for reasons that perhaps range from an excess of sensitivity to a shortfall of fortitude.

The problem, Caddell concluded, was Hart himself.

MEMORANDUM

TO: Gary Hart Date: Sunday—April 1, 1984
FROM: Patrick H. Caddell
RE: CRISIS

Summary
One can conclude that the problem is not the "message" but the "messenger." While moving more in agreement with Hart's "new leadership, new ideas" positions, the voters have been focusing more on Hart the candidate. . . . They are uncertain or ambivalent when it comes to voting for Hart the *potential president*. . . .
A Candid Review of the Campaign to Date
We can no longer ignore or downplay the critical problems that confront the Hart campaign. I know your instinct will be to reject or disregard the analysis that is being offered. However, I urge you to approach this with an open mind.

. . . First, Gary Hart has become the issue—frankly, somewhat sooner than I would have hoped. . . . Second, the campaign has been unable to coordinate its message, the schedule, its media, its field operations, and its politics in a coherent and strategic manner. . . .

The loss of Illinois, which revived Mondale, was totally unnecessary. . . . The first "ad" mistake was the most grievous act of what, in truth, were a series of actions by the campaign that were made without a strategic framework. . . . Finally, the Vrdolyak episode was the result of the failure to have an agreed-upon strategy, a total breakdown of communications including your lack of knowledge about the precarious Hart position in Illinois. . . .

Everyone has become a media expert including you. . . . I do not know how Ray [Strother, Hart's ad specialist] keeps his sanity. For weeks it has been nightmarish. . . . In all my years in politics, I have never seen anything approaching this chaos. . . .

Finally, your own role in the media has been nothing short of incredible. You write spots. You decide what spots should be produced or not. You have final approval over trafficking [purchases of airtime for ads]. You make these often arbitrary decisions without benefit of any presentation of needs, goals, strategies, or targets. Too often, you are tired or unfocused. . . . You may be concerned that you will get burned again, a la Chicago. . . .

. . . If the [Hart] campaign is unmanaged, disorganized, ineffective, amateurish, but devoted, then it is because you chose for it to be. Frankly, I believe that you want a weak campaign [staff]. If you wanted something different, then it would be so.

Despite your protestations to the contrary, you want to be the campaign manager as well as the candidate. . . . You want to shape the strategy, determine the efficacy of the message, and control the media. There is no way, at a national level, that a candidate, buffeted in the hurricane as he is, can have the perception necessary to adequately handle these functions and still be an effective candidate.

PART FOUR

TEN

VICTORY BEFORE KICKOFF

VIDEOS

The odyssey of the Olympic torch flickers across the nation's television screens in the spring and summer of 1984, as the symbolic flame slowly makes its way across America, borne by patriotic volunteers. The flame, the runners, and the spirit are cheered each day by Americans along the route and those watching at home.

President Reagan is visibly and apparently genuinely moved as he is celebrating Father's Day by taking the network-news cameras with him to a special Olympics, the International Games of the Disabled. Americans in their living rooms join their president in this moment of special poignancy as they share in the courage of these handicapped athletes from around the world.

The Statue of Liberty, wrapped in scaffolding, is seen in the early-morning light, and the camera closes in on a jackhammer worker . . . then a worker on the great lady's face . . . then a riveter . . . a grinder . . . and a guy spraying liquid nitrogen on the statue's face . . . and finally a guy pouring a beer—and all the while the song is heard: "This Bud's for you/ You know America takes pride/ In what you do."

A bugler's "Taps" pierces the silence of Memorial Day at Arlington National Cemetery, its call both reed-thin and resonant as it filters into the homes of America; and the camera closes in on President Reagan, who is using his presence and leadership to help the nation find honor in the dark memories of its too-recent past. The Vietnam War's Unknown Soldier is being laid to rest, and his people, painfully wiser, are learning that it is okay to remember and honor, even as they maintain their unspoken vow: Never again.

The Statue of Liberty once again joins Americans in their homes, as a television camera closes in on those now-familiar views of the symbolic lady encased in scaffolds and braces. Again there is music, this time soft and orchestral, as the announcer is heralding a product other than beer: "It was a dream that built a nation, the freedom to work in the job of your choice, to reap the rewards of your labors, to leave a richer life for your children and their children beyond. Today the dream lives again. Today jobs are coming back, the economy is coming back. And America's coming back, standing tall in the world again. President Reagan, building the American dream."

The heroism of Normandy is remembered—President Reagan has brought the old soldiers and the young daughter of one who couldn't return to that beachhead in France as, together in tears, they remind Americans back home of the greatness and glory that is theirs. . . . The Fourth of July is celebrated—in a down-home, upbeat, festive, and folksy day at the Daytona International Speedway, as the president parties with his own special-interest group, those just-plain-Americans who love a good stockcar race and a president who cares enough to share their good times.

The Olympic torch again, its odyssey not yet completed, is being carried down a country road; a father and son stop their farmwork to watch and pay tribute. It is a small, touching, patriotic gesture that is witnessed by no one but the runner and of course the camera crew from the beer company's ad agency, which is filming this new commercial in order to ride the same patriotic wave that Ronald Reagan has been riding and fomenting for some time.

They are all together, at last, at the Los Angeles Olympics. The torch is atop the Coliseum. Mary Lou Retton is atop the balance beam. Greg Louganis is atop the diving board. And President Reagan is on top of the world, officially opening the 1984 Olympic Games as the crowd cheers. Night after night, victory after victory, Americans watching on ABC are serenaded by Ray Charles singing "America the Beautiful." As United States victories mount, "Go for the gold!" threatens to overtake *e pluribus unum*—and in this nation that plays its politics like sports, it is no surprise when its president transforms that sporting chant into his political slogan. "Go for the gold!" becomes the number-one crowd pleaser of Ronald Reagan's campaign-rally speeches.

That was the summer of 1984. It was a red-white-and-blue time when the television news looked like the television beer and car commercials, and the beer and car commercials looked like the Reagan campaign, and they all glowed with the reflected patriotic neon of the Olympics. It got so that Mondale campaign manager Robert Beckel couldn't stand to turn on his television set in the spring and summer of 1984, because every time he did, he could see all too well just what was happening. And that is why Beckel was moved to observe, in a voice mixed with anguish and admiration: "They created the American mood of 1984."

While Beckel's plaint may well have given the Reagan strategists a bit too much credit, it is true at least that they tried mightily to feed and foster that mood, and did their job well. All summer long it had gone like that—actually it began in the spring—as Ronald Reagan's strategists worked like none have before to make him as one with the American people. Fostering patriotism was, after all, his stock in trade in all his years as an actor and all his years as a politician. The creative skills and the use of symbolism of the Reagan advisers and the president himself built upon a confluence of events such as the fortieth anniversary of the Normandy invasion and the Olympics. It produced an atmosphere that would cause *Time* magazine—right smack in the middle of the fall presidential campaign—to produce a cover story that celebrated the new mood by turning its cover into one of those "heart" bumper-sticker slogans: "I Love U.S.," a story about "America's Upbeat Mood."

"It was the greatest public-works program by . . . government and private industry," is how Beckel described the summer-long efforts much later. "It affected everybody. You saw it on TV every day in every way—the news, the ads, the soaps. When Budweiser ran that series of ads on the Olympic torch, I, myself, was taken; when the Brannigans stopped work in their fields, I was moved—I stopped work at my desk for a moment, out of respect.

"The most memorable—the most unbelieveably well-done TV they did—was when they went to Arlington and did the Tomb of the Unknown Vietnam Soldier. It was perfect—absolutely perfect, the bastards." He lowered his voice and added a final observation (it is the sort of notation that is a bow to bitter fruit and of course makes no difference, but it would be too much to expect a losing campaign manager to resist): "And it was all done at government expense."

While Labor Day marks the traditional kickoff of fall presidential campaigns, the fact is that presidential elections in the television age have often been pretty well determined by the events that took place during the summertime and were spread by television throughout the nation, live and in color, taped and rebroadcast, night and day. But in those elections of the contemporary past, all of these were events that *happened to* a campaign—calamities and blunders that hurt a campaign.

The 1968 race was altered decisively by those catastrophic clashes of demonstrators and authorities in the streets of Chicago during the Democratic Convention; Hubert Humphrey spent all fall trying to regain the support that had cost him. And the 1972 race was doomed (although it is doubtful it could have succeeded under any circumstances) by the debacle in which Democratic presidential nominee George McGovern had to replace his chosen running mate, Thomas Eagleton, after his history of mental illness leaked out following the party's convention. Both of those gave the nation the presidency of Richard Nixon. Similarly, the 1980 election was won by Reagan primarily because of what happened to President Carter's campaign when those helicopters crashed and doomed the rescue mission to free the Americans held hostage in Iran. Night after night Americans continued to be reminded that Carter was presiding over a nation held hostage by those nightly numerical references in Walter Cronkite's news show or Ted Koppel's *Nightline* broadcasts.

But the Reagan campaign of 1984 showed that a shrewd and politically sophisticated group of strategists and a willing and communicatively sensitive candidate can manipulate the messages of the spring and summer so they work *for* their campaign. They showed that it is possible to use the mix of television news and ads to in effect achieve victory—or at least lay the groundwork for victory—before the traditional Labor Day kickoff.

This crucial public mood of patriotism and optimism was designed and nurtured by Reagan's top strategists—James Baker, Michael Deaver, and their associates on the White House staff—plus the group of some forty Madison Avenue advertising-agency brainstormers who called themselves the Tuesday Team (named for Election Day) and worked to produce commercials to sell Ronald Reagan as skillfully as they had sold Campbell's soup, Prego spaghetti sauce, Pepsi-Cola, Gallo wine, and Yamaha motorcycles.

The mood was fostered as well by the Madison Avenue types who never left their commercial accounts and who continued to push America's patriotic buttons to sell the products that were their accounts: Budweiser and Stroh's beers, Northrop airplanes, Prudential-Bache and their rock, M&M's ("real American value"), and Remington products ("proudly made in the U.S.A.").

And it was fostered as well by television's communicator decision-makers, the most influential and successful of them being Roone Arledge, ABC's president of news and sports (at the time, that is; he has relinquished the network-sports presidency since he made ABC preeminent in that field). Arledge is the master of innovation who set the standard for television sports coverage with his *Wide World of Sports* and for nightly in-depth news coverage with his *Nightline* show, that late-night monument to television news and public service at its best starring Ted Koppel. So too, it was Arledge's network coverage of the Olympics that in tone and content gave the nation a very pro-American, superpatriotic coverage that ran consistently true from musical theme to event coverage to analysis and commentary. It was a production well done, and captivating to watch; but it was a production done live and in color, mainly in red, white, and blue.

Michael Deaver said that watching the way the Democrats conducted their televised primary-election debates convinced him of the direction the Reagan news and ad-message campaigns should take. "I thought the way the Democrats handled the primary situation was abominable," said Deaver. "It was far too scrappy and disagreeable. No one emerged as acting presidential. The business of Hart and Jackson and Mondale . . . and Dan Rather sitting around a table as equals [in the New York primary debate moderated by Rather]—I mean, it blew my mind. I would never have let my candidate sit around a table. Even a nonpresident, absolutely not! Absolutely not! . . . It was shouting and arguing and even when they sat on a stage eight across . . . [they] shouted and argued and yelled at each other."

If that is what the public was getting from the Democrats—political harangues and lectures about what was wrong with America—then the Reagan campaign would give the public just the opposite. Deaver recalled one meeting of the Reagan strategy-makers in Baker's White House office. "We decided early on that the best thing we had going were all these guys [the Democrats] screaming and scratching. . . . While all these people are fighting, we've got to go with nice old couples walking down the street eating ice cream cones, and kids waving the American flag, and people buying houses, and more people getting married, and more people believing in America again . . .

"We felt not only because of the Olympics, but a feeling we got through [polling] research . . . that this idea of making people feel good was the way to go. As long as it worked, we ought to use it forever. . . . That's the Reagan constituency; all we were trying to do was show that visually."

The orchesteral theme music, soothing and uplifting at the same time, plays in the background, and the scenes that drift through the Reagan ad are done in soft-focus photography, which complements the soft-sell messagery. First there is an ideal factory, then people working, a cowboy dusting himself off, people getting married, people building a house.

ANNOUNCER: It's morning again, in America. Today more men and women will go to work than ever before in our country's history. With interest rates at about half the record highs of 1980, nearly 2,000 families today will buy new homes, more than at any time in the past four years. This afternoon, 6,500 young men and women will be married, and with inflation at less than half what it was just four years ago they can look forward with confidence to the future. It's morning again, in America. And under the leadership of President Reagan, our country is prouder and stronger and better. Why would we ever want to return to where we were less than four short years ago?

CAPTURE THE FLAG

The television screen was awash in a sea of red, white, and blue, as thousands of Democrats put down their Mondale, Hart, and Jackson placards and began waving American flags instead. "That's our message strategy of 1984," Mondale campaign manager Bob Beckel beamed as he watched the Democratic Convention finale play on television. "In 1968 and 1972, Americans saw Democrats burning flags on television. Now they see Democrats waving them."

The Mondale campaign's private polls had, of course, told them the same things the Reagan polls had been saying about how they could best win back the presidential votes of America's middle-class, blue-collared people who deserted them in 1980 and white-collared young urban professionals who in 1980 had opted not to vote at all. The campaign of 1984 would show how, with lack of internal discipline and lack of attention to detail, this strategy concept would get lost in the cacophony of the Mondale band of message-makers. (The tip-off of the inability of the candidate and his message strategists to sense public response and feed it accordingly should also have been evident from the outset of this convention that he controlled. For Mondale, in his desire to show he could be a strong party boss, had fired party chairman Charles Manatt on the eve of this convention in Manatt's home state of California, and tried to replace him with Jimmy Carter's friend, Bert Lance, whose reputation had been smudged by scandal stories about banking and financial improprieties. Mondale, predictably, had to cave in and reinstate Manatt when his own party balked. Not since onetime Cleveland Mayor Ralph Perk enlivened an otherwise routine dedication ceremony by inadvertently setting his own hair on fire with a blowtorch has a politician managed to transform so manageable an event into such a flaming embarrassment.)

RECAPTURE THE FLAG

President Reagan's chief of White House advance personnel, Bill Henkel, remembers how he was watching the Democratic National Convention at his home in suburban Virginia, "chuckling and chortling that they were undone," when he saw on his television screen that red-white-and-blue flag-waving finale the Democrats had staged on their last day in San Francisco.

Henkel stopped chuckling and chortling. He started fuming instead. "I felt they were desecrating the flag!" Henkel said, his eyes blazing and shaking his fist even months later. "This is a highly personal, loyal, emotional response to something. But I know I wasn't alone. . . . I felt wounded. I mean I felt that they had taken our symbol, which, you know, frankly, the president deserved. I really did. I think a lot of us just felt that. Not because he's the president, but I think he truly believes in the flag and in so many of the fundamentals and ideas that are so symbolized by the flag.

"It had a lot of the trappings and appearances of something that we would have produced and orchestrated. . . . I probably went to bed that night with a case of nerves. . . . It's so interesting how the whole thing unwound so rapidly for them."

* * *

Deaver convened meetings and Henkel said plans were drafted to "get back on the TV and . . . recapture the flag" for Ronald Reagan. They decided to put their plan into effect immediately, at a rally in Austin, Texas. "The way we did the events was designed to recapture the flag," Henkel recalled. "We were going to use an awful lot of flags and red, white, and blue."

The Reagan officials vowed to plan this recapturing gambit down to the last detail. There was a memo from campaign manager Ed Rollins to White House adviser Richard Darman on whom the president should appeal to in Texas and what he ought to say there.

> REAGAN/BUSH '84
>
> MEMORANDUM FOR DICK DARMAN
> FROM: Ed Rollins
> SUBJECT: July 25–27 Speeches
>
> Following are my recommendations for the tone and content of the President's speeches next week.
> TEXAS
> TARGET AUDIENCE: Traditional Democrats, recent Texas residents.
> TONE: Future-oriented, attack on House, youth oriented.
> CONTENT: Use the "choice of a new generation" theme to highlight the differences with liberal Mondale agenda and Reagan agenda, with strong emphasis on the economy and high technology. . . . Unabashedly say we are in Texas because we love Texas and have a Vice-President who really understands Texas. . . .

The Reagan campaign budgeted $1,740 for signs and flags alone for this rally, and—in what was sure to be a photo opportunity that local television and newspapers could not resist—they had arranged to have Houston Oilers' star running back Earl Campbell there to present Reagan with two Stetson hats. It turned out Campbell couldn't make it at the last minute, so the advance man on the scene substituted two Houston Oilers cheerleaders—in their gridiron-scanty costumes—instead. Indeed that caught the eye of the television and newspaper camera people, who used the shots of the president with two sexy-looking Houston Oilers cheerleaders, but Henkel caught hell from White House chief of staff James Baker. "You know, we were very, very precise about any image or picture that we put out," Henkel said.

The rest of the campaign, Henkel said, was as much as anything else a reflection of Mike Deaver's red-white-and-blue admonition that no one would ever be allowed to "out-patriot" Ronald Reagan.

OLYMPIC FEATS

Among the ample skills that have enabled Roone Arledge to become the greatest innovator of television news and sports is a certain sense of just how seemingly unrelated things play off each other, and how these things all come together in the public mind.

Which is to say that Roone Arledge knows an orgy when he sees one. And especially when he caters one.

"It was just an orgy of patriotism by the time you put it all together," Arledge said as he looked back on Ronald Reagan's summer of '84, and the Olympic Games coverage that helped make his day. ". . . It really started with the torch across the country. That really got people involved and really . . . from town to town . . . inspired the [patriotism] idea."

Arledge conceded that Reagan surely went for—and won—the gold in that spring and summer of White House–planned events that culminated in the Olympic Games: from the thrill of United States victories to ABC's "America the Beautiful" Olympic theme; from sea to shining sea.

"I was concerned . . . at the opening ceremonies that you give the president his due—he's there and he's the president and you talk to him—but you don't turn this into a political event for him. What happened after that, with all the American victories and the frenzy . . . it became overwhelming. But the fact that Reagan would have benefitted from all of that was just an extension of the summer. I mean, he benefitted from going to China. He had benefitted from [seeing] the pope. He had benefitted from—you name it and they had it. . . . There is also just no question that what further added to it was all the [patriotically flavored] commercials.

". . . And this was just the climax. I don't think they ever anticipated it would be quite as powerful as it was."

As Roone Arledge explains it, the Americana of the Games just got away from them. Nobody meant it to happen, it just did. First of all, there were two separate simultaneous broadcasts, he said. "We did two separate feeds. We had one for the United States and one for the rest of the world. The [feed for] the rest of the world was totally neutral, you take whatever you want. If you're in Britain you take all the things the British are interested in and the sports you care about—you don't take baseball."

The American feed was unabashedly American. About the theme music: " 'America the Beautiful' we had played at every Olympics since Innsbruck in 1976. I first heard that record by Ray Charles right after the Munich [games] and I made a note then to use it in the future, partly because I thought it was great and it was during that period when black artists were not saying very many things about the United States that were any good. But also it had a beat at the beginning which, ironically, came right out of our Olympic [music]. We had ta-ta-dum-dum-ta-ta, and the opening of 'America the Beautiful' is da-da-dum-dum-dum-dum, and when I first heard it, it was just a natural.

"And we used it and everybody loved it. And we used it as a reprise for a salute to all the American athletes. . . . In the past, because American athletes have never been as successful as they were here, we usually ended up at night with an anthem and showing the gold medals. But the first day of the Olympics [boycotted by the Soviet bloc], I think we won seven gold medals. . . . And it became obvious that we couldn't play the anthem every time an American won, because nobody else won!"

"God, it was awful." Peter Jennings, the gifted ABC News foreign correspondent who graduated to anchor, was recalling what had seemed like the longest and most professionally unpleasant interview of a distinguished career. His, after all, had been a career that had led him into the practice of broadcast journalism in tough places, not the least of which was that danger zone when Arab commandos took over the Munich Olympics.

"Interminable! Interminable!" He winced as he sat in his modest ABC News office and reflected upon three minutes of airtime at the Olympics—but not *that* Olympics. For he was talking not about the 1972 Games, where he and his crew had crouched and spied, live and in color, upon the Palestinian terrorists in their evil act; he was talking about the 1984 Games, where he'd sat upright and interviewed President Ronald Reagan. And it was his own act at the 1984 Olympics that he found so distasteful.

The ABC News chiefs considered it a public-relations coup to have Jennings interview President Reagan at the opening of the 1984 Olympics in Los Angeles. Roone Arledge, president of ABC News and ABC

Sports, had passed over Jim McKay and the other ABC sportscasters and inserted Jennings, who was the least known of the three major network-news anchors, into that moment in the national spotlight. The ABC hierarchy considered it an image-boosting move that could only help the ratings of Peter Jennings's news in the battle with Dan Rather's news and Tom Brokaw's news.

Jennings considered it a professional trap. He was worried that he would wind up looking like a naïve adjunct of the Reagan reelection juggernaut for conducting what would have to be a softball interview in the middle of the presidential campaign. He worried because this was a rare chance to interview a president who was running for reelection by running from the media, and whose strategy called for avoiding press questioning in a campaign that emphasized pageants over policy. He was worried, he said, that he would look like "a wimp."

He did. Jennings came off sycophantic and substantively lightweight in his interview with Reagan at the Olympiad. But it is to Jennings's great credit that he recognized the danger beforehand, and he candidly acknowledged the result afterward. Said Jennings:

"I had some very ambiguous feelings about that [interview]. . . . I had them before and I had them afterwards. ABC . . . had the rights to the Games and the opening ceremonies . . . and somebody decided in management that it would be wonderful to have the president interviewed—I assume it was Roone. And I don't find the idea bad—except that it was in the middle of a campaign and I was assigned to interview him. It was going to be three minutes and I knew exactly what was happening. Here you have what is in global terms a nonpolitical occasion, with the president of the largest free country in the world opening what turned out to be great Games. But it's also right in the middle of a political campaign.

"So how could I look like anything but a wimp either way? I couldn't say, 'Mr. President, the Games are opening, but what are you going to do about arms control?'

"Conversely, if I went the other way and said, 'Mr. President, aren't these games just wonderful? Isn't this the best thing that's ever happened to you?'—how could I avoid doing anything but play right into the center of the president's campaign? . . .

"God, it was awful! My wife and I sat outside our hotel in Los Angeles for about two hours trying to devise a set of questions that would be both political and benign. And it was awful!"

Meanwhile, back at the White House, while Jennings and his wife were putting themselves through angst, the Reagan, Deaver, Henkel & Company were salivating at the political prospect of putting the president into a made-for-television noncampaign setting—right in the middle of a campaign. Months later, when asked how important Reagan's appearance and interview at the Olympics were to his campaign, Henkel said: "Oh, very—imagine the audience! . . . There is only one president, and we can truly put the president above any kind of partisan activity when he is president of all Americans. . . . Hell, you talk about reinforcements!"

The televised interview of Reagan at the Olympics was one of those things that is viewed as a great public-relations move by both institutions. "We'd been involved in the Olympic thing for at least a year," said Henkel. ". . . I'm sure we offered it [the interview] and I'm sure they requested it.

The White House officials were aware of rivalries within the network, as ABC sports officials did not want to let a newsperson like Jennings into their jockular domaine. As Henkel recalled: "There was some controversy within ABC, to be honest—I know this for a fact—over who would do the interview. Jennings is news and . . . at ABC Sports . . . they weren't wildly enamored with the idea of Jennings sharing the interview. . . ."

But the concerns of the White House centered not on who would conduct the interview but what he would be asking. The White House officials sought to get the subject matter of the questions approved in advance—and they wanted assurance that the questions would be related to Olympics and world sports, not politics and world policy. "You can never dictate what the questions will be," Henkel said. "But I mean, we made some representation that we felt that the interview should be on the Olympics—what was happening that day, and not suddenly in the middle of the event get into a—you know—Beirut question, or, 'Are you going to get reelected, Mr. President?' Or something like that.

"So I think there was a tacit agreement among everyone. . . . Everyone sort of agreed that the spirit of this was not going to be an interview. It didn't need to be an interview."

ABC's Roone Arledge saw it that way too. "We debated whether we should interview him or not," Arledge said. "My concern was twofold. One was that we had just had a full summer of giving him a free forum. And I was concerned that they might turn it into a Reagan political thing. But he was very restrained and he didn't do that. The other was just that it intruded, that if you're not going to do a news interview . . . then it's intruding on a ceremony that people really want to watch. And why do a meaningless interview with the president? So we tried to kind of walk the line halfway between. . . . We didn't want him making a political statement, and we, on the other hand, had kind of an understanding that this was not a [news interview]. So there was no contention about it.

"Millions and millions and millions of people were tuned in to watch the opening ceremonies of the Olympics, not to have a political speech or a drilling by a correspondent. One of the concerns we originally had was whether Peter ought to be in a position of doing a softball interview with the president. . . . We decided . . . it was really a ceremonial appearance."

Arledge's decision to have his news anchor do the interview did not meet with rave reviews from his fellow news presidents at the other two networks. "It seems to me that if the White House came and said we'll allow this man to be interviewed but only about sports, at that point Curt Gowdy does the interview and the anchorman steps aside," said former CBS News president Van Gordon Sauter.

NBC News president Lawrence Grossman stopped short of pointed criticism, fashioning instead a response right out of the Gertrude Stein protocols. "I don't know the ground rules Jennings had," Grossman said. "I think newsmen should be newsmen but the Olympics are the Olympics." And of the Olympics, he said, "That's not journalism. It's not done by the news division, it's done by the sports department and there's rooting and cheering. . . . ABC was following the national mood. People were interested in what the American athletes were doing and the Olympics were staged like a big patriotic extravaganza."

(The combined lure of the sports spotlight and the presidential aurora eventually proved irresistible to NBC too. As part of its broadcast of pro football's Super Bowl in 1986, NBC had its anchor Tom Brokaw interview Reagan in another session done more for ratings public relations than for news, as Brokaw played the event more to show rapport with a president than to elicit news from him.)

ABC'S INTERVIEW AT THE OLYMPICS PRESIDENT REAGAN AND PETER JENNINGS LOS ANGELES, JULY 28, 1984

The flags of 140 nations are parading in colorful spectacle in the background, and a capacity crowd is cheering, as the camera starts wide to capture the panoply of it all and then zooms in tight to capture the president of the United States and the anchor of ABC News.

PETER JENNINGS: We're honored at the twenty-third opening of the Olympic Games to have President Reagan not only open the games but join us for a few minutes. Mr. President, back in '32, President Hoover thought it was a silly idea to come and open the Games and he didn't. How do you feel today?

PRESIDENT REAGAN: Well, maybe the world has changed somewhat since then . . . [he lapsed into a lengthy observation on how "the history of the Olympics is tied to peace and the ancient Greek city-states . . ."]

JENNINGS: Did I hear a rumor earlier that you said you had never seen the spirit of America expressed so well as down there on the field?

PRESIDENT REAGAN: Well, I think that there is a great patriotic feeling that's sweeping this country and it bodes well for our future. And I think it was expressed here today. I think it's not only patriotism for our own land, but you saw this great American crowd here and their response to the visiting athletes from other countries. I just feel proud to be down there with all those wonderful young people on that field representing a hundred forty countries. I bet if we turned some of the problems of international relations over to them, they'd solve them before tomorrow.

JENNINGS: Are you sad the Soviets are not here, sir?

PRESIDENT REAGAN: Yes, I think it would be far better for the world if they were. But I think they're the losers.

[There were other questions: "Do you think these games can add to international peace?" and "How can you get politics out of sports?" And then there was a round of thanks, and ABC's Olympics microphone was handed back to Jim McKay.]

Months later, Jennings was asked what he had been thinking about as he was doing that interview with the president at the Olympic Games. He looked as if he had just been sentenced to a life of migraines. "Interminable! Interminable!" he said. "I could hardly wait to get back. . . . You feel like a fool, to be honest."

The ABC News anchor, a journalist of considerable accomplishment, added that one reporter covering the Reagan White House at the time, Lou Cannon of *The Washington Post*, "subsequently said that was one of the great sycophantic interviews of all time. And I wrote him a note and I said, 'Jeez, I really have to agree with you'—

which is an awful position to be in." He shook his head and repeated, "Awful position to be in."

According to Roone Arledge, it could have been worse. "The network wanted to have a promotion theme for the fall entertainment program in which all the [ABC entertainment] stars came on in all the station breaks [during the period of the Olympic Games] and said, 'Let's go America.' I said we don't do that. Sports is not quite like news but there's a journalistic function there, and it's one thing if Al Michaels gets carried away at a hockey game and says 'Do you believe in miracles? Yes!' or whatever. But it's something else for us . . . to be rooting so openly for a team when you're covering an event. . . . There's got to be some semblance of objectivity. I tell you, it's just going to backfire against you.

"And I found I was the only voice at the network and I finally got that killed. And if that had gone in the middle of all this, I shudder to think—!"

ELEVEN

FALL CLASSICS

America takes a day off on the first Monday of each September, and once every four years, while their countrymen take their leisure, two politicians take to the hustings. They put themselves through the motions of what has become a made-for-television ritual—the official kickoff of a presidential campaign that has, of course, been off and running for some time.

So it was that on Labor Day, 1980, the incumbent Democratic president, Jimmy Carter, and his Republican challenger, Ronald Reagan, found themselves placed in front of strategically selected backdrops for this video occasion. Labor Day, 1980, would test the proposition that incumbent presidents have a huge and perhaps decisive advantage over their challengers when it comes to manipulating their way to visual glory on the television news.

Both campaigns approached the official kickoff with finely honed game plans:

Jimmy Carter's White House experts, under the direction of media master Gerald Rafshoon, had gone to great lengths and considerable expense to provide their leader all the Rafshoonery they could muster to remind Southerners that this president was one of their own. They had concocted a Southern-fried picnic and set it deep in the heart of the South, at Tuscumbia, Alabama; they had ordered up colorful balloons that would soar skyward on command, a band to play "Hail to the Chief" and "Dixie," and a famous singer, Charlie Daniels, to draw a crowd and pack the park. They had also arranged with the networks and the Secret Service to permit a network camera crew to get one of those aerial shots that would capture the grand panoply of it all.

Ronald Reagan's presidentially untested crew, led by Michael Deaver, had reserved a piece of New Jersey that is called Liberty Park, which gave the challenger the Statue of Liberty to use as a backdrop and a talking point; he also had a supply of oversized American flags, the blue sea, and a veritable flotilla of boats flying still more American flags. And they had two special touches: To add to the luster of liberty, they had delivered the father of Polish Solidarity leader Lech Walesa to stand beside Reagan; and to counter the age issue (a problem even then), they had arranged for the sixty-nine-year-old challenger to doff his jacket and tie and stand there in his white shirtsleeves.

On television that night, America saw a presidential challenger at his cinematic best. The sea sparkled; the flags billowed; the candidate radiated John Wayne's strength and John Kennedy's youth as he stood there with the breeze touseling his dark hair and fluttering his shirt, which was unbuttoned to the chest, and which gleamed extra white against nature's aqua-blue backdrop. And the candidate turned and looked out at the harbor right on cue as he said, "The lady standing there in the harbor has never betrayed us once, but this administration has betrayed the working men and women of this country."

And on television that night, President Jimmy Carter's campaign kickoff began with that aerial shot of a huge crowd of forty thousand. That, plus the correspondent's explanation of what viewers were seeing—that one third of the crowd was leaving the picnic grounds early, having heard Charlie Daniels sing and choosing not to stay to hear their president, who was about to speak.

Sooner or later, most presidential candidates and strategists come to the realization that Labor Day kickoffs are remembered more for their fumbles than for producing big scores. In 1980, Ronald Reagan's crew showed it could easily match television-news managing wits with the powers of the incumbent's White House. But even at that, Reagan's 1980 kickoff execution was not perfect. For later in the day, Reagan went to Detroit, and in the course of saying how glad he was to be there, he ad-libbed that his opponent was "opening his campaign down in the city that gave birth to and is the parent body of the Ku Klux Klan." *Fumble!* The media pounced on that one along about the second and third days, after the Carter aides brought it to their attention by howling in agony—like wrestlers slapping the canvas in feigned pain—that Reagan had slandered all of Dixie. Reagan, who'd had a campaign history of gaffes committed while daring to talk extemporaneously, apologized; and that limited it to a minor flap.

In the campaign of 1984, both candidates had resolved to learn from the recent past. Reagan, a ward of his White House aides, operated on a controlled-environment strategy of taking no impromptu questions and leaving nothing to extemporaneous chance.

Walter Mondale, meanwhile, vowed frequently and fervently that on Labor Day he would "hit the ground running."

Americans tuning in to their television news on Labor Day saw that Walter Mondale seemed to have hit the ground by planting his first step firmly on an upturned rake. It was a momentum stopper unparalleled in the course of presidential-campaign television—and it was self-inflicted.

Labor Day, 1984, stands as one of those special days in the course of campaign television that demonstrates many things at once about the way candidates campaign for television and the way television and newspapers cover them.

It is one of those days that students of politics can cite to illustrate the difference between political aides who are woefully inept and political aides who are extraordinarily ept. And it is one of those days that students of media can cite to illustrate the difference between the way television covers political news and the way newspapers cover political news.

The Mondale advisers can be seen failing to understand even the most basic aspects of just what it was that television journalists would focus upon as the subject of their nightly news story; they lost control of their message on the one day when they had weeks to prepare for it and no outside interference to mar it. The Reagan advisers can be seen at their cinematic best.

Many of television's most famous and influential journalists and executives can be heard making their case vehemently that this was a perfect example of a time when it was appropriate that compelling visual scenes dictate the shape of the nightly news story. They say that only television reported the real story of Labor Day, 1984, while print journalists missed the point because they concentrated on what the candidates said, instead of how they looked.

The story, as the nation's major newspapers presented it, was about the candidates outlining their fall campaign themes. It was Reagan spelling out the themes of optimism and a promise of a "great crusade" while standing in the midst of a huge rally in Orange County, California. And it was Mondale spelling out his theme of fairness and his charge that Reagan caters to the rich and ignores the rest, as the crowd cheered him on at a Middle America rally in Merrill, Wisconsin. The stories in all the major papers were heavy on themes and quotes.

The three major networks were also in agreement—but with each other, not with the newspapers. The story on television was Reagan getting off to a spectacular start and Mondale getting off to a horrendous start. It was Reagan standing in the midst of a pageant of Grand Old Party spectaculars in Orange County, California, gazing out at a huge crowd as balloons of red, white, and blue ascended and skydivers trailing smokestreams of red, white, and blue descended, and speaking several sentences about optimism. And it was Mondale walking with union officials and Democratic politicians along sparsely populated Fifth Avenue in Manhattan—a "puny" start in front of an "embarrassingly small crowd"—because his aides had him attend the annual Labor Day Parade before making that major campaign kickoff speech in Wisconsin, a speech the networks barely mentioned.

In the print media, the *Los Angeles Times* account, by staff writers Maura Dolan and Richard E. Meyer, was typical of the way the major newspapers handled Mondale's day. It began:

> Democratic presidential candidate Walter F. Mondale and his running mate, Geraldine A. Ferraro, swept across the nation Monday from New York to Southern California and officially began their fall campaign by accusing President Reagan of serving "all the people in his country club" at the expense of the rest of America. . . .
>
> [In the fifth paragraph it mentioned the parade.] In New York, only scattered clusters of people showed up as they walked 16 blocks in the city's annual Labor Day Parade.

And the *Dallas Morning News*'s Washington bureau chief, Carl P. Leubsdorf, began his report with:

> Merrill, Wis.—Democratic presidential nominee Walter Mondale launched his general election campaign Monday by calling on President Reagan to "tell the truth about the future" and urging voters to "stop, look, and listen" before they make their decision. . . .

[And in the fourth paragraph] First, Mondale and Ferraro marched through virtually empty streets in midtown Manhattan as they became the first Democratic candidates to attend New York's Labor Day parade since Hubert Humphrey did in 1968.

Here, in contrast, is the way the television networks began their Mondale reports. All of them featured similar visual scenes that were a stark contrast to those spectacular aerial shots and wide-angle shots and behind-the-presidential-earlobe shots of the Reagan rally.

The networks' Mondale reports began with Mondale seen walking down an empty Fifth Avenue in Manhattan, at the head of a parade that was small but still large enough so that the participants seemed to outnumber the spectators.

SEPTEMBER 3, 1984
NBC NIGHTLY NEWS

LISA MYERS: Mondale could only hope that the embarrassingly small turnout at New York's Labor Day Parade wasn't an omen. Way behind in the polls, doubted by members of his own party, he and Ferraro wanted to restore confidence and convey a sense of optimism. Instead, they opened their campaign to empty streets. Mondale's aides attributed the poor turnout to a nine o'clock start on a holiday morning. Then it was on to rural Wisconsin, where it sprinkled on Mondale's parade and poured on his rally. But that didn't dampen the spirits of a large and enthusiastic crowd. . . .

ABC WORLD NEWS TONIGHT

BRIT HUME: If you saw Walter Mondale and Geraldine Ferraro coming up Fifth Avenue this morning, it all looked and sounded the way a Labor Day Parade should. But in fact there was almost nobody lining the street, and no wonder, when you got past the band marching with the candidates, there wasn't any parade either. This is what is called a media event and the candidates went along with it to the point of going into the reviewing stand for a while even though there was nothing to review. But they didn't stay long. It was on to Merrill, Wisconsin, population 9,500, where there was a real crowd and a real parade. When it came time for speeches, though, there was real rain. And before she was finished, Ferraro was wearing both a raincoat and cap. But that didn't stop her from pouring it on the president for his comments linking religion and politics. . . .

CBS EVENING NEWS

SUSAN SPENCER: The band tried its best. But, for a campaign with nowhere to go but up, New York City's Labor Day Parade was a puny way to start. The candidates waved bravely, but neither the campaign nor big labor had produced much of a crowd to kick off their underdog effort. Even Mayor Koch was among the missing. But Mondale and Ferraro were determined to prove that, starting today, this is a gangbusters national effort, that they offer a clear alternative to President Reagan and Vice-President Bush. Next stop on their cross-country Labor Day blitz—the tiny town of Merrill, Wisconsin. . . .

The Reagan campaign entourage had checked into their hotel in Salt Lake City for the night, and about half a dozen aides had gathered in White House chief of staff James Baker's hotel suite to hoist a few beers and celebrate a good day of pageantry. The television set was on, and when the late-night news came on, the Reagan men watched the reports about Mondale's day in disbelief. "It was a disaster! A disaster!" said William Henkel. ". . . It was really extraordinary. I could not believe it. . . ."

Neither could the Mondale officials, who had finished their day in Long Beach, California, where the rally microphones had conked out, forcing Mondale to use a bullhorn in his effort to unseat the Great Communicator. They reflected back on all that had gone wrong, from Long Beach all the way back to "On the Beach," those desolate streets of Manhattan. Hours later, days later, months later, and even years later, the Mondale advisers of 1984 still blame each other whenever the matter is mentioned.

Richard Leone was Mondale's message czar, the senior adviser charged with the responsibility of seeing to it that the Mondale message got communicated properly, especially on the nightly news. "I was focusing on Merrill, Wisconsin," Leone later explained. "That was supposed to be the centerpiece of our day. That was what we expected the networks to focus on." The New York parade was just something they had agreed to belatedly, as a sop to the AFL-CIO, after the Wisconsin planning had begun. Mondale's campaign chiefs insisted the Labor Day Parade had to be early enough to get him to Merrill on time; advance aides moaned that this would mean a small crowd. And amazingly, the top advisers said they didn't care, because Wisconsin was the key event. "Nobody ever took charge of the parade," said Leone, who had no better explanation for having lost control of Mondale's message. Neither Leone nor any other advisers ever envisioned that the networks would build their stories around that New York parade as long as they had compelling pictures, whether of huge crowds or no crowds at all.

Many of the most prominent people in network-television news say in overwhelming numbers that they are convinced it was television, not the newspapers, that found the real story of Labor Day. And often they make their case with considerable fervor.

The camera shots of Mondale leading the empty parade, they say, captured with perfect symbolism all that was wrong with Walter Mondale and his campaign—the inability to communicate, the inability to lead. And they were not at all bothered by the fact that they failed to communicate the themes of Mondale's day, or by the fact that they had let sloppy staffwork by Mondale aides and a chance rainstorm all but drown out the campaign kickoff message of the candidate himself. And they were not bothered by the inherent unevenness of the Reagan and Mondale stories—Reagan receiving the sort of beautiful and artistic coverage that could pass for a campaign commercial, Mondale receiving the sort of downbeat treatment that was hard to overcome.

Listen to the views of the people who had made the decisions—the executive producers of the three network evening news shows.

"Television did a much better job than the newspapers," said Paul Greenberg, who was executive producer of the *NBC Nightly News* during the campaign of 1984. ". . . I mean the point of that was not just to pick on Mondale, the point of that was that they didn't know what they were doing. They screwed up. . . . The fact that they were at the parade at the wrong time was indicative of something that was going to plague them throughout the campaign. . . . It's not just pictures, it's more than pictures. . . . This is the guy [Mondale] that's going to run against this other guy [Reagan]—and this other guy's got the power of the incumbency, he's got the balloons, he's got the helicopters, he's got all this stuff. And they're walking down Fifth Avenue with three people! . . . You learned more from that television piece . . . I mean you saw a dynamic there. And that's one thing television can give you. It can give you a kind of . . . experience."

William Lord, executive producer of ABC's *World News Tonight:* "It was a huge embarrassment [for Mondale] and a perfect television story. It would have been far wiser for them to have started their campaign off in the Midwest. Then we would have been confronted with the only substantive Mondale appearance of the day. And then we would have had to deal more with the speech instead of the foolishness of the New York effort. . . . In retrospect, wouldn't it have been nice to have then pointed out that this embarrassment overshadowed the words they had been working on for so damn long for the public to hear?"

Lane Vernardos, executive producer of the *CBS Evening News* throughout the 1984 campaign: "I think you have to start off with the basic fact that we deal with pictures and these were, for whatever the editorial content might have been, these were essentially picture events. They were the traditional kickoff of the campaign. . . . When the producer and the reporter sit down to conceive a piece given the material they have . . . sometimes the consideration has to be how are we going to use . . . the crappy material and pictures we have? . . . The single most compelling picture of the piece was the pullback from them marching along and waving at people who weren't there."

Listen now to the network-news executives.

"Let me be critical about the print world," said Edward Joyce, who served during the 1984 campaign as president of CBS News, comparing the television approaches to the newspaper approaches that stressed the content of the two candidates' speeches. "I think that's reporting by handout, basically. The speeches are handed out, and that's easy. . . . Here's what I believe—I didn't used to feel this way, but as I get older and see more campaigns I do think the conduct of a campaign is one of the ways you ought to measure a candidate. . . . You certainly want someone in that kind of job that knows how to handle the staff, can assemble a staff and knows how to run things. . . . If the Mondale campaign was being kicked off with a Labor Day Parade . . . and it was a dismal failure . . . that was I think a significant story."

And Van Gordon Sauter, who preceded and followed Joyce as CBS News president, and who supervised Joyce's operation of the news division from the corporate headquarters during 1984: "I think the television coverage was right on target. Print did what it did well—it runs transcripts of speeches. It doesn't catch the reality of people, places, and mood nearly as well, and that will always be the case. . . . The picture does it better. The picture with the correct narration does it better. . . . I thought the [television] coverage . . . was quite reflective of the reality. What Mondale had to say about Reagan hardly constituted news. . . . It was not new. . . . Look, Reagan was not participating in a screwed-up parade and it was not raining on him. I mean, it's just that real. As I said, television correctly portrayed the reality of the Mondale and Ferraro camp on that one given day—on a very symbolic day."

And listen to the views of a network anchor.

"It's a classic example of how the information spectrum in America works," said Tom Brokaw, anchor and managing editor of the *NBC Nightly News*. "It has a lot of different parts, not always complementary . . . radio, magazines, newspapers, television. . . . You get a transmission of the experience through television of what his day was like. It takes you there. I am a camera. I have followed Walter Mondale all day long. And what happened here in New York was symptomatic of the problems that he had had before opening the general campaign and the problems that followed it. So what I'm saying . . . is that we probably wouldn't do it a different way again, because we're giving you . . . the whole fabric of the story. . . ."

Of all the television news decision-makers and on-air talents interviewed, only three voiced real opposition to the way the networks played the Labor Day story. They happen to be two of the most prominent people in network television: ABC News president Roone Arledge, *CBS Evening News* anchor and managing editor Dan Rather, and NBC News commentator (and former anchor and managing editor) John Chancellor.

Roone Arledge remembers watching his network's coverage of the Labor Day events and being troubled by the inherent unevenness of the two pieces. "I thought about it at the time, and I thought . . . it was unfair to Mondale," said Arledge as he sat in his offices atop the news division he directs. Arledge concedes many of the points his subordinates made are also valid—that Mondale was "hoist on his own petard" because the reason he had to be on Fifth Avenue so early in the morning was so he could get to Wisconsin and California on time; and that perhaps incidents such as that do help people make their decision about whom they want as their president.

"But my feeling at the time was that we didn't give him the benefit of the doubt. We made it appear as though no one turned out in New York because he had no support [in New York]. I don't think we played it as a gaffe as much as we played it that his first appearance was before an empty house—there was no enthusiasm, no support, and very few people. And I think if we had put it more that a scheduling screw-up had forced an embarrassing situation [it would have been better]. . . .

I think we attributed the wrong reasons to what we should have known. . . . On the evening news, there was no question that the walk up Fifth Avenue was portrayed as a disaster—not of scheduling, but of influence."

The networks do two news shows each evening—one at six-thirty P.M., and one at seven P.M. (it may be just a replay of the earlier show's videotape, or it may have some portions of it updated or modified as new information comes in or second-thought judgments are made). Arledge said he had seen the second news feed that evening too late to have any changes made in the wording of the reports. So he said he called up the folks at *Nightline*, "And I think as a result we did *Nightline* [on this subject at eleven-thirty P.M.]"

The CBS Evening News with Dan Rather was without Dan Rather on Labor Day, 1984. Bill Kurtis, then the host of the morning news show, was filling in and so Rather did not have a chance to put his ideas and objections into practice. Rather said he does not fault television's coverage for what it did air as much as he would fault it for what it left out. "The way Mondale, his staff, and campaign handled Labor Day . . . told us something about where his campaign had been, where it was, and where it might be going. Told you something about his qualifications for president, if you will. . . I do think it was a telltale and seeing picture. . . . What it amounted to was an inept effort to deal in symbols. . . . [And] one of the qualifications of leadership is to understand the symbols of leadership."

But Rather added that CBS should have gone beyond the story it aired. "We should have gone further that day," he said. "Ideal, perhaps, would have been to do exactly what we did that day—the parade, then Wisconsin—and come back behind it or later in the broadcast" to cite the major substantive points that Reagan and Mondale made. "If you're talking about nirvana, that probably would have been ideal," Rather said. "And if your argument is that newspaper coverage was better that day than ours, I probably wouldn't argue with that."

That is precisely the way NBC's John Chancellor saw it too. "The print versions on Labor Day were much more respectable to the process," Chancellor said. ". . . I keep saying that nobody in America should not watch television—but equally, nobody in America should not read a newspaper. Because the technical limitations and strengths of these two ways of transmitting information are complementary. . . . Different people do it different ways. Again, if *Life* magazine had been a weekly, *Life* magazine probably would have covered the story the way the networks did. Because *Life* would have had—I'd bet a thousand dollars—*Life* would have had the parade that fizzled in New York. They would have had a wide shot, showing Mondale in the middle of the street and the empty sidewalks. Right? So you are getting down near the bone marrow when you are talking about this difference."

There were, of course, a number of different ways that the television networks could have given due emphasis to the parade Mondale's aides bungled in New York while still giving Mondale his due for having a small-town Middle America kickoff that came off very well despite the rain, and also giving him the same break the networks gave Reagan—the chance to deliver his campaign-kickoff message to the nation.

One way would have been to begin their pieces with the Merrill, Wisconsin, rally and then look back to the fact that Mondale's day had gotten off to a lonely start. Another would have been a television version of the way *The New York Times* played the story, in which the parade was a local happening even for the globally sophisticated *Times*. Correspondent Bernard Weinraub began his story this way:

"Walter F. Mondale and Geraldine A. Ferraro opened their fall election campaign together today on sharply contrasting notes. The canyon that is Fifth Avenue in Manhattan was disappointingly spare of spectators when the candidates were there in the morning for a Labor Day parade, but a midday rally in a small town in Wisconsin was ebullient."

ON BEING SCOOPED

Two days after Labor day, Dan Rather was very much back on the job and at the anchor. And as he sat under the lights delivering the news to America, he had his eye on Ted Koppel.

Discreetly in front of Rather are three television monitors: One shows his news and the other two show the competitions'. And during a commercial break as he was doing the first of his two back-to-back news shows, he noticed that on the ABC monitor, Ted Koppel, who was filling in for Peter Jennings, was doing a story that he did not have. It seemed to be a big one, and that gets a competitor like Rather mighty steamed.

He couldn't hear what Koppel was saying, but he could see that in the glass-walled "Fish Bowl" his producers were looking a bit frantic; Rather quickly got a fill from executive producer Lane Vernardos during the commercial break. Koppel was saying this:

KOPPEL: ABC News has obtained a copy of the speech that Walter Mondale plans to deliver tomorrow here in Washington before a convention of the Jewish service organization B'Nai B'Rith. If delivered as prepared, it is a ripsnorter of a speech in which Mondale accuses President Reagan of creating a holier-than-thou climate by gift-wrapping political issues in the name of God. For some time now there have been predictions that Mondale would really hammer away at the separation of Church and State issue. Tomorrow's speech is clearly it. It says in part, "There are some in our midst today who insult religion by seeking to invoke God for political ends. And yes, Mr. President, I'm speaking to you." . . .

To a newspaper correspondent watching Koppel's newscast that night, the report only seemed bizarre. In a political campaign there are always drafts of speeches floating around—usually made available surreptitiously by the speechwriter—and most of them never wind up being delivered by the candidate as they were written, if they are delivered at all. For there are often competing drafts, done by other speechwriters as well. Generally, it is a good rule to follow that a campaign speech is not news until the candidate says it—or at least until the candidate says he is going to say it. But that is the view of a newspaperperson not under the gun, not pressed for time, and not feeling competitively threatened by the Koppel report. Meanwhile, back in the Fish Bowl —and at the anchor desk—the CBS journalists, who were among the most capable and savvy in the business, were of another frame of mind.

Lane Vernardos describes the action: "I was pissed and I was—not quite panicked—but I thought here we are, the first real week of the campaign and we're getting our nuts handed to us by ABC on a story that we should have known something about. So I was yelling at the people in Washington, our Washington producer. I was yelling at Richard [Cohen, the senior political producer]. And Dan was fit to be tied. He was really mad. Because we'd been beaten. We thought we'd been beaten on a story. It never occurred to us that—as I recall, the subtlety of [it being a] 'draft' was lost on me. What was on the screen, as I recall, were strong quotes on the screen with quotation marks around them, which means, to my untrained eye, 'Somebody said this.' "

We switch now to Dan Rather with more of the story: "It is . . . my nature, which I don't always like . . . that anytime anybody else has anything that appears to be of substance that we don't have, I want to know that they have it . . . and I want to know why we didn't have it and/or why we shouldn't use it. I have no apology for that. First of all, I couldn't apologize, it's not my nature. . . . I don't want to be a guy, when somebody beats us on a story, to just shrug my shoulders and say, 'Well, we'll be able to do it tomorrow.' That's not my idea of how to do this."

Rather recalls Vernardos coming over to his anchor desk during each commercial to explain—very calmly and matter-of-factly—that they are checking the story, trying to match it, and will slip him a note if and when it is done—either for the six-thirty P.M. news show, or the seven P.M. show. "One of the requirements of an executive producer of this broadcast is he has to be ducklike," said Rather. "All feathers have to be in place above the water. Underneath, he has to be paddling like hell."

CBS never matched the ABC story, and there is good reason for that. The ABC exclusive is still exclusive—because not even Mondale matched the story. What ABC had was a draft of a speech Mondale never gave. The next night, Koppel, who is one of journalism's most talented and classy practitioners, went on the air and apologized forthrightly.

KOPPEL: Well, the speech that Mr. Mondale actually delivered today was, as you've heard, on the same general subject—but in no other way resembled—the speech from which we quoted. What we obtained was a draft that had been solicited by the Mondale campaign but never used. We got that draft from a political source friendly to the Mondale campaign, someone who believed in fact that Mr. Mondale would deliver that speech. We could, and should, have checked with the Mondale campaign. We did not. We can only apologize to Mr. Mondale and his supporters.

In the course of presidential campaign history, the episode had absolutely no lasting significance; but it remains a fascinating sidelight showing the inner workings of network news.

THE CBS PLAN

At CBS News headquarters on West Fifty-seventh Street, at all levels from president to anchor to on-camera journalists to off-camera journalists, it was known simply as "The Plan." From Dan Rather on down (and, in some cases, on up) all players had come to understand that CBS was going to make a dedicated effort in Campaign '84 to avoid the mistakes that they felt had plagued television journalism for years. They were going to at last follow through on some of those suggestions and complaints that had come out of that unique CBS postmortem on the 1976 campaign. They were going to try to resist, with all due willpower, the lure of great pictures as the driving force behind doing a story. They were going to resist the efforts of the politicians who would try to manipulate and shape their news coverage by providing irresistible videos even when the news was highly resistible and exceedingly thin—or nonexistent. They were going to be especially wary of the media masters of this manipulative art, the current residents of the Reagan White House West Wing. They were going to make daily decisions about the news value of what the politicians were doing.

CBS News was often successful in sticking to this plan—even when under considerable pressure, most of it generated from within, as correspondents and field producers chafed upon seeing their competition getting pieces on the air while they were told "Thanks, but no thanks" by their colleagues at West Fifty-seventh Street.

The plan at CBS was that on the days when the story did not merit a full piece from the correspondent and the two minutes or more of pictures that go with it, Dan Rather would just do a brief mention—maybe thirty-seconds long—of where the candidate was and what had happened there. Brief video footage, or perhaps even just a still photo, would be used. And the airtime saved would then be used for in-depth pieces devoted to a campaign issue or, most often as it turned out, a campaign trend.

NBC News also used brief voice-over reports from anchor Tom Brokaw on many days when there just was not a true news story. They did this with about the same frequency as their counterparts at CBS, although, according to interviews with the network's top decision-makers, NBC did not put itself through the rigorous internal review and debate process that CBS did, nor did NBC promulgate what was recognized top to bottom as a plan.

ABC News, meanwhile, pursued a more straight-ahead approach, dedicated to the proposition that the network ought to have its star White House correspondent Sam Donaldson, who is a very talented and telegenic journalist, on the air every night. That meant that Donaldson would do a Reagan piece each night, and Brit Hume would do a Mondale story. There were very few nights when those two were not on the air with pieces of their own. And most often, as the ABC officials concede, the Donaldson and Hume pieces consisted solely of reporting from those two journalists. NBC and especially CBS would package their pieces in a more complex fashion, inserting interviews done at other locales, which added a new dimension to the topic under discussion.

"Sam is a major star and we want him on the air as much as we can," said ABC News executive producer William Lord. He said there is no document that ABC has that states that Donaldson must be on the air each night. "But what I will say, and the surveys told us this —and it kind of surprised us—is that we are now the network of correspondents, not the network of anchormen." That is to say that unlike the Dan Rather news and the Tom Brokaw news, ABC is noted more for its Sam Donaldson reports than anything else.

There is another reason why a Reagan White House story might get on the air if Donaldson is at the post and the same story might not get on the air if Donaldson is otherwise occupied and a backup correspondent is there, Lord conceded. "Yes," he said, when asked if that happens at ABC, "because Sam comes at you like a freight train and says 'Look what I got.' 'Here's what I want to say.' And he's been quite successful for a long period of time. Sam and I have fought many a battle and we know each other's territory and turf, and we know how to deal with each other."

Donaldson, meanwhile, modestly downplays the possibility that his star status contributes to the network's desire to put him on the air each night. "Oh, bullshit!" Donaldson demurred. "Let the record *record* that I said 'Bullshit!' in answer to that declaration of yours."

Meanwhile, back at CBS, the infighting at times got fierce. At one point during the early-fall campaign, senior producer for politics Richard Cohen wrote a pointed memo to Dan Rather and other decision-makers complaining that CBS was "abdicating" its responsibility to cover the news fully by sticking to its plan. And on another occasion, Rather and Cohen were said by several sources to have been at odds repeatedly and vociferously, when Rather asked Cohen to step into the conference room with him to talk it all out. Cohen confirmed the account. "You can understand it," Cohen said. "Dan at six o'clock at night sort of goes into a new mode of getting ready to go on the air —reading copy and really trying to get into it. And we were still arguing about the political coverage, because I was like a goddamned dog grabbing onto somebody's pants and wouldn't let go. Trouble was I was a little terrier. I needed a Doberman and all I could find was a Welsh terrier.

"We went into the conference room, sat down, and he just sort of turned to me and said, 'Okay, what do you want to do? What are we doing wrong?' And I said, 'There's a double standard operating here.' I said we were doing the president's work. [Cohen made the case that more often it is the Mondale story that gets folded into the Reagan story—and a check of the CBS logs shows that was the case, as twenty-five times in the fall the Mondale correspondent did not get on the air, compared to eighteen times for the Reagan correspondent.] I said both guys are newsworthy; even if one is newsworthy because he's bad, he's still newsworthy. We're not being fair."

Cohen said he closed by saying, "We are abdicating our responsibilities as journalists." Rather nodded, said they would be "open-minded" about what Cohen had been urging, and Cohen said he felt he'd had a good hearing; and they went back outside into the work area to continue their joint efforts at putting out the news as the red camera light blinked on and Rather began to broadcast.

Given Cohen's view that it was Mondale who was getting hurt, it is interesting to note that at the White House, Reagan's top advisers were frequently furious at their inability to get CBS to show the picture events they had concocted to further the president's political fortunes. It became a subject of West Wing meetings and even memos.

CBS's producer at the White House press corps, Susan Zirinsky, had long since established herself as an impassioned pleader for more airtime and better display. And she was perhaps even more upset than the Reagan officials at the fact that some of her best- and highest-quality efforts were not getting on the air—because it was decided in New York that what the president had been saying was not new.

"This is a producer's network—there's no getting around that," said Vernardos. "Zirinsky dealt directly with the Fish Bowl," while at the other networks it would more often be the correspondents such as Sam Donaldson at ABC or Chris Wallace at NBC who would deal with the decision-makers in New York under similar situations.

"She lobbies very heavily for her stuff. . . . Zirinsky is very possessive. It's a personal affront. When she doesn't get on the tube that night it isn't that Lesley [Stahl] didn't get on the air, *she* [Zirinsky] didn't get on the air. It isn't Bill [Plante] whose piece got passed, it's Susan's piece that got passed; and she gets really pissed about that. And hurt. I don't think she'd admit to it."

She does. When the Fish Bowl passed on a piece Stahl and Zirinsky wanted to give them out of a rally day at Buffalo and Endicott, New

York, Zirinsky admits that she was "pissed." She elaborated: "I was a little distraught because it was early on—what's it going to be later on? I figured this was going to get worse. And I was right!"

The White House officials, meanwhile, decided to check with Zirinsky to find out why CBS had not put the Broome County, New York, piece on the air in full video, as it had not done with other pieces in September. According to William Henkel, a member of his advance team, Charles Bakaly, spoke with Zirinsky about it, and then wrote a memo to Henkel—which Henkel duly forwarded to chief of staff James A. Baker and Michael K. Deaver.

THE WHITE HOUSE
WASHINGTON

[Henkel's handwritten
forwarding notation:]
JAB/MKD
FYI

September 14, 1986

MEMORANDUM FOR WILLIAM HENKEL

FROM CHARLES BAKALY

SUBJECT SCHEDULING OF EVENTS FOR NETWORK COVERAGE

Network decisions as to the content of their broadcast are not definitely made until airtime. . . .

In the case of the Broome County event, CBS made an editorial decision not to air a CBS White House correspondent produced piece. The time of the event was not a factor at all.

The crucial issue is: "Is the event newsworthy?" With the polls the way they are it is not surprising that the nets are reluctant to air well-produced events with large supportive crowds that end up looking like political commercials and not "news." . . .

It appears that CBS has made an editorial decision regarding the reporting/airing of Presidential events.

The key is to make news. An important issue was raised by Mr. Baker at our recent press meeting concerning the press created impression that the President is detached from people, real people. To counter this, we should actively and regularly seek opportunities for the President to make unannounced visits to different

groups. . . . Unannounced events have always yielded good coverage. . . .
[Below that was a handwritten addition:]
My CBS contact states: Time had nothing to do with not getting Endicott on the air! An editorial decision by New York and Rather. CBS has met and decided it does not want to air our "commercials," i.e., slick rally events without news. The last two nights CBS used Rather voice-overs, not pieces sent in by their W.H. correspondents.

A PROUD MOMENT

White House advance chief William Henkel found himself in Memphis early in September, and it didn't take him long to realize he had a problem. His political-strategist superiors at the Reagan White House and campaign had given him his orders: Create a visually great event in Memphis. It had to be Memphis, they said, because polls showed it represented a place of great potential for cutting into traditionally Democratic votes.

But as Henkel made the rounds, he could see the problem clearly—there was nothing to see. Oh, there's plenty for a tourist to see, but nothing for a network-television camera to see that would make for great symbolic video politics. Henkel had hoped the Federal Express headquarters would do the trick, it being an example of an all-American company that made a quick success of itself in the capitalist tradition of the country and its president.

"But Federal Express was visually dead during the daytime," Henkel said.

So the chief of advance called his political superiors and informed them that he was not going to do what they wanted. He was leaving Memphis and would try Nashville. Memphis would make for terrible national network television, he said. He explained: "We just did not ever want to take a public-relations or TV hickey."

There is a lesson in this for the Mondale officials: The Reagan political strategists understood and accepted the decision of the advance chief without further discussion. They understood what the Mondale officials never understood when their advance people tried to tell them about that Labor Day Parade in New York: that there is a larger need and a greater political good than the mere politics of one city or region or interest group.

In Nashville, Henkel eventually found his way to the Grand Ole Opry. He still did not know what he wanted to do when someone told him it was approaching singer Roy Acuff's eighty-first birthday. *Bingo!* Henkel said he knew at once, and within hours a grand birthday bash had been created: complete with a cake and confetti and Minnie Pearl and Lee Greenwood to sing that country song that became a Reagan campaign theme, as Reagan himself stood there celebrating and joking and beaming.

ABC and NBC used the occasion to do pieces about how the event was the epitomy of the all-video Reagan campaign, dodging the tough issues like the deficit and taking no questions. ABC also used a long piece from the Mondale campaign, with the candidate standing in a sweaty barn in Tupelo, Mississippi, fielding questions at length on every tough issue, attacking Reagan for the policies he created and the answers he was not giving.

CBS did none of the above. The Nashville event was a classic television nonevent, the network decision-makers said. And Mondale did not really break new ground. So Dan Rather just did short explanations of what went on at each event, with a few seconds of sound and picture from each. Then they turned the rest of the political segment over to veteran correspondent Bob Schieffer, who did a lengthy and well-done look at the campaign in the South and how it was shaping up.

Zirinsky, meanwhile, was in Nashville, in tears; and Stahl was every bit as frustrated and just a bit more composed. She had proposed just the sort of package that the other two networks wound up airing. "The pictures were UNBELIEVEABLE!" said Zirinsky. ". . . This was the manipulation by the White House campaign. Pretty pictures. Good about yourself. No issues. And everybody loves it. It was a great way to illustrate it!"

Meanwhile, back at CBS, the denizens of the Fish Bowl told her they were going to pass. "I said, 'You're kidding!' And they said, 'No.' I was furious. I was close to tears—as a matter of fact, I probably was in tears that day." (Her opposition duly noted that indeed she was.)

Chris Wallace's NBC piece and Sam Donaldson's ABC piece were similar and both were strong.

SEPTEMBER 13, 1984
NBC

CHRIS WALLACE: The president kept refusing today to get specific about how he would cut the deficit. But there were numbers he did want to talk about—new polls that show him leading Mondale by as much as sixteen points.

[Reagan was shown saying "Goody!" about the polls and making a joke about Minnie Pearl's hats being like his opposition's promises: "They both have big price tags hanging from them." And then he was shown amid a shower of confetti and singing and celebration.]

WALLACE: And back at the Opry, the president's men put on a show, complete with flags, confetti, and the unofficial campaign theme song. What the president has done very skillfully is to wrap his campaign in what appears to be a new wave of good feeling about this country, so the Democratic attacks against him are made to seem almost unpatriotic.

ABC

SAM DONALDSON: The president failed again today . . . to say exactly how he intends to reduce the deficit, if not through higher taxes. None of this talk about deficits and taxes and such is the essence of the Reagan campaign. The essence of the Reagan campaign is a never-ending string of spectacular picture-stories created for television and designed to place the president in the midst of a huge throng of wildly cheering patriotic Americans . . . God, patriotism, and Reagan. That's the essence this campaign is trying hard to project.

The Reagan White House officials, meanwhile, were thrilled to have this latest in their "never-ending string of spectacular picture-stories." And they were unperturbed about the fact that the correspondents were pointing this out as they showed this latest of their video spectaculars.

(In a rare instance of commonality, officials at the Mondale campaign, the Reagan White House, and the networks reacted with equal measures of snickering and amazement to a George Washington University study that concluded that television had no impact on the 1984 presidential race. The study analyzed only the transcripts of the spoken words of the network-news anchors and correspondents and concluded that they had been tougher on Reagan than on Mondale. The study then concluded that since Reagan won in a landslide, television coverage must have had no effect on the voters. What the campaign and television people found so amusing, of course, was that the university's experts might just as well have been analyzing radio, because by omitting the pictures, they were overlooking the one essential property of television and the one essential tactical advantage Reagan's campaign had over Mondale's.)

For William Henkel, the event and what happened there took on special meaning when he received what he considers the highest form of compliment. It occurred as he was watching the show along with his boss, James Baker.

"The one time that I knew we did something really right was when Donaldson came up. . . . I mean the confetti was falling and everything was coming together. And he came up and he said to Baker and me: 'This is absolutely shameless! Have you no shame?'

". . . It was meant as a compliment, in its own way. . . . It was one of my proudest moments."

TWELVE

THE OTHER END OF THE FUNNEL

Monday, September 17, 1984, had just tumbled out of the television set in Mike and Sue Talbot's family room in Hanover Park, Illinois. It was the first and biggest day of Walter Mondale's Foreign Policy Week, according to the master plan of his advisers. The Talbots and fourteen of their friends and neighbors had seen the day unfold in a special videotape that compiled the campaign-news coverage of the three major networks and inserted a Mondale commercial and a Reagan commercial in between each show.

The viewers at the Talbots' had seen network-news reports covering the speech that was the centerpiece of Mondale's strategy. It was a torrent of strong attacks on the Reagan foreign policy, charging that the president had shattered respect for America around the world. But the newsclips showed Mondale delivering his speech in a bland tone, seeming to lack not only passion but even conviction. He was seen delivering the speech while standing in front of a colorless backdrop, a gray wall in a Cleveland meeting hall, an unimaginative setting for a speech Mondale would have liked voters to remember.

The television set was switched off after Monday's news and ads, and those in the Talbots' family room were asked to write down the one scene that they most remembered having seen. More than half the people listed the same thing out of that patchwork video quilt of news and ads and special-feature reports. But no one cited Mondale and his foreign-policy pronouncements. Instead, this is what they remembered most:

Vice-President George Bush standing in the Orange Bowl in Miami, where the stands are exploding with the emotions of nine thousand Cuban refugees who have just been sworn in as U.S. citizens—and who, overflowing with tears of joy and pride in their adopted country and its leader, are chanting "Rea-gun! Rea-gun! Four More Years!"

They remembered the Cuban-Americans who spoke of their love of their new country, sometimes with tears streaming down their cheeks, as they stood in a line outside the Orange Bowl to register as Republicans in time to vote in November.

It was a visually compelling—unforgettable—scene. And tucked into those memorable pictures was a message quite contrary to the one Mondale was pushing. That slice of news, a spectacular Reagan campaign production that the White House maintained was not even a campaign event (and hence was paid for by the American taxpayers), was far more memorable than any foreign-policy event they would see in that week of news and ads in this, Walter Mondale's Foreign Policy Week.

Reality, as it poured out of the Funnel and into the Talbots' family room during the fall of 1984, was that Democratic presidential nominee Walter Mondale's best efforts to close the gap on the Great Communicator were being doomed by a great failure to communicate. A close look at that reality and how it shaped the views of the electorate is essential to understanding the presidential electoral process that has become the Great American Video Game.

The various "public opinions" that eventually would turn up listed in those weekly public-opinion polls in 1984 could be seen as they were being formed in the Talbots' home in Hanover Park. And, of course, so could the result that turned up everywhere on the first Tuesday in November. It was possible to understand why the polls were going to show what they did just by spending a little time at the Other End of the Funnel, in Hanover Park, Illinois.

In the autumn of 1984, in that pleasant middle-class suburb northwest of Chicago, well out past O'Hare Airport, Mike and Sue Talbot and their neighbors and friends watched the presidential campaign unfold its realities—in the form of newscasts, campaign commercials, and candidate debates.

The people at the Talbots' were a sampling from a number of so-called voter groups: Democrats, Republicans, Independents; senior citizens, middle-aged, and young; males and females; marrieds and singles; blue collars and white collars; well-to-dos and not-doing-wells.

They were chosen not by scientific sample but by common-sense proportioning. For the goal here was not to create a national survey but just to see how people's opinions shifted (if they did) based upon watching that assortment of political information and images that comes pouring out of the television sets daily, news and ads as they are seen in no particular order amid the casual settings and the familiar disorder of the home.

On one September evening, for example, sitting in comfortable family-room chairs and nibbling on snacks, the Talbots and their friends watched that specially prepared videotape that consisted of a week's worth of campaign coverage from the three major networks, with one Mondale and one Reagan campaign ad interspersed between each network's nightly show. On other nights, the group also convened to watch the two presidential debates.

On each occasion they talked about what they'd seen and heard and how they felt about the race. And at the end of each session they cast votes for president, as though each meeting were Election Day, to see whether opinions had changed. Because each session was being treated as Election Day, those undecided were told they would have to make a choice—they were, after all, already in the "voting booth"—but they were allowed to add a question mark beside their candidate's name to indicate that they were not yet firm in their decision.

In this look at the Other End of the Funnel, it quickly became clear that Walter Mondale was failing to communicate his policies in all policy areas—foreign and domestic.

Those watching a week's worth of campaign news and commercials at the Talbots' home in mid-September found Mondale's foreign-policy message unmemorable, his economic message incomprehensible.

ON FOREIGN AFFAIRS

The day after Mondale's major foreign-policy address was drowned out by George Bush's Orange Bowl spectacle, Mondale tried once again to pour his foreign-policy themes through the Funnel.

His strategists had wanted to show him outlining his policy views before a young and enthusiastic crowd—the Reagan campaign, after all, was having such success in packaging youthful enthusiasm for the nightly television news in their rallies (where admission was by ticket only). And so they put Mondale in a rally at the University of Southern California, an unusual choice because it is one of the state's more conservative campuses (it was, for example, the alma mater of the Nixon White House's young upwardly mobile corps of true-believing followers that included Ronald Ziegler and Dwight Chapin). Not surprisingly, Mondale was heckled unmercifully at USC. And of course Mondale's slice of television news that night was not Mondale on foreign policy, but Mondale battles young hecklers.

So much for Mondale's foreign-policy week on television.

ON DOMESTIC AFFAIRS

The Funnel had emptied its week's worth of news and ads, and night after night, when Mondale was not pursuing foreign policy, he was back to pushing that same message he'd been trying so hard to make the staple of his campaign since Labor Day: the horrendous Reagan budget deficit, and the fact that he had put forth a plan to cut it and Reagan had refused to spell out his own cure.

"We'll make Reagan eat his deficit," Mondale's message czar Richard Leone had vowed, and his television ad creator, Roy Spence, had promised the same thing.

So they put Mondale out there to do his assault on the deficit armed with a series of visual props—charts and gimmicks. But the charts were so complex, they were incomprehensible to the glance that television afforded; and the gimmicks only seemed puzzling and pointless, like the time he stood beside a huge "ReaganCharge" card (it was supposed to be a play on MasterCard, an implication that we're living high now but we'll have to pay up later—get it?).

What they had given the nation was a made-for-TV docudrama that could have been titled *The Pedagogue versus the President*. For night after night, Mondale was seen out there on the stump trying to educate the public in nine weeks about the dangers of the deficit that they had not come to understand (let alone fear) in the previous nine months of campaigning.

Meanwhile, in this mid-September week, no sooner had Mondale's antideficit video bombardment stopped than a new battle erupted among the Talbots' guests.

The people gathered in that family room at Hanover Park were sharply divided over whether Mondale had actually put forth a plan of his own, or whether he was just saying he had. And they were unclear about just what such a Mondale plan might be—raise taxes only for the rich, or for everybody?

Morrie Oldham, the accountant who says he is neither a Democrat nor a Republican, said he was troubled by Mondale's promise to raise taxes. He was sure he saw Mondale come out with a plan a week ago promising to cut the federal deficit by raising everybody's taxes. "He's detailed his program," said Oldham. ". . . I'm hearing higher taxes, plans for higher taxes."

Joe Martingello, the brake-parts shop manager who says he is a middle-of-the-road Democrat, said that he missed Mondale on television last week, but he saw him this week and he saw no specifics, no plan. "You say Mondale had a plan," said Martingello. "But I don't see a plan come out of what I've seen in a week of television. I do not see Mondale with any plan whatsoever. . . . I see him talking about a plan, but I do not see a plan. . . . He's always attacking Reagan but he doesn't come up with any better ideas."

"No, he said *cut* taxes," said Mary DeFranze, a mother of three who was studying computer science and considered herself a conservative Democrat who was leaning toward Mondale. "He said he'd cut the defense [spending to balance the budget]."

"No, Mondale said tax *increases*," countered Oldham. "I don't want my taxes raised. . . . And that's why I think I'm for Reagan."

And Martingello maintained, "I wasn't paying attention that week. . . . This week I was watching and I heard Mondale talk about a plan, but I haven't seen one. . . . What I have heard him say tonight—I don't like him. I guess I'm for Reagan."

The Mondale message was muddled.

For Mondale to cut into Ronald Reagan's lead, it was clear that he would have to regain the confidence and support of the people who should have been his to begin with. That included people like the accountant, Morrie Oldham, who after all had voted in past years for Lyndon Johnson, Hubert Humphrey, George McGovern, and Jimmy Carter. And it included blue-collar worker Joe Martingello, who sometimes doesn't vote, but who did after all vote for George McGovern in 1972.

And mainly it meant he would have to win the vote of Monty Clark, a forty-year-old schoolteacher who said often throughout the fall that he really wanted to vote for Mondale but couldn't quite bring himself to do so as he watched the campaign unfold on television. Clark was a former local-chapter president of the American Federation of Teachers, which was endorsing Mondale; he kept agreeing with Mondale on all the major issues, but he kept wavering between Mondale and Reagan, because in the end he would come back to the proposition that the American economy *was* back and things *were* better.

"I'd really like to vote for Mondale, you know," said Monty Clark. "I'd really like to. . . . But things are better now—the economy is better. . . . The inflation rate is down and it needs to stay down. . . . And we need a few years to kind of stablize that, and then I would be for more social programming and more welfare and some of the things that Mondale's for. . . . So I'm leaning toward Reagan."

By the end of the campaign, Mondale would fail to win the support of Monty Clark and Morrie Oldham and Joe Martingello and a young worker in his shop, Chris Evans. And he would come close to losing the votes of several others who were Democrats but were not sure Mondale could be a good president, and who would back him reluctantly in the end.

There are times in every presidential campaign when the news breaks favorably in the direction of one candidate's message strategy and against the other's. Those are the times when the success of the candidate is determined by his or her ability to take advantage of that break and convert it into significant gains.

This week of September 17 was a week when the news broke in favor of Mondale. And, as the Talbots and their friends and neighbors looked on, it turned out that Mondale was singularly unable to capitalize on his own good fortune, not in his responses on the trail or in his ads.

A look at the week's news and ads stands as a primer of what not to do.

This was, for example, the week when the television news—which gets public high marks for credibility—reported that the end to economic good times might be at hand. CBS treated the story with greater depth than the others.

CBS NEWS
WEDNESDAY, SEPTEMBER 19, 1984

DAN RATHER: Seen from one point of view, the U.S. economy is booming back and the future is bright. From another, an economic downturn already has set in and the only question is how far down does it turn. That is the context as some economists tonight are revising their predictions of economic growth downward. This comes in the wake of the latest evidence that the economy in the third quarter may be cooling more than some economists anticipated. The Commerce Department said housing starts for the month of August plunged 12.8 percent. Ray Brady reports.

RAY BRADY: Not since the recession of late 1982 have so few houses been started. For the second month in a row, builders slowed up construction and took out fewer permits to build houses in the future. Treasury secretary Regan predicted today things won't get much worse.

DONALD REGAN: And I think builders may get up their courage and you may see that the . . . starts aren't going to go below what they are at the current moment.

BRADY: But if builders are losing courage, it's because potential home buyers are losing out. They can't buy because of high interest rates.

JAMES CHRISTIAN (of the U.S. League of Savings Institutes): About 88 percent of American households cannot afford to buy a medium-priced home at today's fixed-rate mortgage rates. . . . It's hard to see the basis for any significant decline in interest rates.

BRADY: Analysts say every time mortgage rates go up one percentage point, more than three million Americans are priced out of the market.

Chris Evans, who was twenty-one and a worker in the brake-parts shop where Joe Martingello works, had sat silently through most of the evening of watching and discussing the news and ads. He had come to the session wondering why he was even there, feeling, he said, that he didn't know anything about politics and wouldn't have much to contribute. His turned out to be one of the most helpful contributions of all. For that news item prompted the reserved Evans to speak out. He voiced the one concern that had been bothering him most—and it revealed a central strategy for attacking the deficit that somehow had eluded the Mondale ad-makers and was missing from their array of sophisticated television commercials.

"I have a sense that things are better, yeah," said Chris Evans. "But I know that someday I want to own a house—and how am I going to do that with the interest rates the way they are? You know, one-thousand-dollar-a-month mortgages. And I really don't see anyone saying anything that would sway me to one candidate or another."

Evans spoke haltingly and he rambled a bit unsurely as he talked; yet his message was more to the point than Mondale's. "I would be for a guy who is going to work and do things for people my age," he said. "There is nothing for me, I don't think. I mean, if I work hard, I'm going to make it. But with interest rates where they are, I think a president needs to work on getting interest rates down."

Just before that CBS report on the economy, the group had seen Walter Mondale's ad that attempted to address the issue of people owning their own house.

MONDALE AD

[A small house is seen from the outside, its windows lit on a quiet summer night.]

ANNOUNCER: After you work a lifetime to pay off your house, you expect to be free and clear. [Then the White House is seen and the baffling figure of $18,000.]

ANNOUNCER: But in another house, there are plans today to put you $18,000 in debt. Your share of Mr. Reagan's deficits.

[The little house is seen again, and crickets are heard.]

ANNOUNCER: But when Mondale moves into the White House, he won't forget about your place. He'll cut spending, close tax loopholes, and put new taxes in a trust fund to pay off Reagan's debt. Let's stop mortgaging America.

That was it. The Mondale people pitched their home-ownership ad at those who already own homes. They built their case around a calculation about how $18,000 is each household's share of the federal deficit—although it was never clear how an $18,000 figure was supposed to scare somebody who already had a mortgage much higher than that.

After Chris Evans spoke, those in the Talbots' family room were asked what they remembered about Mondale addressing those concerns. They didn't remember anything about it. Then they were asked if they remembered anyone talking about the subject. Mary DeFranze remembered that there was one ad—but she wasn't sure whose it was. "I remember the one with the crickets," she said. "I can't remember what the message was. . . ."

A woman interjected: "The houses or something?"

A man asked: "Taxes?"

"No, it was a comfort, though, a comforting thing," said DeFranze. "It was something to do with comfort . . . it was an old white house, it was a white house in the dark with the lights on." She said she thought the ad might have been one of Reagan's.

That Mondale "Little House" ad is worth recalling to make still another point. For it contained a brief mention of a "Trust Fund," and no doubt there are few Americans who were around during the presidential election of 1984 who will know what that is about.

The Trust Fund idea was considered by virtually all of Mondale's political and public-opinion experts to be the key to making a success of Mondale's controversial crusade to cut the deficit by raising taxes. The only problem was that the candidate remained unenthusiastic—opposed deep down, in fact, his former advisers say—and his issues experts had resisted the idea all along. So the idea of solving the Reagan deficit with a Mondale Trust Fund never really became part of the public consciousness, and Mondale never really gave his party even a chance of recapturing the White House.

The reason Mondale's public-opinion advisers (including Peter Hart and later Patrick Caddell) and his message advisers (including Richard Leone and Roy Spence) all argued so strongly that a Mondale Trust Fund was needed was because the people just didn't trust Mondale Democrats to cut the deficit if they were given more tax revenues. They believed the Mondale Democrats would probably spend more if given more. (Remember Monty Clark's comment at the Talbots' that Mondale's social- and welfare-spending programs would be good at a later time; that was the perception of Mondale's program even though he was not saying it.)

The Trust Fund idea was akin to Fritz Hollings's old across-the-board-spending-freeze idea in that it was intended to ensure that new tax revenues would be set aside solely to retire the deficit, and that there would be no new spending increases. "We had trouble getting the Trust Fund approved by Mondale," said Leone. The spending freeze was something he would not buy. Leone recalled the time that Mondale's campaign chairman, James Johnson, and he took Mondale for a walk in the Minnesota woods just before the fall campaign in one last attempt "to get him to go for the [spending] freeze . . . one last pitch. . . . And Mondale made all of the good, sound arguments—given his beliefs—about why that [freeze] might tie his hands . . . and he talked about specific programs . . . which were cut by Reagan and would have been hurt. . . . And he was just willing . . . to take the political damage rather than compromise on what he believed in. . . . I remember it quite well. . . . He said, 'It's just not right. I'm not going to do it.' And I remember looking at Jim and we just shrugged and went on to chat about something else."

Leone hesitated, then added: "You know, Mondale is an interesting person, because he can be intensely political and then just refuse to budge on something when he understands the political consequences. . . . There are many endearing things about him that hurt him."

Still, the results of the Mondale campaign's own surveys continued to make compelling arguments to the candidate and his strategists to pursue the Trust Fund. The case for them was studded throughout the three-inch-thick volumes of focus-group reports that were done for the campaign by MRK Research, a Boston firm headed by Edward J. Reilly (the fellow who had also been the pollster for WBZ-TV back in the primaries). The reports were given to Mondale and several top-level strategists and were treated within the campaign as closely held documents.

> "This trust fund idea makes sense."
> —Strong Mondale (Teacher)
> September 7, 1984
> Clifton, New Jersey
>
> . . . Key Findings
>
> . . . The Trust Fund concept continues to receive high marks from respondents. The need to put the "Mondale Trust Fund" into the lexicon of this election is paramount. The Trust Fund also needs further explanation. This should become an idea that people feel they understand. Paid and free media should be used extensively to explain it during the next two weeks.

In the category of Mondale's missed opportunities to communicate the deficit problem is the case of the one visual-aid chart that he never used.

> MRK/RESEARCH
> Strictly Confidential
> FOCUS GROUP RESEARCH
> MONDALE/FERRARO CAMPAIGN
> August 30, 1986
> Chattanooga, Tennessee
> Stamford, Connecticut
>
> . . . Trust Fund
>
> In all four groups, all respondents reacted with strong support for this concept. They really liked the idea, it was easy for them to

understand, and it gave them a sense of hope in tackling the problem.

. . . Representative Quotes

"That's the best thing I've heard all night. Put the money aside and we can start to pay this thing off."

—Undecided (Auto-insurance claims adjuster)

It was not a campaign secret from a "strictly confident" source—it was published in *The Washington Post* on August 11. It seems that about the time the Mondale advisers were walking their boss through the woods, hoping to get him to see the forest from the trees on the Trust Fund and spending freeze, a group of Republican aides were also at work trying to find a clever way to help their side ward off whatever the Democrats planned to throw at them on the matter of the Reagan deficit.

They hit upon the idea of comparing the Reagan deficit to what the Carter-Mondale administration's deficit would have been—if only Carter-Mondale had defeated Reagan-Bush back in 1980. These Republican staff members of the House Budget Committee feared that the Democrats would make great political capital by reproducing an existing House Budget Committee chart that showed projections for the Reagan deficit climbing to $248 billion by fiscal year 1987. So they decided to substitute bars labeled "Carter-Mondale" for the bars labeled "Reagan" to project what would have happened if Carter-Mondale policies had been allowed to continue through the 1980s, using Congressional Budget Office computations.

But the chart the GOP aides produced would have been political disaster-at-a-glance. For their calculations showed that while the Carter-Mondale policies would have produced a deficit that rose to a peak of $149 billion in fiscal 1983—the Carter-Mondale deficits then began falling sharply!

Their chart showed the Reagan deficit bars climbing steadily to $248 billion in fiscal 1987. But it showed the Carter-Mondale deficit bars descending like steep steps down the walkway of prosperity. The deficit bar for fiscal 1984 plunged to $111 billion; the deficit bar for fiscal 1985 stepped down to $83 billion; the deficit bar for fiscal 1986 stepped down still further to $63 billion; and the deficit bar for fiscal 1987 plunged again until it looked like a manageable little step of just $39 billion—a minuscule drop of red ink in the federal bucket compared to their own chart's side-by-side projection of a $248-billion deficit under Reagan that same year.

Compared side by side, those Republican-prepared Carter-Mondale and Reagan deficit bars for fiscal 1987 looked like the Plains, Georgia, train depot being dropped alongside the World Trade Center towers of Manhattan. The Republican staff aides discovered even worse news: For their charting showed that in fiscal 1988, the Carter-Mondale policy projections would have produced a deficit of just $11 billion. And in fiscal 1989—when the projected Reagan deficit would be an astronomical $326 billion—the Carter-Mondale policies would have given the United States an $11 federal-budget surplus!

The Republican budget staff aides did the only politically honorable thing they could do in such graphic circumstances, the *Washington Post* story back on August 11 reported. The Republican aides declared their own chart inoperative and went back to the drawing boards for the good of the Grand Old Party. They couldn't change their calculations; but they could undergo a change of chart. And that's what they did—they scratched out those last, offending, descending bars of the Carter-Mondale years and stopped their chart graphically short, so that the comparison ended in fiscal 1984.

The *Washington Post* article was published complete with the Republicans' "Before" and "After" charts. It remains an interesting sidenote that the Mondale strategists never found a way to pour any of that into the Funnel so it would reach the fourteen voters gathered at the Other End in the Talbots' family room, where Mondale's deficit-based campaign message never really caught hold.

While the economic news was breaking a bit in Mondale's favor, the international news carried the potential of an even bigger—but painfully tragic—break against the conduct of American policy in Lebanon.

ABC NEWS
THURSDAY, SEPTEMBER 20, 1984

PETER JENNINGS: It has happened again. The American Embassy is attacked in Beirut. Americans and Lebanese die.

CBS NEWS
THURSDAY, SEPTEMBER 20, 1984

DAN RATHER: It has happened again. Another terrorist bomb attack against an American target in Beirut. And once again it was a bomb-filled vehicle driven by a person bent on death, his own and others. And once again, he succeeded.

NBC NEWS

TOM BROKAW: Another tragic Beirut bombing, this one at the American Embassy Annex. Two Americans and twenty-one others are dead.

With these strikingly similar introductions from their anchors, the networks once again had to pour new but too-familiar pictures of death and disaster into American homes. Once again, the United States government was shown to be improperly prepared to safeguard the security of its own installations in Lebanon, despite a similar attack from a truck filled with explosives that had killed more than 60 people—17 of them Americans—a year and a half earlier; and despite the bombing of the U.S. Marine barracks that had killed 261 marines as they slept just a year earlier.

Mondale was shown that night taking the high road. "We stand behind the president in taking appropriate acts to punish those that are responsible for these wholly inexcusable acts of violence," he told the cameras.

But Americans were reacting with more anger and frustration. On NBC, Marvin Kalb, the distinguished veteran of diplomatic reporting, concluded his piece with phrases reminiscent of the darkest days of Carter's hostage crisis in Iran:

KALB: The signs tonight are that the administration is leaning against military retaliation, even though senior officials say that once again the U.S. looks helpless against terrorism and its policy in Lebanon looks pathetic.

But Friday was a new day, and Mondale faced the cameras with a new tone.

NBC NEWS
FRIDAY, SEPTEMBER 21, 1984

TOM BROKAW: When news of the attack first started coming in yesterday, Walter Mondale said that it was a time to stand behind the president. Well, today he had a much tougher tone and sharp words for the president.

MONDALE: But after a fourth time, and after one thorough commission, and now after the recommendations of the State Department, and after a public threat, and after a fairly identifiable problem—it was almost certain that it was going to be in a car or a truck loaded with demolitions coming at you through—driven by a fanatic—not to have the barriers in place; not to have that gate there . . . not to have some steel reinforcement; not to have the best, the trained marines there, armed the way they should be, I can't—I found that going beyond what was acceptable.

In Hanover Park, they tended to blame American officials—but not the president—for the slipshod security precautions that continued at American installations in Beirut. But they also volunteered concerns about the different approaches Mondale took to the problem in the news that week.

Bud Cherry, who favored Reagan, but not enthusiastically, from the outset, brought it up. "I'd like to change the direction—I'm more confident about my opinion about Reagan," said Cherry, who owns that brake-parts company where Joe Martingello and Chris Evans work. "It was something Mondale did . . . he said, 'I stand behind the president.' Then the following day on the news, he was a little ambivalent about how he stood behind the president. . . . He kind of rehinted that it was maybe the president's fault that those people died."

Cherry said it reminded him of something he thought he saw in Mondale when he was responding to those hecklers at USC. "That same Mondale . . . I've seen a very vulnerable person at USC. He exposed a side of himself that was—he really got out of control. He was very vulnerable to being out of control. . . . I saw that person as cracking under the pressure." (It must be noted that others in the room viewed that USC incident quite differently. Sue Talbot, who is the bookkeeper of the family's truck-parts company and who favored Mondale, said: "I got a very different feeling about it. I thought he showed some spirit.")

Whether Bud Cherry's conclusions are right or wrong, his comment illustrates the most valuable service that television provides for the American voters. It enables them to make that very personal judgment that they seek most of all. It enables them to take the measure of the candidate—to make that very personal determination as to which candidate will be the sort of president each voter wants in the White House.

In the fall of 1984 it was not really Teflon that protected Reagan from suffering damage inflicted by terrorist bombings overseas. Reagan had long ago carefully cultivated an image that he was at one with America's fighting men overseas. He had nurtured that image with ease, for it coincided so clearly with his own heartfelt beliefs. Moments such as that poignant classic at Normandy had left him with a residue of oneness with the American military people and the civilians at home that no terrorist's bomb could crack.

So too voters seemed willing to forgive the president for misdeeds (and marginal political deeds) they believed his subordinates probably committed. So it was that when there were reports that the heckling of Mondale had been orchestrated by Reagan campaign officials—and a low-level Reagan California operative was quoted on CBS as having admitted to orchestrating that USC heckling of Mondale—the Reagan aides for once had no qualms about letting reporters near the president so they could ask him the obvious question and he could give his best aw-shucks reply.

SAM DONALDSON: Your people aren't organizing that, are they?
PRESIDENT REAGAN: Sam, good Lord, no.

Those gathered in the Talbots' family room found it very plausible that Reagan aides had done just what was reported, but that Reagan himself did not give the orders or know anything about it. And they tended to accept the spirit of his answer as being true even if they believed it was technically wrong. No blame.

And then there was the time when the president announced a package of loan guarantees and loan deferrals for farmers on the eve of his campaign swing through Iowa, where farmers were angry. The reporters were let into the photo opportunity in the Cabinet Room so they could ask the question about whether this was being done for campaign politics. "Now, I know that none of you standing over there on that side of the table are going to believe this—it wasn't done with that in mind. It was done because there are people out there that need help."

The Talbots' family room erupted in hysterical laughter, as clearly no one seated on that end of the Funnel believed it either. But then again, no one held it against the president. It was, after all, just politics. "It's an election year and the program is probably needed," said Mike Talbot, who was decidedly for Mondale and was no Reagan fan.

"Maybe it's a shame they waited until an election year to do it. . . . If Mondale was the incumbent he would have done the same thing."

Talk to any political strategist schooled in the television age and he or she will explain at once how the key to winning major races is to have the message that is projected on the TV news be in synch with the message that is projected in the candidate's ads. Their shorthand way of saying it is that the "Free TV" must be in synch with the "Paid TV"—consultants talk like that.

One ad that people especially remembered seeing was one for Mondale that warned about the dangers of building an economic upturn on huge deficits. It featured a roller coaster—the ad put the viewer into the roller coaster, and as it climbed slowly the announcer talked about how America was climbing a mountain of deficits. What will happen when it reaches the top? The ad asked the question as the roller coaster—with us inside—began hurtling downward.

"It gives me a feeling of fear," said one woman at the Talbots'. "Fright," said a man. "A scary feeling of 'Oh, my God!' " said a third. All of that was just what Mondale's strategists wanted to convey. The ad was done by media consultant David Sawyer, an outsider who was brought into the Mondale camp to prepare some ads, and who had done the primary media campaign for John Glenn. It successfully conveyed a sense of fear of the Reagan deficit, which Mondale was also trying unsuccessfully to convey on the evening news.

Judy Cherry, who serves as bookkeeper for her husband's brake-parts company, leaned toward Mondale but was never completely sure about it. She said she was very concerned about nuclear weapons and she wished Mondale had addressed that issue in one of his ads. But Mondale had. He did it in an ad that featured a man digging a hole in his backyard as his children watched. The announcer said that Reagan's undersecretary of defense had once said that in case of nuclear attack, "everybody's going to make it if there are enough shovels to go around. Dig a hole, cover it with a couple of doors, and throw three feet of dirt on top." The ad went on to say that "Mr. Reagan has opposed every nuclear-arms agreement since the bomb went off. No wonder he's never achieved one."

It turned out that everyone in the room remembered having seen that ad featuring a man digging a hole, but no one thought of it in terms of the nuclear-weapon issue—the visual imagery was so removed from that. People thought maybe it had something to do with the economy—"You know, digging yourself into a hole," said one.

* * *

But it's not always the vivid and memorable ads that work best. Consider this exchange. Many of those in the family room agreed with Mike Talbot's observation that he found rather insulting those Reagan feel-good ads—the ones that proclaimed, "It's morning again in America," and consisted solely of soothing, uplifting music, soothing soft-filter cameos of Americans waking up, going to work, lifting new housing frames into place, getting married, and smiling all the while. "The thing I didn't like about Reagan . . . was that he never gets down to issues. I mean everything is just water-clear in his commercials—the kind of sweet music that lulls you. . . . It doesn't come down to anything that really has to do with issues."

And that prompted Judy Cherry to say something that had virtually everyone in the room nodding their heads in agreement. "Truth is, I don't see the ads," she said. "I block them out completely. When I walked in here tonight, I couldn't have told you what anybody's ads were. And when I looked at them [tonight] I knew I'd seen them all before."

About twenty minutes later, she was explaining that she thought she favored Mondale, even though his candidacy did not excite her. "But you know," she said, "I have to say that *things are better now*, economically. In my neighborhood, for instance, there are two new houses going up."

And as she spoke, she illustrated her remark by opening her hands, palms outstretched, and pushing them up and away—just as those actors in the Reagan commercials had done when they were tilting into place a wall frame for a new house as the Reagan announcer was explaining how *things are better now*.

INTERLUDE: THE AGE OF REAGAN IN THE TELEVISION AGE

He was seventy-three. And as he stood before the klieg lights and the nation, debating Walter Mondale for the first time, Ronald Reagan's most ardent supporters watching in Mike and Sue Talbot's family room in Hanover Park, Illinois, were stunned to see that he looked—and mainly he acted—every year of it.

They discovered new doubts about their leader that night, and they discovered new virtues in his opponent. For Reagan had seemed stumbling and rambling; he had seemed lost in his answers and even in his rehearsed closing statement. Mondale had seemed crisp and confident, knowledgeable about the issues and authoritative in his views. Pollsters and pundits generally fail to measure properly the effect of a debate on a campaign. They ask the question, Who won the debate? which is politically meaningless, for elections are not won or lost by rounds; they should ask questions that will indicate how this latest campaign event affects the way individuals plan to vote.

As the first presidential debate of 1984 was viewed by the gathering at the Talbots', no votes actually changed—but a lot of opinions shifted. Those who had cast mock votes for Reagan a week earlier, after watching the campaign unfold in the form of television newscasts and commercials, were still writing down "Reagan" on this night's sample ballot—but now they were adding question marks beside his name to indicate that they were suddenly unsure and undecided. Those who a week ago had voted for Mondale but had added question marks of doubt beside his name, now were voting for Mondale with new assurance—and without the old question marks.

October 7, 1984, marked a milestone of sorts in the history of televised presidential debates. In 1960, the first-ever televised presidential debate, between Kennedy and Nixon, showed how the general tone, appearance, and persona of one candidate can be decisive in the television era, as Kennedy was credited with having emerged as the favorite of those who saw the debate on television, but not those who heard it on radio.

In 1976, the debate between Carter and Ford on foreign-policy issues showed how the aftermath of a debate can be more decisive than the debate itself. Doubts about Ford were raised not really during the debate, but during the days of controversy that followed, as Ford repeatedly refused to admit he had misspoken when he had declared that Poland was not dominated by the Soviet Union; that became the main topic of news for days, reminding voters of a gaffe that they had not caught or had not cared about on the night of the debate.

But the first presidential debate of 1984 was something else. For, viewed from the Other End of the Funnel, the event showed for the first time how a televised presidential debate can be seen clearly altering opinions among voters and raising new doubts where none had existed—before any of the instant analysis and commentary can be heard from the television and print journalists.

Listen to Sanford Johnson, who works as a marketing expert for a chemical firm and calls himself a conservative Republican, as he spoke about Reagan's performance just after the television clicked off on the night of that first Mondale-Reagan debate:

"It was apparent that he was not as confident or sure of himself in this particular debate. That raises the question that maybe he is getting a little bit too old and his mind isn't as sharp as it ought to be." Johnson put a question mark beside Reagan's name and said he wanted to watch the next debate and the rest of the campaign on television very closely before deciding whether Reagan was really up to the job and deserving of reelection.

Dian Johnson, an artist who calls herself an Independent and "somewhat of a conservative," agreed with her husband's analysis—but said the debate moved her from a tentative and unsure Mondale voter into a confident Mondale voter. "I took away the question mark," she said as she cast her ballot after the debate. "I think Mondale came off a bit more calmly than Reagan and I think he played a very good political role. . . . I . . . didn't think I saw or heard Reagan really answering anything."

Adam Silverstein, a retired senior citizen and a liberal Democrat firmly for Mondale, recognized what he felt were all-too-familiar symptoms of advancing years. "I think Reagan is past his peak of his efficiency—I know that because I'm pretty close to the point he's at," said Silverstein. Would he have those doubts even if he had come to the debate favoring Reagan? "To be honest with you, I think I would have. But you see, I didn't expect him to be as hesitant, seemingly bereft of all direction there for a few times. I never expected that."

Around the room there were nods of agreement. "I noticed that too," said Monty Clark, the schoolteacher who had come to symbolize the essence of Mondale's campaign problem. His political demographics indicated that Mondale should have had his vote long ago—he was, after all, a Democrat and a former local chapter president of a teachers' organization that had nationally endorsed Mondale. His political emotions indicated the same—when Mondale had delivered his ringing debate summation calling on Americans not to mortgage their children's future, Clark, a normally undemonstrative man, had pumped his right fist in the air for approval. But then Clark wrote Reagan's name on his mock ballot, explaining that he was not yet convinced to come home to his party's fold this year. "I'm a Democrat and it touched a cord in my heart," said Clark. "But I don't think I can afford it right now. I don't think the nation can afford it right now. Four more years from now, I thnk we can afford it."

But Monty Clark conceded that along with all of the standard tug-of-war between heartstrings and purse strings, there was this new matter that was now worrisome: Reagan's age. "I noticed that a little bit four years ago, but it was much more pronounced tonight," Clark said. "When he [Reagan] didn't have a script in his mind, he was in much more difficulty. Mondale looked like the standout tonight."

On Tuesday, October 9, 1984, two of the major television networks—CBS and ABC—discovered the issue of Ronald Reagan's age. They discovered it by reading page one of that morning's edition of *The Wall Street Journal*:

NEW QUESTION IN RACE:
IS OLDEST U.S. PRESIDENT
NOW SHOWING HIS AGE?

REAGAN DEBATE PERFORMANCE
INVITES OPEN SPECULATION
ON HIS ABILITY TO SERVE

The article by *The Wall Street Journal*'s top-flight political reporters, Rich Jaroslovsky and James M. Perry, probed precisely what its headlines promised. It quoted university experts on aging, raising the specter that "mental impairment" could occur in a man Reagan's age in the next four years and urging that Reagan submit for regular tests to see if senility had set in.

That evening CBS and ABC did lengthy pieces of their own examining the question of whether America's oldest president was too old for the job.

The CBS story, incidentally, cited two experts—Dr. Lawrence Klein, of Georgetown University Medical School, and Eugene Jennings, a psychologist and management expert from Michigan State University—both of whom had been cited in the *Wall Street Journal* article.

CBS NEWS
TUESDAY, OCTOBER 9, 1984

DAN RATHER: One issue that President Reagan can't diffuse with a policy change is an issue that went unspoken but not unnoticed during his showdown Sunday with Walter Mondale—the issue of Mr. Reagan's age. Does it affect his performance as president?

Will it in [the] future? Since Sunday, the issue and those questions are being talked about more. Bill Plante reports why. . . .

BILL PLANTE: In Sunday's debate, the president stumbled, hesitated, and sometimes appeared to be groping. . . . The oldest man to ever serve as president has always relied on humor to diffuse the age issue. [Reagan is shown joking about his age.] Lines like that, plus all the pictures of a robust Mr. Reagan swimming or clad in jeans on the back of a horse, have so far cancelled out any signs of aging such as his deteriorating hearing or occasional dozing off. Statistically speaking, doctors say that people Mr. Reagan's age are approaching a difficult time.

DR LAWRENCE KLEIN: People reach seventy-five, eighty years old, the prevalence of chronic disease goes up, the prevalence of dementia goes up. Of course, some people do quite well in that seventy-five to eighty to eighty-five range. . . .

PLANTE: . . . Still, the president's performance on Sunday has caused doubts among some longtime supporters such as psychologist Eugene Jennings, a management expert.

EUGENE JENNINGS: Well, based upon what I saw, and knowing what he was like four years ago, I think aging is having an effect.

ABC News took a different approach. First its correspondent James Wooten, a respected veteran of political wars and White House campaigns, pointed out in very up-front fashion that Washington was suddenly buzzing about the president's age—and that the buzzing had indeed been touched off by the *Wall Street Journal* article. Wooten confined his report to the political questions about Reagan's age. And then—in a most unusual segment—anchor Peter Jennings interviewed ABC's medical editor, Dr. Tim Johnson, who offered his own rather provocative comments about the condition of this president he has not personally examined. The introduction to the whole issue was done low key by Peter Jennings, who noted simply that in some countries, such as the Soviet Union and China, age has seemed a prerequisite for high office, and he asked: "Should age be a factor in determining leadership?"

ABC NEWS
TUESDAY, OCTOBER 9, 1984

JAMES WOOTEN: This was one of those rare days in schizophrenic Washington when the whole town seemed to focus on one thing—Ronald Reagan's age. It all started with this morning's *Wall Street Journal*. . . . The question may be fairly simple. Is Mr. Reagan, the oldest man ever to serve as president, too old to serve four more years? . . . Even some of his loyalists concede that he didn't seem up to snuff in the debate.

[Visuals: The screen shows an example of Reagan flubbing in the debate, and nodding off during an audience with the pope at the end of an exhaustingly scheduled European tour. And then there is that famous scene from an impromptu press conference in which he is prompted by his wife, Nancy, and he repeats the answer exactly as she whispered it.]

REPORTER: Is there anything you can do to get them to Vienna?

PRESIDENT REAGAN: Uh . . .

NANCY REAGAN (whispering behind her husband): We're doing everything we can.

PRESIDENT REAGAN (out loud): We're doing everything we can.

Then came that Jennings interview of the network's own doctor, who had made a house call to the anchordesk.

JENNINGS: Dr. Tim, if some people in the audience did see the president more faltering, more uncertain, and looking old, does that really tell us anything?

DR. TIM JOHNSON: I don't think so, Peter. I think one has to make a very careful distinction between various aspects of aging. . . . President Reagan appears to be in good physical health from all we can gather. There are other processes that might be more associated with changes in mental acuity. But even those do not necessarily signify aging. A person may, for example, have always stumbled while trying to think or speak on their feet. And what we're more interested in is any change for them. Finally . . . there are other kinds of changes that have nothing to do with either physical ability or mental acuity. Such skills as judgment and instinct and intuition.

JENNINGS: Let me interrupt you for a second. You're saying that if the president was faltering and uncertain on the television it is not necessarily a reflection on his ability in other areas.

JOHNSON: Not necessarily, but obviously cause for concern. . . . With increasing age there is clearly an increased statistical risk for both physical and mental problems. Ten percent of people who reach seventy-five have significant mental impairment. Having said that, the other side of the medical coin is that there is no good way to predict in any individual case what's going to happen or how fast anything might happen.

JENNINGS: The president said in the 1980 campaign that if he became president he would take regular tests for mental agility, or, as he called it then, senility. Is that something that he should do, or any man seventy-three in that job should do?

JOHNSON: . . . I personally think that those are tests we would apply to anybody we suspected of having some mental problems or some aging associated with mentation and maybe we should apply to a president as we would to anybody else.

NBC News with Tom Brokaw did not do a story on the issue of Ronald Reagan's age. It was a decision carefully arrived at, a decision not without considerable internal debate.

"We all thought the *Wall Street Journal* story was fascinating, but it was a far reach, we thought, from there to Ronald Reagan's state of Alzheimer's," said Tom Brokaw. "And one of the things that we're extremely conscious of in this media is that it's different if you write that kind of story in the newspapers, where people can go back and reexamine, and you can write with great care and caution and spell it out in a way that it's understandable. . . . Television, by its very nature . . . is so ephemeral—it's instantly here and it's instantly gone. What's left very often is buzz words. Senile. Too old for the job. That kind of thing. And there was no hard medical evidence that Ronald Reagan had lapsed into some serious or even minor medical problem. I mean, he didn't perform very well in the debate, but that could be for lots of reasons.

"I thought it [the *Journal* story] was within the bounds of responsibility—just inside. . . . But it would not have been for us to pick that up and go with it because I know how it would have landed in the living rooms of America."

Joan Carrigan, NBC News's senior producer in charge of political coverage, remembers that the *Wall Street Journal* article had caused quite a stir around the newsroom in Rockefeller Center. "By the time I got in in the morning there were calls—'Let me see *The Wall Street Journal*'—from people . . . not even directly involved in the campaign. That caused quite a sensation. There were other producers saying 'Maybe we should do an age spot.' 'Maybe we should do a piece on Reagan's age.' 'Have you seen *The Wall Street Journal*?' It went on all morning.

"I thought it was a terrible idea. To me that piece was indefensible.

And Chris [Wallace, NBC's White House correspondent] called me and said, 'Everyone's talking about this and do you think we ought to do it?' And I said, 'No, I don't.' And he said, 'I think both of the other two will.' And I said, 'I hope they do.'

"I was reminded about Eugene McCarthy's quote about blackbird journalism—when the one flies away they all fly away. I thought the *Wall Street Journal* piece, built around men who'd never met Ronald Reagan, making all these suppositions and generalizations about people at this kind of age, and linking that to his performance in the debate and his potential for deterioration—I didn't think that met any of the standards we're obliged to meet.

"I think that his problems in that debate had been well examined. And the leap to sort of having your house media doctor sit on the side and discuss senility in people his age . . . just to leap right on a *Wall Street Journal* story which really had no foundation . . . I just thought it was a low point. And I'm glad we didn't have anything to do with it.

"Everybody raised the question about whether it should be done and I made my case and it was accepted. . . . I made the point that if the polls were to show, if there were some data that people were very concerned about Ronald Reagan's age. . . . But we had no evidence that people out there were saying 'I think maybe this president is too old.' "

Carrigan makes a strong case about the merits of not doing the story without any evidence of people's concerns. But, of course, the evidence was out there—it was there in the Talbots' family room in Hanover Park, for example; but a news organization would not know that unless it had gone out to the Other End of the Funnel in search of the evidence. The strongest possible story would have been to report the genuine concerns of voters watching the debate and then report the way the experts addressed those concerns.

But the dilemma of television is a very real one, for Brokaw's point is indeed well taken about how the medium leaves impressions that may well drown out the most diplomatically crafted and carefully nuanced verbal explanation. For Brokaw's erstwhile rival at ABC, Peter Jennings, discovered for himself what Brokaw had meant when he said, "I know how it would have landed in the living rooms of America."

Here is Peter Jennings, recalling the way his network's piece landed in America's living rooms: "We went out of our way that evening to make the point that age had nothing to do with influence, opinion, perspicacity, et cetera. But in the course of the piece about the president . . . we showed the picture of the president nodding off . . . during the pope's visit. I mean, people were outraged! And I sat here for hours answering the telephone calls of people. And I kept saying to them, 'Didn't you hear what I said? We had our medical editor on, Tim Johnson, to talk about age and ability.' Nobody heard it. I was flabbergasted! I shouldn't have been flabbergasted, but I was. And I would say to people on the phone, 'But let me tell you some of the things we said.' And of course then people on the phone would get very sheepish and say, 'Oh, yeah, but well, yes, you should have showed that picture.' "

The age of Reagan stands as an example of one of those times when network television takes its journalistic cues from the newspapers. But one of the more interesting developments in recent years is that network-television news has matured to the point where it is generating its own trend stories far more often than it used to, without waiting for some print journalist to discover a trend.

That was what some of the best correspondents at each of the networks were in fact assigned to do—to work on those longer-range trend stories that try to get behind and go beyond the nightly news. That was the role played skillfully in 1984 by correspondents such as Bob Schieffer and Bruce Morton of CBS; Ken Bode of NBC; and Richard Threlkeld, James Wooten, and Sander Vanocur of ABC.

ABC's World News Tonight executive producer William Lord acknowledged that it was the *Journal* story that moved ABC to do the Reagan age story. "It was the *Wall Street Journal* piece that got us going," he said. ". . . Yes, we were concerned about the stumbling of the president . . . and analyzing it. But that *Wall Street Journal* story hit the nail on the head and they woke everybody up."

At CBS, Lane Vernardos, executive producer of *The Evening News with Dan Rather*, said CBS had been talking about doing a piece on Reagan's age on Monday—the day before the *Journal* story appeared. "But the *Wall Street Journal* piece clearly gave us impetus. . . . You know, if you wake up in the morning and at your doorstep is the *Wall Street Journal* piece on the president's age . . . you know that you're not the only one who's going to see that piece and if . . . some other network wasn't already working on one, you're damn sure they're going to start working on one.

"I was a little uneasy about the [CBS] piece just because we had no cooperation from the White House; they wouldn't provide any kind of spokesperson, which is their wont, of course. . . . And the result of the piece was journalistically correct. . . . But we caught a load of shit for that one. The phones didn't stop."

Anchor Dan Rather's concern was that CBS did not do the piece on Reagan's age earlier, that the network had to be bolstered by the *Wall Street Journal* piece into doing a story he thought should have been done, and which they had talked about, earlier. "We probably should have done something before the debate," said the CBS anchor and managing editor. ". . . And I don't think it speaks very well for us. . . . There are a lot of reasons why we didn't. And among the reasons—not the only reason, but among the reasons—is that we were afraid. And I don't like it when we're afraid of anything."

Rather believes it is quite proper to go to the experts—in this case the doctors—to discuss the difficult issue of old age in a world leader, just as it was shortly after the election when the White House revealed that Reagan had cancer. "I think it's quite a legitimate journalistic technique, and I think it might be irresponsible not to go talk to those experts and say, 'You haven't examined this patient . . . but you have seen thousands of these kinds of cases, Doctor, and so tell me the important things to know.' Nothing wrong with that. . . . So it was with the debate thing. There wasn't a thing wrong with going to the doctors. You've got to. . . . I think it was good coverage, legitimate coverage . . . and I think we did it pretty well."

I'M OKAY, YOU'RE OKAY

That soft, gliding sound that could be heard in Hanover Park, Illinois, on the night of October 22 was the sound of Ronald Reagan's voters sliding smoothly back into the fold. In the second and last debate of the 1984 presidential campaign, Reagan had let his people know that he was okay, after all. And they had moved almost as one as they found their faith and returned to the fold.

Walter Mondale had burst onto the television screen looking like an aged Rocky Raccoon with a bad case of insomnia; the big "key light" that was to illuminate Mondale had been deliberately set low by his own adviser (much to the astonishment of the network pool producer, David Buksbaum of CBS), and it had given Mondale such dark circles and puffy bags under his eyes that he looked about as old in the second debate as Reagan had acted in the first debate. And once this foreign-policy debate had begun, Mondale had inexplicably slipped back into that low-keyed, cautious mode that he sometimes favored.

His answers were competent but not crisp, lacking in spark and not really memorable.

But none of that mattered anyway. Because the view from the Other End of the Funnel in that first debate had made it clear that this second debate would be only about Ronald Reagan. Those who wanted to support him—but who had some doubts about his age and his competence—were looking only to see that their leader was okay. Reagan was, and once their faith was restored they returned to Reagan without reservation.

Sanford Johnson, the marketing specialist and Republican, pronounced himself pleased. "I thought Reagan did much better than in the last debate," he said. "He seemed more relaxed . . . well rested." He cast his mock vote for Reagan, unequivocally.

Morrie Oldham, the accountant and Independent, pronounced himself relieved. "Had Reagan fallen on his face, hemmed and hawed in his answers . . . I think I would've been really worried." He too cast his vote for Reagan.

Monty Clark, the teacher and Democrat, pronounced himself satisfied—sort of. "I found myself kind of rooting for Reagan," he said. And he found himself voting for Reagan too.

Mike Talbot, truck-parts company owner and Mondale backer, pronounced himself surprised. "I think that Reagan did a lot better than I thought he would do. He looked a lot better than he did in the last debate." Talbot stayed true to Mondale. But as he looked around the family room in his home, he did not need George Gallup and Louis Harris to tell him that his candidate was done.

THE FINAL DAZE

The Mondale/Ferraro campaign was making one last effort to call Democrats like Monty Clark to come to the aid of their party. They did it with a round of ads aimed at portraying the election as a contest of Feel Good versus Feel Guilt.

MONDALE AD

[An invitation is received in the mail.]

NARRATOR: Reverend Jerry Falwell and President Reagan cordially invite you to join their party on November 6. Here's all you have to believe in:

WOMAN: The secret war in Central America.

MAN: New Supreme Court justices must rule abortion a crime even in cases of rape and incest.
WOMAN: No Equal Rights Amendment for women.
MAN: No verifiable nuclear freeze. What kind of party is this?
NARRATOR: Think about the people who have taken over the Republican party. They want their new platform to be your new Constitution.

In the final days, CBS stopped doing those special-project pieces and started doing very straight, short daily stories on the campaign efforts of the candidates that day, with the emphasis on hard news and not analysis.

"It was the last week of the campaign," recalled Lane Vernardos, executive producer of *The CBS Evening News*. "Dan [Rather] and I felt fairly strongly that okay, we've given this campaign our best shot, we've analyzed it as best we could. . . . Let the candidates speak. Let's not paraphrase them as much as we have during the course of the campaign. Let's give them their thirty-five-second sound bites every time they go out. . . . Let people out there hear what these [candidates] . . . are saying as the campaign comes down to the wire."

At ABC, they continued their straight-ahead reporting, covering each candidate daily. Brit Hume, whom the Mondale camp always considered to be fair even when he was being tough, made no effort to pull his polling punches in characterizing Mondale's prospects. On the last Thursday of the campaign, for example, Hume reported on a day in which Mondale drew a huge crowd in Manhattan by beginning his piece like this: "If the polls are right, Walter Mondale's about to get blitzed. He might as well have gone over Niagara Falls in a barrel, but he flew down from Buffalo to New York City."

At NBC, meanwhile, Mondale correspondent Lisa Myers continued her tough assessments of Mondale right to the end. One week before the election, after Tom Brokaw announced the latest NBC News–poll results giving Reagan an "overpowering" twenty-four-point lead, Myers opened her Mondale coverage in Duluth by saying:

"Having finally escaped the shadows of Hubert Humphrey and Jimmy Carter, having silenced cries of wimp, Mondale came home to ask those who know him best to save him from further indignity—from what could be the worst defeat in the history of presidential politics. . . . With polls so bleak he no longer discusses them, with his situation deteriorating by the hour, Mondale asked for one final favor [a victory in his home state, Minnesota]."

The Mondale campaign had been unhappy with the coverage NBC's

Myers had given Mondale all year and especially during the fall. "The Mondale people . . . were very unhappy with NBC," Brokaw conceded. "They felt they'd been covered far too close and Mondale himself acquainted me twice and Jim Johnson [Mondale's campaign chairman] a number of times. Once just before the New York primary in a one-on-one interview I had with him [Mondale], they cleared out the room so that he could talk to me. And he thought that he'd been getting unfair treatment from us. He thought that Lisa was—I guess the upshot of it is that [he thought] Lisa had it in for him." When Mondale had given details of his budget plan, for example, "she described what would happen if the Mondale budget were enacted and he thought that she'd cooked her figures. That kind of thing."

Once, Brokaw said, Mondale had spoken to him about this during the primaries. Said Brokaw: "He said to me, 'Jimmy Carter even called me the other day to say to me that when he was at the White House, NBC was the fairest of the networks—and he just can't believe what you guys are doing to me.' I mean that was the quote."

Brokaw gave Mondale and Johnson his home phone numbers, in Connecticut and in New York. "They called me in Connecticut and they called me at home here. Fritz was really angry. Jimmy was . . . 'God Tom, did you see tonight? Well that just isn't fair. . . .' So I'd call Lisa and I'd say, 'They've raised this, so you go over and talk to Jim Johnson about it. Because in my eye she's a very good reporter and I wasn't going to put any heat on her."

Meanwhile, back in the Chicago suburbs, Monty Clark was having one last attack of second thoughts. He saw Mondale's "Invitation" ad. Said Democrat Clark: "That had to have been a pretty powerful ad. Not only did it make me think of the potential dangers of the Republican party but at school I had a lot of people—teachers . . . in the teachers' lounge—saying they hadn't realized Reagan was really that close to Falwell until they saw that ad. I hadn't realized the danger of the Supreme Court being loaded by them."

He added: "What did affect me was the newscasts. They reported it the way it was—that Mondale didn't have a chance. But it was almost a self-fulfilling prophecy. It kind of took the wind out of my sails. . . . It'd be like casting a vote to the wind."

On Tuesday, November 6, 1984, Monty Clark voted for Ronald Reagan, as did millions of other Democrats and labor-union members.

THIRTEEN

CAMPAIGN BY TV: DON'T MAKE AN ISSUE OUT OF IT

Joan Carrigan works at the upper levels of a state-of-the-art industry that does its communicating in living color but too often does its thinking in black and white.

Late in a day of discussion about the decisions she made as NBC News's senior producer in charge of campaign coverage in 1984, Carrigan turned off the videotape machine and took on the question she and most people who work in her industry at any level, network or local, have long ago grown defensive about answering—because it is always asked. It is the question about the issues: why television seems to cover them superficially, at best.

She answered the question by rephrasing it: "Should we be in the role of the great instructor of the electorate?" she asked. "Or should we be covering the news?"

That is the dilemma as Carrigan and most of the decision-makers in her industry see it. It is the first of a series of misperceptions that leads the industry to produce at far less than capacity. For the real role of television news should be to report what is really going on.

This means reporting not just what the politicians choose to say for their microphones to hear, or reporting just the events the politicians contrive for their cameras to see. Reporting what is really going on means reporting the truths about some policies that the politicians would prefer left unsaid and unseen. It means laying out the alternatives for all to see, even when the politicians prefer to keep the most painful alternatives to themselves. It means reporting not just what the polls say people want to hear about the news, it means reporting all the news—all that is going on.

For all of their innovative new graphics, for all of their chroma-key computers, for all of their sophisticated satellites, their high tech and lofty intentions, America's television networks really did not take one giant step for mankind in explaining the issues of 1984 to the voters. They did not cover themselves with journalistic glory in showing voters just where the candidates stood on the crucial policy questions (or stooped to duck them, as was occasionally the case).

Network television's coverage of issues was at times impressive, but mostly uneven and haphazard, in 1984—and not all the steps the networks took were in a forward direction.

Consider NBC.

Back in 1980, anchor John Chancellor assigned himself the mission of conveying the issues to the public. And he went out and did it in a way that was not very glittery but was very informative, in both the primaries and the general election. "In 1980, what we did was that we developed a questionnaire of I think thirty questions. And I went around on weekends and nights and at various other times and put the same questions . . . in the same order to everybody—to Bush, to Reagan . . . to Phil Crane, to everybody. And then . . . instead of editing each candidate and saying [in one night] this is where George Bush stands on gun control, abortion, all the questions that you would ask—what we did was say, 'There are five Republicans who are in the primaries and here is how they stand on gun control.' And then you'd get five of them giving those thirty-five to forty-five-second answers. And you could see the difference."

Indeed you could. In the primaries, with Democrats Edward Kennedy and Edmund G. (Jerry) Brown pitted against the incumbent, Jimmy Carter, and with those Republicans pitted against each other, it was possible to see how each handled a given issue, one topic each night. And it was even possible to take the measure of each in terms of those intangibles that have to do with communicating and leading—the viewers could see the way the candidates handled themselves and the sense of confidence and commitment they had as they addressed identical questions.

During the primaries, the *NBC Nightly News with John Chancellor* packaged and delivered to the public pieces of about three to four minutes each that showed the candidates staking out their positions on inflation, the Equal Rights Amendment, abortion, the hostage crisis in Iran, plus their explanations of just why they are running and what they think about the way the incumbent is handling the job.

During the fall, the *NBC Nightly News with John Chancellor* cut and spliced interviews with Carter and Reagan and presented its viewers packages in which the candidates spoke to the issues of Israeli settlements in the occupied West Bank, the Equal Rights Amendment, the role of the clergy in politics, American military readiness and the Rapid Deployment Force program, taxes, the environment and Alaskan-oil exploration, the status of Jerusalem, foreign policy, and the proper role of government and government programs.

These issues pieces did not always make for great television, but they did make for great public service as the nation's democracy went about its quadrennial business of testing its working parts. "I thought it was a very useful thing to do," said Chancellor.

NBC did not do it that way in 1984. The issues were treated in a less coherent and less frequent manner. Chancellor, no longer a decision-maker on the *NBC Nightly News*, contributed only commentaries to anchor Tom Brokaw's show.

"I'm a complete outsider and that's the way it ought to be," said Chancellor. "You don't want an old anchorman hanging around the water cooler saying, 'I think you kids aren't doing it the right way.' Times change. They may be doing it the right way."

The decision-making was being done in part by Chancellor's former field producer back in 1980—Joan Carrigan. And it turns out she has some definite views about the way her former boss approached the issues in Campaign '80.

"I thought, frankly, that was just old-think," Carrigan said of the way Chancellor covered the issues. ". . . In 1979–1980 . . . we had done the routine, in my view, knee-jerk approach. . . . I thought it was just something people [in network television] did routinely.

"They did it without thinking. And it was time to stop doing it because the issues were very well understood. The polls showed that the people in large, large numbers, on almost every single issue, disagreed with Ronald Reagan. And they [the polls] also showed that it had absolutely no bearing on why they were voting.

"Given that reality, isn't it a waste of time to rehash what people have demonstrated they understand and have demonstrated they don't believe has any bearing on their vote? I mean, so why should we do it in the context of the election campaign?"

Follow the reasoning of this chief planner of NBC's political coverage of 1984. It is a classic illustration of circuitous logic: (1) NBC was not doing extensive pieces on the candidates' positions on the issues and the consequences of those policies; (2) the viewers were thus underinformed at the time they were having to make their choice; (3) so viewers were telling pollsters they favored Reagan, but their decisions were based on those other aspects—persona and charisma—that the network was showing them; (4) but when asked, they would also take positions on the issues that were different from Reagan's; (5) and meanwhile, back in the newsroom, NBC was concluding that if people were choosing Reagan even though they disagreed with him on the issues, then that must mean that issues do not matter—and so there is no need to better inform the public about them.

That is why, Carrigan explained, she did not push to have NBC do a special series on the issues. Her view is not unique among network decision-makers—just her candor is. Carrigan's thinking seemed representative of the way most network planners approached Campaign '84, as she talked candidly about why she felt it was unnecessary to do a series on the issues at campaign time, that time when most people are focusing for the first time on their choice for president.

"I didn't assign it or ask for it or suggest it," she said about a series on the issues. ". . . I think it may have come up in one meeting, but I may have said what I said to you. People were quite satisfied that we had covered the issues in terms of regular news coverage continually. I mean, whether it was arms control, or whether it was Star Wars, or whether it was tax policy, for example—all those things we'd been doing our job on . . . just as a public-policy matter. And . . . it wasn't particularly relevant to drag them out and put them in a campaign framework because they really didn't exist in the campaign framework. The candidates were succeeding or not succeeding really on other grounds."

Carrigan was told that what people were demonstrating they did not understand about the deficit in the fall of 1984 is itself astounding. "But that's not because we haven't spent hours telling them," she countered, referring to the past years of coverage of daily budget battles. But the early stories on the deficit were done months and years earlier, when people were not focusing on the election of 1984. Carrigan was asked why NBC did not put greater emphasis on reporting about the deficit and other issues that the candidates for president were running on during the fall campaign period.

"Well what were they [the candidates] running on? I mean, that's what the question is. I mean, Ronald Reagan was running on America's back and optimism and those crybabies who don't understand anything and who don't believe in personal initiative and who ran this country into trouble all these years. 'We've had enough of them and we all understand them.' I mean, that's what he was saying.

"Walter Mondale's main point was Ronald Reagan is out to lunch, doesn't understand the future, isn't the proper person to take us where we have to go, doesn't understand the constitutional limitations such as religion and other things. And is not telling people the truth about the financial realities we're facing as a nation. And that he has not been pursuing peace in our time the way he ought to be. The whole area of arms control has been neglected by this administration. . . . They've been spending all that money in the Pentagon that they should have been addressing to other needs and reducing the deficit.

"Both of those cases were covered and covered and covered. We would do that when there was a news reason to focus on it." What Carrigan was saying, in effect, was that they would cover those issues only when one of the politicians chose to talk about it that day. And then they would report only that politician's positions, rather than comparing and contrasting them with his opponent's, and adding in what the experts were saying about each.

There was another reason Carrigan gave for not doing many separate stories on such issues as the environment. She called it "Judicial notice and the law." She explained:

"If you come into court . . . the judge will take judicial notice of certain absolutely known facts such as the sun rises in the east. You don't have to bring in an expert to establish that. Any moderately informed American, anyone who's a semiregular part of our audience, knows that Ronald Reagan's record on the environment is what it is. They know about the scandals at EPA. They know there's been criticism from within the Republican party. They know where the Sierra Club stands. And it used to be that [network television] people would do the takeout [lengthy piece] even if the issue was irrelevant in the campaign and had been done to death. . . . We always did issue pieces. We didn't do it this time because it really didn't seem necessary, new, or relevant and, as I say, all of the studies that were done indicated that people understood. . . . And it wasn't the basis on which they were making their decision. They said they were making their decision because Ronald Reagan had done a good job, or he made them feel good, or they didn't like Jimmy Carter, or . . . Walter Mondale was boring . . . or just seemed to them like a hack politician, or listened too much to the special interests. . . .

"So why do it?"

Carrigan had two other points to make, both of which also brought her right back to that same conclusion. One point was that perhaps newspapers should do stories on the issues, while television should not. She said:

"There's a difference between television and newspaper. If I were working in a newspaper I would find it much more proper to do those takeouts, give people who wanted to spend time informing themselves in that way . . . the opportunity. But the evidence is that, first of all, it isn't news and no one is saying that it's news; and second is that people aren't interested."

And this in turn led her into her second point—and it is perhaps the most important factor of all, as the networks see it. It is that stories on the issues can be dangerous to the health of a network's ratings.

Carrigan said candidly and openly what most network officials will say only privately:

"We have a captive audience; we're forcing them to watch this twenty-two minutes. . . . And if we had done a three-minute piece on all of these issues . . . if you were at home and we went into our issues—Reagan and Mondale on the environment—I think you'd have switched the channel during the three minutes. Because you know about Mondale and Reagan on the environment. You'd have gone over to see if Bruce Morton [of CBS] had a provocative piece on something else.

"I don't think you'd have stayed with us."

WHEN THEY WERE GOOD, THEY WERE VERY, VERY GOOD

The grand paradox of 1984 is that when network television chose to highlight campaign issues on the nightly news, it did the job wonderfully well. When they put their hearts and minds and high tech to it, the three major networks produced pieces that covered the issues with greater depth, clarity, and viewer interest than ever before.

When they were at their best, the networks succeeded in part because of the greater technological capability to use graphics to illustrate, and thus simplify, the complexities of subjects such as the economy. Their coverage of the issues suffered not in quality, just quantity.*

One special series that was perhaps the best in-depth approach to an issue in the entire year of prime-time network news was NBC News's massive and impressive look at "The New Cold War." As NBC News officials saw it, the series was deliberately not related to the presidential campaign; it just happened to air during the fall campaign period. "The New Cold War" stands as an example of the best that network television can accomplish. And despite the concerns voiced by Carrigan (which are in fact shared by many in network television), the cold war series was neither deadly dull nor detrimental to the health of NBC's ratings.

NBC decided to deploy its major news talents, both on camera and off, in an all-out assault on a single but vast topic. The network then coordinated the finished product so that viewers of news in the morning and night—on the *Today* show and the *Nightly News*—would be informed in depth about just what had been happening in this vital area: relations between the Soviet Union and the United States.

NBC's John Hart and Garrick Utley carried the brunt of the on-camera workload in this series that ran from September 7–24: Hart examined U.S.-U.S.S.R. relations in the twentieth century; Utley reported on the ethnic, cultural, and political diversity of the Soviet people; Fred Francis looked at Soviet influence in the Caribbean and Central America; Utley again on Soviet history and the way the Soviet media covers the United States; Hart again on U.S.-Soviet cultural exchanges; Utley on Soviet domestic problems; Frank Bourgholtzer on successors to Soviet leader Konstantin Chernenko; Tom Brokaw on U.S. and Soviet conventional military strength; Utley on the Soviet economy; Utley on Soviet approaches to child-rearing, divorce, and teenage problems; Hart on Soviet emigration; and Hart on shared concerns and mutual fears of people within the two countries.

This commitment of network-news resources, a commitment both deep and wide, was made by NBC not in conjunction with the pres-

*According to research done at the Gannett Center for Media Studies at Columbia University by David Bushman, who is himself a journalist, ABC, CBS, and NBC aired a total of just thirty-four separate pieces that were devoted to a close look at specific campaign issues during the period from Labor Day to Election Day. That turned out to be just eleven or twelve from each network during that sixty-four-day period. This is, as Bushman cautioned, a very subjective statistic because it does not include most of the instances where the correspondents dealt with foreign- or domestic-policy matters as part of their daily stories from the campaign trail. But it is a good indication that there surely was more to be done.

idential campaign but in spite of it. There was no attempt to link the documentary effort with the views and policies of the candidates, but rather there was a conscious decision not to do that. The decision was unfortunate because the public could have benefitted from a good look at just what a Mondale presidency would be likely to produce in this crucial area as compared to an extended Reagan presidency.

As anchor Tom Brokaw's explained, no one at NBC ever thought of the cold war series as part of the campaign coverage—and, in fact, the network would have been happier to air the series at a time when there was no campaign.

The idea grew out of a proposal made by Brokaw at the first network editorial-board meeting convened by the new NBC News president Lawrence Grossman back in June 1984. "I had been for some time thinking that at NBC News . . . we ought to take an important issue and do it on all of our programs for a week at a time and tie it to a documentary so that you have a kind of one long fabric that everyone can deal with," said Brokaw. "I raised that [at the meeting] . . . and frankly I said we ought to do it on the American automobile industry, because we knew that they were coming up with Japanese quotas. . . . And then, as we got into it, we couldn't sustain it. And it was Tom Pettit [then a network vice-president, who has since returned to the role of network correspondent in Washington] who said, 'You know, we really ought to do it on the state of U.S.-U.S.S.R. relations. That has more meaning.' And everybody said that's a terrific idea.

"And then, two or three weeks into it, one or two people said, 'Gosh I wonder if that won't be too provocative in the middle of a campaign?' And everybody agreed that you couldn't let the campaign ambiance, if you will, dictate your editorial decisions about what was plainly the overwhelming political dilemma that this country faces How are we going to get along with the Soviet Union? So we just pressed ahead to do that. And we didn't do it in the context of Mondale's or Reagan's campaign. . . . Just the nature of the problem."

Paul Greenberg, executive producer of the *NBC Nightly News*, said, "I would say it was happenstance [that the cold war series ran during the fall campaign]. I don't think it got in the way of the fall campaign," he said. It certainly did not. Network officials would be well served to look at it the other way around; for that series demonstrated to NBC and its competitors the sort of approach that, with a little planning, can be adapted to produce a major thematic companion to television's coverage of presidential campaigns.

That approach could be utilized by television networks to bring to campaign coverage the sort of documentary brilliance that television does best. The all-out commitment to the presidential campaign of correspondents expert in policy, not just politics, could usher in a new era of in-depth coverage of the Great American Video Game. For television could highlight, in compelling and comprehensive fashion, just how the paths of foreign and domestic policy can be significantly redirected by the choice the voters will make.

THE ISSUES AT A GLANCE: FOREIGN AFFAIRS

On their nightly news shows, the three major television networks did seven campaign-issues pieces devoted to comparing the views of Reagan and Mondale on foreign affairs during the fall campaign coverage, according to researcher Bushman's analysis. ABC's Richard Threlkeld did two of them, both strong and informative pieces.

Threlkeld, who is titled chief correspondent at ABC News, was ABC's designated hitter on all issues. His campaign assignment was to do pieces that ABC labeled "Issues '84," in which he focused on topics both foreign and domestic. On September 28, timed to coincide with Reagan's meeting with Soviet Foreign Minister Andrei Gromyko and his speech to the United Nations, Threlkeld aired a piece examining American and Soviet relations that gave strong (albeit fleeting) representations of the Reagan and Mondale positions on how to deal with the Soviets.

ABC NEWS SEPTEMBER 28, 1984

THRELKELD: Five weeks ago in Dallas, the Republican party warned America that the Soviet Union is a threat to freedom and peace on every continent. Last Sunday the Republicans' standard-bearer, who's characterized the Soviet Union as an evil empire, shook hands with the Soviet foreign minister for a full twenty-three seconds. And Monday he surprised the United Nations by giving Moscow a sort of verbal bear hug.

REAGAN: For the sake of a peaceful world, let us approach each other with tenfold trust and thousandfold affection.

THRELKELD: Getting along with the Russians and getting agreements with them has preoccupied each of Mr. Reagan's predecessors. But he hasn't shown much interest in this sort of thing till now. Is it just politics?

MONDALE: Gone is the evil empire. After four years of sounding like Ronald Reagan, yesterday morning he tried to sound like Walter Mondale.

THRELKELD: Or is it real?

The piece went on to present the views of one expert on foreign policy, *Foreign Affairs* editor William Hyland, who said that a president can't be in that office for months without rethinking "some of his original notions." And then it laid out what each of the parties said about taking on arms control—far too briefly, but at least the positions of both sides were aired.

Threlkeld aired another notable piece on foreign-policy campaign positions on October 28. It was strong and even long by television-news-show standards. But its four and a half minutes was enough time to give only a smattering of comparative views on a few major world issues. And unfortunately, the piece was aired so late in the campaign, by that time the polls were showing that most people had already made up their minds to vote for Reagan. Indeed, the main campaign news of that day, carried much earlier in the show, was that Mondale campaign chairman James Johnson was reported to have told his candidate that Reagan had an insurmountable lead; the report noted that Mondale was now furious about those published reports, but the best face he could place on this obvious debacle situation was to claim that Johnson had only told him Reagan's huge lead made the race "tough."

Now that people had made up their minds, ABC was giving them food for thought on the crucial policy differences in powder-keg places.

ABC NEWS
OCTOBER 28, 1984

[The screen shows the cemetery graves of a marine killed in that barracks bombing in Beirut a year earlier and a soldier killed in the American invasion of Grenada, which occurred later that same week. The cemetery scene remains on the screen as dialogue from the recent presidential debate on foreign policy is heard.]

MONDALE: In Lebanon, this president exercised American power all right, but the management of it was such that our marines were killed; we had to leave in humiliation.

REAGAN: First of all, Mr. Mondale should know that the president of the United States did not order the marines into that barracks, that was a command decision made by the commanders. . . .

THRELKELD: . . . The American peace-keeping mission there failed and left Lebanon worse off than before. Since then, Washington has mostly left the Mideast to its own devices.

Next Threlkeld focused on the triumphantly trumpeted invasion of Grenada:

> . . . The Reagan administration counts the invasion of Grenada as its signal triumph. It foiled an ugly Marxist coup, relieved Grenada's neighbors, and salvaged some frightened American students. No argument here; even Walter Mondale says he would have done the same thing as president.

Then on the semisecret war against Nicaragua:

> . . . Despite Washington's so-called Contra guerrilla war against them, Nicaragua's Sandinistas still go their own irritating way. The Reagan administration has never decided whether it just wants them to stop aiding and abetting the Salvadoran rebels or to try to get rid of the Sandinistas altogether. . . . Walter Mondale says he'd stop the guerrilla war and negotiate with the Sandinistas.

And briefly, on the whole:

> . . . In sum, the Reagan record in those two trouble spots, the Mideast and Central America, and in the world at large, is basically blank, no famous victories, no crushing defeats.
> . . . The choice is important. The next president will have to keep Israel and Syria from going to war with each other, decide what to do if Nicaragua won't behave itself, and how to handle the Philippines if it starts to come undone. . . .

CBS chose to combine much of its issue reporting with its polling, relying upon the CBS News/*New York Times* poll to provide the framework on which to hang a bit of foreign-policy crepe. Prior to the presidential foreign-policy debate, Bruce Morton did the story on "the foreign-policy mood of Americans" in the strong and thoughtful way he does all his work. But the format left him little time to explore the positions of the two candidates, since he was first obliged to tell Americans what they already thought about the two men's views on these issues before he could go on to explain just what those views really were.

All three networks relied on the skills of their top correspondents to fold bits of policy positions into their nightly news stories from the campaign trail. And the network correspondents covering the two presidential candidates did that job as skillfully as it could be done in this a-phrase-here-a-sentence-there approach to the issues.

Not all good efforts made it through the Funnel, however. When President Reagan went to Bowling Green State University in Ohio, his strategists had him working hard to try to ease the concerns that were showing up in some of their private polls that many people viewed him as too hawkish and most likely to push the United States into a war. So Reagan delivered a speech that was chock-full of expressions of peace and conciliation toward the Soviets. And CBS News correspondent Lesley Stahl noted that in her piece and wrote in her closing line that an indication of Reagan's new emphasis was the fact that he used the word *peace* twenty-three times in his speech. But back in the Fish Bowl, the producers ordered the kicker changed; it struck them as editorial and a bit flip, although it seems an effective way to make that point. Both Stahl and Susan Zirinsky, her producer on the CBS White House team, fought with New York to keep the original ending, but finally lost. "That one drove 'Z' nuts," said Stahl. She went on to describe a process in which CBS correspondents submit their scripts for approval by the producers in New York. The process she described puts the work of the correspondents under far greater control by the New York producers than the work of correspondents at the other two networks, especially ABC's Donaldson, who would often do his story without having had his script approved at all, having mastered the knack of being conveniently on deadline, writing up to the last minute.

"Did I feel pressure? Sometimes I felt my pieces were softened," said Stahl. "And I was very frustrated by it when it happened. . . . It's one of the great frustrations of my life that I have to go to so many people. It drives me nuts. It drives me crazy. I can't stand it. I mean, I pass my script in to one producer who gives it to another, who sends it to New York. He gets it back, gives it to her, she gives it back to me. And I wrote it. And if I want to defend something—they want to change something and I want to defend it, 'Here's why I wrote it that way'—it goes back to her, back to him."

Another closing comment on a Stahl piece that floated through the Fish Bowl and poured through the Funnel provoked considerable displeasure from one of those viewers at the other end. The viewer happened to be Van Gordon Sauter, overseer of all that was CBS News. After having ignored the October 23 anniversary of the tragic bombing in Beirut, and keeping the press away from the president so that he could not be asked about that day of tragedy, the White House went all-out to celebrate another one-year anniversary the next day: the invasion of Grenada. They held ceremonies at the White House, seeing to it that some of the American students rescued there were flown in for the event, as was the father of a serviceman killed there. Reagan, once again at his poignant best, paid tribute by addressing himself to that father. Stahl's piece ended like this:

PRESIDENT REAGAN (at the White House ceremony): You asked him, "Sean, was it worth it?" And, "Yes, Dad," he answered. And you asked again, "Would you do it again?" And he looked up at you and said, "Hell yes, Dad." [Applause was heard.] A few months ago, Sean died of his wounds. But he, Sean Lukatina, gave his life in the cause of freedom." [The screen dissolves from Reagan to footage of the father placing flowers on his son's grave.]

STAHL: Left unsaid, that Sean Lukatina was a victim of friendly fire. He was in a command post that was strafed by a U.S. Navy jet which had been given the wrong coordinates. Lesley Stahl, CBS News, the White House.

Sauter was said to have been furious at that closing comment by Stahl, whom on other occasions he made clear he considered a most talented and accomplished correspondent. Zirinsky acknowledged this displeasure from the top, saying, "Sauter hated that piece." Stahl said she simply would not discuss the matter. Zirinsky did not see the closing line in terms of emotionally insensitive impact regarding that father and the life and death of his son. She saw it in its political terms—Reagan's unmistakable effort to make political gain out of that incident of war, and his willingness to use these American heroes for his purposes.

"I thought that piece was very fair," Zirinsky said. "It was a little emotional heartstring. . . . But, I mean, if Ronald Reagan is going to take an incident like the Grenada operation and pay tribute to a soldier and never mention that he was killed by American forces, that to me has to be pointed out in the editorial scheme of things." That is true, but the manner of the serviceman's death could have been covered by just mentioning it parenthetically in introducing the event, rather than as a jarring concluding comment.

THE LATE SHOW: ISSUES FOR INSOMNIACS

Because television journalists and decision-makers know they will inevitably be asked why television does not do a better job of covering the issues, they develop a few stock replies, and the gist of their responses is that sooner or later television does get around to covering most issues.

Indeed it does—later. Usually just before midnight, in fact. In the fall of 1984, those people with nothing better to do as the midnight hour approached could turn on their television sets and catch up on the issues, in varying degrees of depth. Their choices ranged from Johnny Carson and his monologues to Ted Koppel and his nightly guests to Dan Rather and his Monday-night specials. Each came with its own special rewards and its own manner of dealing with current events and candidate views in the election year. And each had a certain effect in the shaping of public opinion.

The shows of Koppel and Rather also left their network executives with the satisfied feeling of knowing that they could point to those offerings as examples of how they had covered the issues, even if they had done so in those late-night time slots which have far fewer viewers than the evening news programs.

Every weeknight of the year, in his *Nightline* show on ABC, Koppel treats the nation to a consistently high-quality look at a major issue or trend. Koppel and ABC have taken that original format, pioneered by Public Broadcasting System's Robert MacNeil and Jim Lehrer in the *MacNeil/Lehrer Report*, and infused it with Koppel's own timing and tone to set a substantive news standard that is the envy of ABC News's competitors. "It's a very successful broadcast in its editorial sense," said CBS News's Van Gordon Sauter.

For those who cared, *Nightline* offered searching looks into arms control and Star Wars, policies in the Mideast and Central America, all manner of domestic and foreign issues, and various themes including religion and politics, the new wave of patriotism, terrorism, the troubled steel industry, and much more.

For all its excellence, *Nightline* also opted for one very questionable show that could have become quite controversial if 1984 had been one of those down-to-the-wire photo finishes instead of a Reagan runaway. For in the last week of the campaign, on November 1, 1984, *Nightline* doubled its time slot to a full hour to present a fifth-anniversary commemoration of the Carter-Mondale administration's darkest days —the hostage crisis in Iran that led to the creation of *Nightline*, and led as well to the defeat of Jimmy Carter and the advent of the Reagan presidency. It was a resurrection of a historic event, and it was justified certainly by the calendar. But it also served to be a far more dramatic reminder of the pain of those Carter-Mondale times than Michael K. Deaver and the Tuesday Team could ever have created had they thought of buying time to do some negative advertising against the Mondale campaign. It was, for example, many times more inflammatory than that Boston television station's minor news piece that used some pictures of the hostage crisis during the New Hampshire primary campaign, the story that caused Mondale and his staff to erupt in such fury. Their wrath was muted this time only by the realization that it really did not mean the difference between winning and losing. Still, Koppel should have delayed his anniversary show one week in order to avoid unnecessary and unfair detrimental impact that the resurrection of that numbing episode (which after all was a problem presided over by Carter, not Mondale) rekindled within Americans.

The show opened with scenes of blindfolded hostages and fanatic Iranian captors as Koppel evoked those memories of the days of "America Held Hostage" in his introduction. "Tonight we'll look back at one of the longest and most painful peacetime ordeals in American history, the hostage crisis in Iran," said Koppel. And the show ended an hour later with Koppel making an extraordinary personal comment—excoriating former President Jimmy Carter at length for having conducted American policy and even his own campaign politics and personal life-style during that year in a way that riveted global attention on the ordeal of the American hostages in Iran.

Said Koppel:

"There were some lessons to be learned from what happened in Iran, and there is good reason to believe that we didn't learn them. Did the media by its pervasive coverage—did we, with our nightly 'America Held Hostage' programs—complicate matters? Probably. Did all the media attention help lengthen the time the hostages were held? Almost certainly. There can be no doubt that America's adversaries always have, and probably always will, take comfort from the public criticism and debate that accompanies every American crisis. All the more reason, therefore, that our public officials exercise extreme caution in using foreign crises for domestic political effect. It was President Jimmy Carter, facing what he believed would be a tough primary campaign against Ted Kennedy, who resorted to the famous Rose Garden strategy, refusing to leave the White House because the hostage crisis was too important, too all-encompassing. It was, said President Carter, the first thing he thought about in the morning, the last thing he thought about at night. Nothing could have pleased or flattered the hostage-takers more. . . . There's only one thing that terrorists cannot abide, and that's to be ignored," Koppel said. "Perhaps it's expecting too much of the media to ignore them, but our leaders should know better."

Meanwhile, CBS was using Monday nights to serve up a weekly fall campaign series of special reports, anchored by Rather and under the direction of executive producer Joan Richman. Eight years after that postmortem at the Plaza Hotel, where the most prominent figures at CBS had complained about their seven-thirty P.M. time slot for the Campaign '76 specials, the network opted to put Campaign '84 where the late show once played, eleven-thirty P.M. to midnight.

The CBS specials of 1984 were substantive and significant, as they blended coverage of domestic and foreign policies with analyses of the horse race itself, and sought to put each in the context of the other.

Perhaps the best piece to air on a major television network in the fall of 1984 on the issue of the federal deficit was carried on the late-night CBS special of October 2. CBS News's Ray Brady was the correspondent.

CBS NEWS SPECIAL REPORT
MONDAY, OCTOBER 2, 1984
11:30 P.M.

RATHER: . . . Mondale has put his tax plan on the table and challenged Mr. Reagan to come forward with his. Instead the Reagan campaign has attacked the Mondale plan as unrealistic and without a prayer in Congress. . . . Yes or no? Is a tax increase needed to lower the growing federal-budget deficit? That's a question Ray Brady has been examining.

BRADY: This year's big tax battle really started here—Vietnam, 1969. President Johnson wouldn't raise taxes to finance an unpopular war. Since then, the deficit has kept going up. And when President Reagan cut taxes without getting big spending cuts in return, the deficit soared. So did its price tag: $500 for every man, woman, and child in interest payments. If the government prints money to pay those bills, it brings back inflation. If it keeps borrowing, interest rates will sail even higher for everyone—government, business, home buyers. That leaves two solutions: raising taxes, cutting spending. An Urban Institute study found Mr. Reagan's tax cuts favored the rich, not the poor, so Mr. Mondale would raise taxes for companies and high-bracket Americans. To Mr. Reagan, higher taxes are a last resort. But many economists say Mondale's right.

[An economist was then shown saying just that. It was Charles Schultze, who happened to be the chief economic adviser in the Carter-Mondale administration.]

BRADY: The president has skirted the deficit issue, saying a growing economy will boost government revenues.

The piece went on to quote Reagan as saying the deficit can be wiped out just by holding down the rate of increases on spending and generating more revenues through economic growth. It quoted Shultze as saying that was flat wrong and Reagan should know it. It quoted Mondale as saying, "You can't hide your red ink with blue smoke and mirrors." And it quoted Nixon-Ford administration economist Alan Greenspan as saying there was a little blue smoke being spread by Reagan, but also by Mondale.

Brady then showed how those budget cuts in scrapping the MX missile, B-11 bomber, and Star Wars would save just $25 billion, while the 1989 deficit was estimated at $263 billion. And then it showed Pierre Rinfret, an economist often cited by Nixon administration officials, as saying that taxes have to be raised and spending has to be cut. And finally, as a graphic pie chart displayed the realities of government spending on the screen, Brady showed how it was impossible to cut the budget significantly "without going into the programs many Americans want."

The Rather special went on to a related segment, as the anchor jointly interviewed a Mondale economic adviser and a Republican senator on the deficit and the tax plans of the two candidates.

While it is to CBS News's credit that it aired a piece as comprehensive as Ray Brady's, it reflects poorly on the network that it could find no place in its evening news broadcast—the prime-time news—for that report.

Dan Rather agrees. "I wish it had been on the *Evening News,*" said Rather. He recalled that "Brady had been aching to do the piece" originally for the *Evening News*. He was worried about the length of it—and Rather recalls telling him to keep working on the piece, "we might find a day when we can let something run a little longer." Rather explained: "You know, we're not afraid to let something run four and a half, five, five and a half minutes on the *Evening News*. We don't do it often. We don't do it often enough." (Brady's piece eventually ran approximately five minutes on the special.) While they were worried the piece might be too long for the prime-time news, Joan Richman approached Rather with the idea of having Brady do a piece for their special. And it was done.

After the special aired, Rather said that he and *Evening News* executive producer Lane Vernardos talked about how the Brady piece had been good and "we need to do a version of that for tomorrow." But then the press of the next day's news pushed aside the idea of redoing the Brady piece in prime time. "I think what happened is the train rolled on," Rather said. "And our intentions got—the news dictated doing the broadcast a different way. . . . It got washed away with the campaign tide."

Rather waxes philosophic about it. "While eleven-thirty P.M. is not prime time . . . the audience is not as large as the *Evening News* . . . but it is a large audience. It isn't chopped liver—as ten-thirty Sunday morning [the time slot for *Sunday Morning with Charles Kuralt*]."

SHORTCHANGING THE DEFICIT

Television's coverage of the deficit issue in 1984 is viewed in two ways by the top people at the networks. Some, mostly executives, say it was adequately covered. Others concede it was not.

"There weren't enough of those [deficit] stories on television," says Sam Donaldson. "That's where I think we were deficient in this campaign."

It is fair to say that neither Walter Mondale nor network television ever found a good way to communicate the problem of the deficit to the voters. The problem as far as television was concerned is that Reagan and his strategists outsmarted them and outmaneuvered them. For television could show Mondale laying out his plan to curb deficits and talking about it, but they couldn't show something that wasn't happening. And Reagan was not giving them anything to take a picture of concerning the deficits, just as he was not giving the public any plan of his own for dealing with the problem. And so television covered what Reagan was doing, rather than covering what he wasn't.

On Tuesday, September 11, Reagan held the only press conference he would hold during the heat of the campaign, an impromptu affair at the White House press room to announce in his new spirit of campaign season peace-seeking that he would be meeting with Soviet Foreign Minister Andrei Gromyko. (He would hold one more on the Sunday before Election Day, at an airport in Mondale's home state of Minnesota, when the outcome of the election was assured.)

While the purpose of that September 11 press conference was to talk with the Soviets, Donaldson took the occasion of this only real opportunity to question the president to press him on his response to Mondale's challenge to put forth his own plan on the deficits. Reagan was pressed three times by Donaldson, and after halting and stumbling and filibustering answers, it was clear the president was saying only that those who want a plan should look at his past budget cuts requested, and that was his only program. That would have included cuts in Social Security and so on.

But that night there was no story about Reagan's deficit and Reagan's lack of a plan other than those cuts in social programs. Not on CBS, NBC, or even in Donaldson's own work on ABC. "You know, that day they had us," Donaldson said. "We got to ask the questions but the thrust of the pieces had to be Gromyko." But Donaldson said he was "shocked" the next day to discover that even *The Washington Post* all but ignored Reagan's comments on the budget and deficit plan, mentioning it only on page A-17, in the last two paragraphs of the continued portion of the front-page story that was all about Gromyko, even though word of the meeting had been out a day earlier. "I was shocked," said Donaldson. ". . . There was no impact either on our network or in your newspaper [the *Post*] about Reagan once again—or for the first time in the campaign—being asked and slipping off the point."

Actually, one major news organization played the story prominently and properly. *The New York Times* did a separate story on Reagan's budget-deficit comments, and played it more prominently than his announcement of the old news that he would meet with Gromyko.

Looking back at the campaign of 1984, Donaldson figures that his network must shoulder a good bit of the blame—and he must shoulder much of it. For he said that his network contented itself too often with doing the most thorough job of anyone on the day-to-day stories, and trying to wrap the facts and failures of the candidates on the issues into their nightly reports from the campaign trail.

CBS, with its planned effort to cover issues and trends, did it better, he said. None dare call Donaldson self-effacing, but there is a candor that has to be admired, as this star of ABC News turns his trademarked critical eye toward the mirror and reports in his familiar outspoken way the warts he sees.

"Well, CBS did that better than ABC did that in the campaign," Donaldson said, referring to the ability to stand back and focus on an issue or a trend. "They would do that from time to time. We almost always relied on the day's story and then a phrase here, and then a piece there, to keep making the point. . . . I repeatedly pointed out during the campaign . . . that he [Reagan] had never spelled out how he would reduce the deficit—but just in a phrase, usually in the context of the day. . . .

"I think we at ABC were deficient and I take, frankly, as much responsibility for that deficiency as anyone else you could point to at ABC. Had I gone to the broadcast [the producers] on any given day and said, 'Today instead of doing what he said and all this, we should do the wider piece, and I should do it'—we probably would have had more of that [holding Reagan accountable for positions on issues such as the deficit].

"But I was tuned, and always have been—which may be revealing more than my inadequacies—to the day's stories. I'm a line reporter rather than [a big picture or put-it-all-in-context reporter]."

It is more than just a style of reporting, Donaldson conceded. It is the fact that being on the television screen each night is the number-one goal of a success-oriented television correspondent, he said. And the only sure way to accomplish that is to do the story about what the president did that day, rather than spending several days trying to put together the story of what Reagan's deficit plans will result in—even though the president won't say so publicly.

Listen to Donaldson's explanation of the facts of life of television stardom and how they at times get co-opted by the Great American Video Game:

"If I can break away my mentality from the so-called day story, I'll go do 'The Presidency' [he was referring to the idea of having one correspondent at the White House assigned not to do daily News stories, but pieces on the shaping and executing of presidential policies on the sort of White House beat, he said, that was once done by *The*

Washington Post] . . . and maybe someone else will do 'Ronald Reagan today said to the businessmen, "Make my day" ' or whatever. . . . But I have a hard time for that because as a line reporter, in all the years I've done it for both here and at WTOP [a Washington, D.C., radio station], I learned that the person who put hands on and was there all the time was the one who was not only seen to be there all the time but who carved out a number-one place [on the beat]. . . . And once you retreated from the rope line, from the briefings, from the North Lawn when the pope is shot . . . in our business someone else is going to do that. . . . In newspapers it's different . . . but on television, it's who the audience sees.

"How many deep analytical pieces did Dan Rather do when he was covering Nixon? Or Tom Brokaw, or anyone you want to talk about?"

Now it is Sam Donaldson who is the preeminent television presence at the White House. And he does it his way. "I think my scripts would explain, you yell a question or you ask a question, and you don't get an answer—and you put that on to show that you're not getting an answer." Donaldson paused to consider what he had just said (the specter of Sam Donaldson pausing in mid-sentence to do anything, especially to reconsider, is an event akin to Refrigerator Perry pausing in mid-sack to perform a *pas de deux*).

"But that's not the same thing as really looking at the numbers and looking at the positions and saying, 'What is the plan to make this whole?' And there is none." Now he spread his hands toward the heavens and bowed his head, slightly:

"But we didn't do any real hard-hitting pieces."

FOURTEEN

REFLECTIONS INTO THE FUTURE

So that's The Great American Video Game, a contest of skill and luck. It is a slow-paced game that takes a full four years to build to a climax and run its course. And it often seems interminable, because no sooner does one game end than the next begins.

The instrument of television has taken control of the presidential-election process. It is the single greatest factor in determining who gets nominated every fourth summer and who gets elected that fall. Some politicians and strategists have shown remarkable skill at regulating and even manipulating the television-news coverage. The most successful of them have also enjoyed a good bit of luck.

Television news has become the greatest force in the nation's presidential process; it also stands as the nation's greatest hope. It remains the only medium that can give the public what it wants most: the ability to take the measure of the candidates for president in those intangible, up-close-and-personal ways that the newspaper page can never fulfill.

This is of great and perhaps even overriding importance, because a vote for president is a special and rather personal thing for many people, a bit like casting a vote for father, or grandfather (or maybe, in the case of John F. Kennedy, a vote for husband). People often find it difficult to sort through the complexities of even the best-explained national issue, to decide which position they believe is right and which they believe is wrong. But they often find it easy to look at the candidates and decide which they would most like to lead the nation through the next crisis, whatever that crisis may be. The task of television-news journalists is to do their journalistic best to tell people what is really going on, to make the issues and controversies as understandable as possible, even as the camera provides the crucial, close, personal insights into the candidates.

When television news fails to serve the needs of people in their living rooms, it is because those in the industry have failed to keep their eyes and minds on their role as journalists. It is often because they have allowed themselves to fall for the traps set by the best of the image-makers and manipulators, people such as Michael Deaver.

When that happens, television news ceases to be an effective instrument for taking the true measure of the candidates; it becomes the instrument of the image-makers.

In The Great American Video Game, the goal of the politicians and image-makers is relatively simple: to design visual settings that will put the candidate and his or her policies in the best possible light, images that encourage television journalists to focus their stories around the photo opportunities provided.

The goal of the television journalists (reporters, editors and producers, and executives) is much more difficult—tougher than that of the politicians or the image-makers, and certainly tougher than that of the print journalists. It is to withstand the designs and schemes of the image-makers and to maintain journalistic control of their news product. It requires an unceasing effort to withstand the temptation to build a story around an event—such as Ronald Reagan's Fourth of July, 1984—simply because it was a day of fascinating pictures. It means they must build the story around his statements that day, relegating the pictures of stockcar racing and holiday spirit to their proper and secondary perspective.

The Great American Video Game will always produce competition verging on warfare between the pols and the television journalists. The task of the journalists is to see that their relationship with the candidates and image-makers remains healthily adversarial rather than symbiotic.

America's television news and its voters do not have to lose every time the Great American Video Game is played.

While gathering information for this book, expressions of frustration and complaint were frequently heard about television's coverage of the 1984 presidential campaign. Among them:

"It was a kind of inane repetition."

"Television . . . ought to find a way to spend more time on issues and less on personalities."

"Network campaign coverage was . . . boring everyone to death."

"I'm sure [ABC, CBS, and NBC] didn't do enough" reporting on the deficit, "because [they] never do."

"I didn't have a feeling that [television coverage was] giving people any kind of overall dimension as to what was happening."

There were all these comments and more—yet there is great cause for optimism in these declarations. Because these frustrations and complaints were voiced not by television's critics but by the presidents of NBC News and ABC News. The first, third, and fifth were volunteered by NBC's Lawrence Grossman during a lengthy interview exploring his views on his network's coverage of 1984 and his hopes for NBC's coverage in future years.

The second and fourth were offered by ABC's Roone Arledge under similar circumstances. And what prompted both of these network-news presidents to speak out was that they were emphasizing their determination to make their network's coverage of presidential campaigns better in future years than it has been in the past—and to be more aware of the ways they are most vulnerable to manipulation by skilled politicians and strategists. That is good reason to be optimistic about what television news can accomplish.

At CBS News, both Edward Joyce, who was president during 1984, and Van Gordon Sauter, who preceded and followed Joyce in that job, pronounced themselves quite satisfied with television's coverage in general—and their network's coverage in particular. They were much more pleased with the results of their organization's journalism than were their counterparts at ABC and NBC. But Joyce and Sauter are both gone from CBS now, having lost out in that network's Star Wars power struggles. But *CBS Evening News* anchor Dan Rather was considerably less sanguine than his then-bosses, as he spoke forcefully and fervently about the need to revise, reform, and even retool to improve shortcomings he acknowledged with a candor that did not diminish the strong efforts CBS News had already begun in 1984.

Behind the examples of television news's failures to resist the enticements of campaign image-makers in 1984, there is also this central reality: There is nothing that television news correspondents or anchors or producers could have done that would likely have altered the outcome of the 1984 campaign. Reagan would likely have won reelection no matter what—even if the television networks had not catered to his made-for-television pageants and his visually compelling ways.

Reagan's campaign hummed in perfect political harmony with its blend of feel-good imagery and economic fact. Beating a president in a time of relative peace and prosperity is as unlikely as it sounds. The unenviable job of having to show the nation that the "peace" was problematic, what with those 261 marine deaths in Lebanon and the efforts to overthrow the Sandinistas in Nicaragua, was left to Mondale and his strategists.

And it was left to Mondale and his strategists to convince their countrymen that the prosperity they felt and saw every time they went to the store was not real, and that a deficit they could not see, feel, or understand loomed as the economic undoing of their children or themselves.

But it is also true that Mondale and his strategists were singularly not up to the challenge of this tough assignment in message politics in 1984. Reagan and his advisers were masterful. And the television networks were often unable to cope with and unable to gain control of their own medium.

Throughout his presidency—and especially in the election year—Ronald Reagan was the Man from Glad, a candidate in a Baggie, hermetically sealed and gingerly lifted from one perfect-for-television setting to the next. His was a strategy steeped in cynicism and arrogance, and bound for success. Walter Mondale and Ronald Reagan worked the election circuit with very different views of what Americans deserve to get in their presidential campaigns; and the nation's television stars and decision-makers found themselves uncomfortably unable to reconcile the disparate campaigns and fit them into a satisfying package they could comfortably call "news."

For Mondale, the medium was a nightly trial by fire; for Reagan, the medium was the massage. Consider this moment of Reagan and television: In a telling and unconscionable burst of cynicism (*chutzpah* says it better), the Reagan media strategists actually ran a television ad in which a woman on the street was marveling over a statistic that of course she had been coached to recite.

REAGAN CAMPAIGN '84 AD

WOMAN: I think he's just doggone honest. It's remarkable! He's been on television—what have I heard? Twenty-six times? Talking to us? About what he's doing? Now, he's not doing that for any

> other reason than to make it real clear. And if anybody has any question about where he's headed, it's their fault. Maybe they don't have a television.

Unmentioned, of course, was the fact that Reagan's twenty-six press conferences was an all-time low in the modern era. Jimmy Carter, who had many other failings as a leader and symbolic pacesetter, held fifty-eight press conferences during the same duration as president.

REFORMS: THE NETWORKS

Lawrence Grossman figures he had a distinct advantage over his fellow news presidents at the other networks during the 1984 season. His advantage: He had just gotten to the job. "So I was looking at this not from the point of view of somebody who was setting policy or direction or emphasis, but as a learning effort," Grossman said. "So maybe I was looking at it more from the point of view of an ordinary viewer.

"It was very clear who was ahead . . . and who was going to win. It was also very clear that it was kind of inane repetition, that we were talking about very small margins of difference [between] . . . what the guy would say on Tuesday [and] . . . what he said on Monday. . . . First we were boring everybody to death—at least, I was bored with it and I'm very interested in politics. Secondly, I didn't feel that we were giving people any kind of an overall dimension as to what was happening. I mean, we were reporting it [and nothing more]."

Grossman said his goal is to figure out "how to make the network news program not a headline production as it always has been, but to use our Ken Bodes and Roger Mudds . . . to get more insight and context and even more history and perspective on what's going on."

Actually, they came very close to discovering that for themselves at NBC in the fall of 1984—only they shied away from taking the logical step that could have greatly improved their coverage and been a model for their competition.

NBC's cold war series showed that there is time enough to present a world's worth of news and then do a four-to-five minute special series later in the show. That series could have been adapted to put the candidates' policies into the context of the cold war, past, present, and future. So too, the networks could have done a week-long series on America's budget dilemma, mixing historical context with computerized graphics; it would have been a major contribution. There is no reason why that sort of story could not be a regular nightly feature of every fall news show on each network—sometimes a policy piece, sometimes a historical-context piece, sometimes a broader perspective on the horse race itself, and sometimes a look at how the candidates perform in a variety of situations—the sort of thing that adds an extra dimension to help voters take the measure of their prospective presidents.

Grossman's own network commentator, John Chancellor, offers a strong suggestion: that the network campaign-trail pieces be shortened to get rid of that nightly analysis and stick to short straight-news pieces. This then would allow for time for regular analytical and extra-dimension pieces, Chancellor said. "You know, we learned in Vietnam in trying to make some sense out of a senseless war—it was very difficult to cover—that it was far easier if we held some footage for a couple of days until an action or a battle was over," said Chancellor. "And then, not try to cover it piecemeal, but to try to do one piece, maybe a little longer, that gave you a beginning, a middle, an end. Provide some context for it. And that would apply to television coverage of campaigns."

Roone Arledge conceded that at his network there was greater emphasis on daily news stories than on contextual pieces. "The classic thing to say—and the true thing to say—is that we ought to find a way to spend more time on issues and less on personalities," said Arledge. He was asked whether he thought he would have had enough good information on the deficit if he had been able to watch all three network-news shows each night. "Probably not," the ABC News president answered.

Along with the emphasis on putting the issues and the race in context, network television must make some rather tough decisions about just what is news and what is not. That was what CBS tried to do in 1984, with mixed results, and it is what all networks will have to do from now on if the campaign strategists are going to borrow from the Deaver playbook in an effort to get the networks to show their cinematic spectaculars, which are heavy on visuals and void of policy.

And former anchorman Chancellor noted:

"I get nervous when I ask myself . . . why were we suckered—or were we suckered? Or what is our function and responsibility in putting on the balloons? And I think you have in television more than you have in print . . . a built-in belief that what the president does is newsworthy, no matter how often he's done it before. I think that's part of a mind-set [of] a lot of network-news operations."

REFORMS: LOCAL TELEVISION

While the nation's major commercial-television networks have worked to apply themselves to campaign coverage and to improve their product,

America's local television has problems that are far more severe. In city after city, primary after primary, local stations have seemed to approach coverage of presidential primaries in a manner that is haphazard at best, and often downright negligent.

America's presidential primaries depend more than anything else on strong local-television coverage to help voters make up their minds. And yet, most local stations seem to do little or no planning and preparation for the campaigns. With them, far too often, it's just: Here comes a candidate; stick a microphone in his face and call it journalism.

Listen to CBS News's Van Gordon Sauter, who formerly headed Chicago's top-performing local station, WBBM-TV, on the subject of local-television coverage of primaries:

"I think local television stations in general have been derelict in their coverage of primary elections. They have a primary role in primary elections and they just have not seized upon that responsibility in the way they should.

"Also, they are missing the boat where they could truly shine. It is a form of politics where they could really fly their banner and show their capacity, and they end up being passive participants. . . . It's the one occasion where they can really show a community that they're a journalistic force.

"I think local television has turned what could be a stimulating and exciting story—the primary election—into a horrendous, dull, repetitive, uninspired event. I think they should say, 'Hey, this is more important than going to the political conventions. This is more important in a peculiar kind of way than election night, where the network really dominates it. And this is the time where we can go out and show this viewing area how sophisticated we are. . . . We can go out and find out what is truly on the minds of the people. . . . And we're going to become the key source of video information about this election. And we're going to make this election interesting—because it inherently *is* interesting.

"It's only dull because we think it's dull, treat it as dull, and convince viewers it's dull."

There are some local stations, such as Boston's two top-rated stations, WBZ and WCVB, that are headed by people (Stan Hopkins and Phil Balboni) who take their job and their journalistic campaign product most seriously. The New Hampshire primary—that first candidate weeder and sorter—will be the chief beneficiary if they are able to deliver on their good intentions.

Local television has to gain at least a modicum of control over its own campaign-editorial product. That means abandoning these silly live interviews with candidates at airports and giving viewers thoroughly edited, well-produced, conceptually sound pieces—perhaps even focusing on local or regional themes and issues.

REFORM: FREE TELEVISION

Changing times and shifting state and regional politics have combined to make the current system of primaries and caucuses a ritual that brings to the presidential-nomination process all of the order and coherence of "The Keystone Kops Meet the Katzenjammer Kids."

Which is to say it is a process that desperately needs to be changed. The selection of the Democratic and Republican presidential nominations begins with two tiny and unrepresentative contests—the caucuses in Iowa and the primary in New Hampshire. Then it degenerates into a helter-skelter affair, with a de facto regional primary in the South, a scatter shot of big state primaries, and the ludicrous climax of primaries in California and New Jersey the same day, leaving it to the candidates to try to crisscross the country in mad dashes, wasting time and money and proving nothing. There is little Congress can be expected to do about each state's primary and caucus calendar. But Congress can—and should—require the networks and local stations to make available to all qualifying candidates a specific amount of airtime for commercials—free commercials. A new law should require that these ads feature the candidate talking directly to the camera—no slick ads, no actors, no narrators. Just the candidate speaking. A number of Western democracies have similar provisions, notably France, West Germany, and the United Kingdom. To qualify for free ad time in the primaries, the same formula could be used that now determines which candidates shall qualify for matching federal funding: The candidate must have raised $5,000 in each of twenty states, in contributions of no more than $250 from any individual. And candidates getting less than 10 percent in two consecutive primaries lose their eligibility.

This will allow candidates to make their best case, out where people can hear it. It will give a Great Communicator hand to those who do not have the luxury of having Mike Deavers to help them get on the nightly news.

It will give a lesser-known candidate with a popular cause just what he or she is seeking—a chance to be heard, to let the voters decide. Television networks and local stations will object, fearing loss of advertising revenue. But Congress can enact such legislation secure in the knowledge that this is one industry it can regulate without fear that Japanese imports will corner the market.

THE GREAT AMERICAN VIDEO GAME OF 1988

"The buzz word of the mid-1980s is *communication*," Gary Hart is saying. He is the only candidate of 1984 who is going to make the run in 1988, and he is talking about what he has learned about running for president in this television age.

Up until now, Hart says, Democrats have paid "more attention . . . to ideas . . . than on stage-managing of the message." He goes on: "I think Democrats are going to have to pay attention to the details, if you will. The lighting, and the backdrops and the [availability of electrical] outlets for television. I mean, it's just a prerequisite. If your face washes out [on the television screen], then people don't probably listen to what you have to say."

Hart says he and other Democrats also went to school on Reagan, Deaver, Henkel & Company, 1984, and they have come away vowing to follow their example of campaign-trail discipline. "It's . . . the discipline about your message. It's saying 'Here's our message for the campaign,' or 'Here's our message today.' "

What's more, Hart says, if he had been the Democratic nominee in 1984, he would have run a different sort of campaign from that which Mondale ran. He would have campaigned against Reagan, Reagan-style. "I would have said, 'Let's keep the number of events small. Let's organize this campaign for television. You know, we're not going to get the votes at rallies, we're going to get them on television. And we don't need to do ten events a day.' . . . That's what I would have said, and I think I could have gotten that to happen."

Meanwhile, when Hart runs his television-oriented race, Dan Rather, for one, will be ready.

"The 1984 campaign was an educational process for the electorate," Rather says. "And they'll be harder to fool next time than they were this time. . . . I think people are becoming much more sophisticated about television . . . understanding not only what we do and how we do it and why we do it . . . but also with the politicians and their staffs.

"But having said all that, there are going to be plenty of days when a Hart or a Kemp or whoever it is in 1988—they and their people are going to walk away from the set saying 'We got you, Dan Rather. We got all our pictures on today and it didn't matter what Lesley Stahl or Bill Plante or anybody else said. We got 'em on today!'

"We're going to be able to resist it only sporadically, and not very well. And I'll feel good on the days when we do resist it. And I'll feel terrible on the days—which will be many more—when we're not able to.

". . . The best we can hope for is some days when they say 'Damn! What's the matter with Rather? He didn't run our housing pictures today,' or 'He only ran 'em for twenty seconds and the other guy ran 'em for two minutes! . . . Damn that Rather!' "

INDEX